POSTMODERNISM

ICA DOCUMENTS

Edited by

Lisa Appignanesi

*'an association in which the free development of each is
the condition of the free development of all'*

Free Association Books / London / 1989

Printed in Great Britain in 1989 by
Free Association Books
26 Freegrove Road
London N7 9RQ

Reprinted in 1993

First published by Institute of Contemporary Arts

Consultant Editor, Geoff Bennington
Assistant Editor, Jane Attala

© ICA and Geoff Bennington, Jacques Derrida, Peter Dews, Kenneth
Frampton, Martin Jay, Philippe Lacoue-Labarthe, Jacques Leenhardt,
Jean-François Lyotard, René Major, J.G. Merquior, Angela McRobbie
Michael Newman, Demetri Porphyrios, John Wyver, 1986.

British Library Cataloguing in Publication Data
Postmodernism. – (ICA documents)
   1. Culture. Postmodernism
   I. Appignanesi, Lisa II. Bennington, Geoffrey III. Series
   306

   ISBN 1-85343-078-1

Printed and bound in the United States of America

POSTMODERNISM

The term 'postmodernism' is ubiquitous in current cultural debate, but its meanings are difficult to grasp. This is in some ways consistent with the deconstructed, fragmented, fleeting versions of the world to which postmodern cultural commentators allude. Here is a collection of documents drawn from a series of events at London's Institute of Contemporary Arts which include contributions from some of the most notable writers on the topic. They address facets of postmodernism in the theory of knowledge, the arts and architecture. Included are debates, interviews and interventions by Jean-François Lyotard and Jacques Derrida among postmodern analysts and careful critical and expository pieces by Martin Jay, J.G. Merquior and Michael Newman (who provides an extended essay on the visual arts and a critical lexicon of terms from postmodernist discourse). The collection is unique in providing an overview of the phenomenon of postmodernism.

Lisa Appignanesi is Deputy Director of the Institute of Contemporary Arts and head of its programme in publishing and television.

Joseph Beuys, The Pack, 1969

CONTENTS

EDITOR'S NOTE

This double issue in the *ICA Documents* series brings together material which grew out of a major conference held in 1985 on the philosophical dimensions of the postmodernist debate, and three autumn seminars from our French Thinkers series, in which public interest extended well beyond the physical capacity of the ICA. We have linked this material into one issue, not only out of expedience, but because we felt that the nature of the intellectual inquiry engaged in by the contributors was not wholly unrelated.

I am grateful to Geoff Bennington for his invaluable help in assembling this issue, and particularly for translating and editing the contributions by Jean-François Lyotard and Philippe Lacoue-Labarthe, and providing essential links in the material. I am also grateful to the contributors who, in some cases, have supplied new papers which give us a fuller insight into the problems at hand.

My thanks, too, to the Collège International de Philosophie in Paris for their continued collaboration with the ICA which has resulted in a fruitful cultural exchange. Jacques Derrida's comments about the potential of the Collège will not go amiss.

Finally, we are deeply grateful to the Service Culturel of the French Embassy and to Gilles Chouraqui for their cooperation and assistance in mounting the live events on which this *Document* is based.

Lisa Appignanesi

ICA DOCUMENTS 4

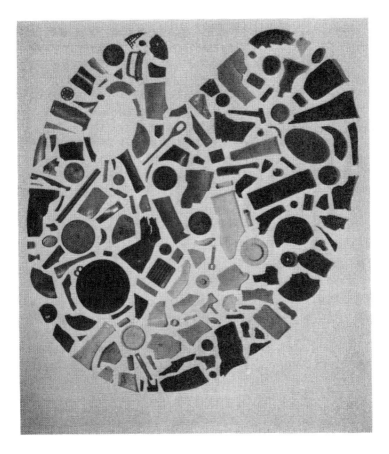

Tony Cragg, Plastic Palette 1, 1985

INTRODUCTION

THE QUESTION OF POSTMODERNISM
Geoff Bennington

The first part of this publication is based on a two-day conference held at the ICA in May 1985, and entitled 'A Question of Postmodernity: The Philosophical Dimension of the Postmodern Debate'. Not all of the texts printed here have quite the same status, however: some are slightly re-written versions of papers read; some are written summaries of more-or-less improvised interventions and responses; some are significantly different from what was actually said; some lightly-edited transcripts of what was said, and some are translated from the French.

The subtitle of the conference indicated that 'philosophical' issues would provide a focus for dicussion: in the event it would probably be more accurate to say that they provided a starting-point for debate. Nonetheless, that starting-point, largely in the figure of Jean-François Lyotard, insisted, persisted and returned throughout in the form of Lyotard's improvised responses to other papers, to other members of the various panels, and to questions and objections from the floor. At risk of apparent unfairness to other participants, transcripts of most of these interventions are included here, because of their considerable intrinsic interest, and because of the way they place and address the philosophical implications of other comments not strictly of a philosophical character. In cases where they respond to questions or comments that it has not been possible to reproduce, I have added a few contextualising remarks for clarification.

A further reason for this insistence on Lyotard is that the impetus for the conference was, in part, provided by the recent publication in English of Lyotard's book *The Postmodern Condition*: for better and for worse, it is this book

which has led to Lyotard's name becoming more widely
known in the English-speaking world, and has associated
that name with the term 'postmodern' in a way which has
possibly given rise to a certain number of confusions, not
all of which are dissipated in the texts which follow. Firstly
and essentially, the 'postmodern condition' diagnosed and
described in the book is not simply synonymous with the
architectural and artistic movement known as 'postmodernism', and which is the subject of some energetic attacks by
various participants in the pages of this volume. In *The
Postmodern Condition* itself, Lyotard is not concerned directly
with questions of aesthetics or of the philosophy of the arts,
but with knowledge and the problem of its legitimation in
'advanced' societies, given a posited collapse of various
traditional 'Grand Narratives' by means of which knowledge had previously been legitimated. The 'condition' that
is described in the book is not, in the first instance,
something that is either advocated or deplored, but a state
of affairs that Lyotard claims to be actual – even though the
book implies strongly that such a condition should not
simply be greeted with indignation, but recognised as
defining the rules to be discovered and displaced in the
conduct of various 'language-games'. (This is a term
Lyotard has subsequently dropped as being too 'anthropocentric'.)

But if this is undeniably the first concern of the book, it
would be foolish to deny all connection with art: Lyotard
has long been involved with the analysis of the contemporary arts, and to this extent his choice of an originally
art-historical term to designate a general 'condition' is
neither accidental nor neutral. And if *The Postmodern
Condition* was indeed an important impulse behind the ICA
conference, Lyotard's exhibition, *Les Immatériaux*, still
running at the Pompidou Centre in Paris at the time of the
conference, was certainly another. Further, the essay
published as an appendix to *The Postmodern Condition*,
'Answering the Question: What is Postmodernism?', does
address questions of art directly (although perhaps less
unequivocally than the translated title suggests: the French
has *'le postmoderne'* and not *'le postmodernisme'*), as do many of
Lyotard's interventions here, notably around the question
of the sublime. And it can be said more generally that the

qualities of flexibility and inventiveness required, in *The Postmodern Condition* itself, of a 'good' conduct of language-games, are, in a certain sense, 'artistic' qualities.

The possibility of confusion stems from the fact that such apparently 'aesthetic' concerns are still not those of postmodernism, and one of the concerns of the 'Answering the Question' essay is to make this clear. Some of the demands the essay begins by citing and goes on to challenge are made in the name of postmodernism seen as a 'transavantgardism'. But against such 'slackening', Lyotard is nonetheless not trying to argue for a totalising and unifying notion of the aesthetic, which he finds in the work of Habermas. What Lyotard *is* concerned to defend is the value of 'experimentation', and this defence, which is closely bound up with an affirmation of Kant's aesthetic of the sublime as against an aesthetic of the beautiful (to which Habermas still subscribes), continues in several of the interventions published here. One result of this line of argument is that the 'post' of 'postmodern' can no longer be understood in a simple chronological sense as 'what comes after the modern':

> The postmodern would be that which, in the modern, puts forward the unpresentable in presentation itself; that which denies itself the solace of good forms, the consensus of a taste which would make it possible to share collectively the nostalgia for the unattainable; that which searches for new presentations, not in order to enjoy them but in order to impart a stronger sense of the unpresentable. A postmodern artist or writer is in the position of a philosopher: the text he writes, the work he produces are not in principle governed by preestablished rules, and they cannot be judged according to a determining judgement, by applying familiar categories to the text or to the work. Those rules and categories are what the work of art itself is looking for. The artist and the writer, then, are working without rules in order to formulate the rules of what *will have been done*. Hence the fact that work and text have the character of an *event*; hence also, they always come too late for their author, or, what amounts to the same thing, their *mise en oeuvre* always begins too soon. *Post modern* would have to be understood according to the paradox of the future (*post*) anterior (*modo*).

It seems to me that the essay (Montaigne) is postmodern, while the fragment (*The Athenaeum*) is modern. (*The Postmodern Condition*, p. 81: translation very slightly modified.)

This much simply to place some warning signs, or recall some distinctions not always easy to perceive in what follows despite the careful explanations in Lyotard's opening statement. To what extent the resulting notion of the postmodern remains inhabited by the connotations of postmodernism or of what-comes-after-the-modern is something for the reader to judge. To what extent, too, Lyotard's 'optimistic' and even militant elaboration of experimentation and the notion of the sublime is vulnerable to Philippe Lacoue-Labarthe's careful critique. *Documents 4* will certainly give a sense of the complexity of the issues involved here, and these few remarks will have served their purpose if they help to hold that complexity this side of confusion.

The second part of the volume is the record of thrée public discussions held at the ICA in the autumn of 1985. Jacques Leenhardt and René Major have provided slightly re-written texts: The discussion with Derrida is a lightly edited transcript of his largely improvised presentation and the questions which followed.

DEFINING THE POSTMODERN
Jean-François Lyotard

I should like to make only a small number of observations, in order to point to — and not at all to resolve — some problems surrounding the term 'postmodern'. My aim is not to close the debate, but to open it, to allow it to develop by avoiding certain confusions and ambiguities, as far as this is possible.

There are many debates implied by, and implicated in, the term 'postmodern'. I will distinguish three of them.

First, the opposition between postmodernism and modernism, or the Modern Movement (1910–45), in architectural theory. According to Paolo Portoghesi (*Dell'architectura moderna*), there is a rupture or break, and this break would be the abrogation of the hegemony of Euclidean geometry, which was sublimated in the plastic poetry of the movement known as De Stijl, for example. According to Victorio Grigotti, another Italian architect, the difference between the two periods is characterized by what is possibly a more interesting fissure. There is no longer any close linkage between the architectural project and socio-historical progress in the realization of human emancipation on the larger scale. Postmodern architecture is condemned to generate a multiplicity of small transformations in the space it inherits, and to give up the project of a last rebuilding of the whole space occupied by humanity. In this sense, a perspective is opened in the larger landscape.

In this account there is no longer a horizon of universalization, of general emancipation before the eyes of postmodern man, or in particular, of the postmodern architect. The disappearance of this idea of progress within rationality and freedom would explain a certain tone, style or modus which are specific to postmodern architecture. I would say a sort of *bricolage*: the high frequency of quotations of elements from previous styles or periods (classical or modern), giving up the consideration of environment, and so on.

Just a remark about this aspect. The 'post-', in the term 'postmodernist' is in this case to be understood in the sense of a simple succession, of a diachrony of periods, each of them clearly identifiable. Something like a conversion, a new direction after the previous one. I should like to observe that this idea of chronology is totally modern. It belongs to Christianity, Cartesianism, Jacobinism. Since we are beginning something completely new, we have to re-set the hands of the clock at zero. The idea of modernity is closely bound up with this principle that it is possible and necessary to break with tradition and to begin a new way of living and thinking. Today we can presume that this 'breaking' is, rather, a manner of forgetting or repressing the past. That's to say of repeating it. Not overcoming it.

I would say that the quotation of elements of past architectures in the new one seems to me to be the same procedure as the use of remains coming from past life in the dream-work as described by Freud, in the *Interpretation of Dreams*. This use of repetition or quotation, be it ironical or not, cynical or not, can be seen in the trends dominating contemporary painting, under the name of 'transavantgardism' (Achille Bonito Oliva) or under the name of neo-expressionism. I'll come back to this question in my third point.

The second point. A second connotation of the term 'postmodern', and I admit that I am at least partly responsible for the misunderstanding associated with this meaning.

The general idea is a trivial one. One can note a sort of decay in the confidence placed by the two last centuries in the idea of progress. This idea of progress as possible, probable or necessary was rooted in the certainty that the development of the arts, technology, knowledge and liberty would be profitable to mankind as a whole. To be sure, the question of knowing which was the subject truly victimized by the lack of development — whether it was the poor, the worker, the illiterate — remained open during the 19th and 20th centuries. There were disputes, even wars, between liberals, conservatives and leftists over the very name of the subject we are to help to become emancipated. Nevertheless, all the parties concurred in the same belief that enterprises, discoveries and institutions are legitimate only insofar as they contribute to the emancipation of mankind.

After two centuries, we are more sensitive to signs that signify the contrary. Neither economic nor political liberalism, nor the various Marxisms, emerge from the sanguinary last two centuries free from the suspicion of crimes against mankind. We can list a series of proper names (names of places, persons and dates) capable of illustrating and founding our suspicion. Following Theodor Adorno, I use the name of Auschwitz to point out the irrelevance of empirical matter, the stuff of recent past history, in terms of the modern claim to help mankind to emancipate itself. What kind of thought is able to sublate (*Aufheben*) Auschwitz in a general (either empirical or speculative) process towards a universal emancipation? So there is a sort of sorrow in the *Zeitgeist*. This can express itself by reactive or reactionary attitudes or by utopias, but never by a positive orientation offering a new perspective.

The development of techno-sciences has become a means of increasing disease, not of fighting it. We can no longer call this development by the old name of progress. This development seems to be taking place by itself, by an autonomous force or 'motricity'. It doesn't respond to a demand coming from human needs. On the contrary, human entities (individual or social) seem always to be destabilized by the results of this development. The intellectual results as much as the material ones. I would say that mankind is in the condition of running after the process of accumulating new objects of practice and thought. In my view it is a real and obscure question to determine the reason of this process of complexification. It's something like a destiny towards a more and more complex condition. Our demands for security, identity and happiness, coming from our condition as living beings and even social beings appear today irrelevant in the face of this sort of obligation to complexify, mediate, memorize and synthesize every object, and to change its scale. We are in this techno-scientific world like Gulliver: sometimes too big, sometimes too small, never at the right scale. Consequently, the claim for simplicity, in general, appears today that of a barbarian.

From this point, it would be necessary to consider the

division of mankind into two parts: one part confronted
with the challenge of complexity; the other with the
terrible ancient task of survival. This is a major aspect of
the failure of the modern project (which was, in principle,
valid for mankind as a whole).

The third argument is more complex, and I shall present
it as briefly as possible. The question of postmodernity is
also the question of the expressions of thought: art,
literature, philosophy, politics. You know that in the field
of art for example, and more especially the plastic arts, the
dominant idea is that the big movement of avant-gardism
is over. There seems to be general agreement about
laughing at the avant-gardes, considered as the expression
of an obsolete modernity. I don't like the term avant-garde
any more than anyone else, because of its military
connotations. Nevertheless I would like to observe that the
very process of avant-gardism in painting was in reality a
long, obstinate and highly responsible investigation of the
presuppositions implied in modernity. The right approach,
in order to understand the work of painters from, say,
Manet to Duchamp or Barnett Newman is to compare their
work with the anamnesis which takes place in psychoanalytical therapy. Just as the patient elaborates his present
trouble by freely associating the more imaginary, immate-
rial, irrelevant bits with past situations, so discovering
hidden meanings of his life, we can consider the work of
Cézanne, Picasso, Delaunay, Kandinsky, Klee, Mondrian,
Malevitch and finally Duchamp as a working through —
what Freud called *Durcharbeitung* — operated by modernity
on itself. If we give up this responsibility, it is certain that
we are condemned to repeat, without any displacement, the
modern neurosis, the Western schizophrenia, paranoia, and
so on. This being granted, the 'post-' of postmodernity
does not mean a process of coming back or flashing back,
feeding back, but of *ana*-lysing, *ana*-mnesing, of reflecting.

ON THE SUBLIME*
Philippe Lacoue-Labarthe

I must ask you to excuse me if I talk in French, and thus expose my typically French linguistic infirmity.

I am, broadly speaking and without going into details, in agreement with the first two points Jean-François Lyotard has just developed. I share this analysis and view of things, and I express my solidarity with the implications or consequences of what he says. I think I can add that this has been so for a long time between Jean-François and myself.

However, in spite of this solidarity, there remains a point of contention between us, which allows a dialogue to begin. This bears essentially on the third point he developed, and more especially on what underlies that development. I'll try to explain what this is about.

First, the philosophical tradition in which I am situated, or find my reference-points, if you prefer, makes me reluctant to accept the scansion of history which is presupposed in Jean-François Lyotard's discourse. By that I mean that if a project is finished today, or no longer sustainable (and the very idea of the postmodern appears to support such a view), it is less, to my mind, the project of the great discourse of emancipation, than the philosophical project *itself* in general, as it was inaugurated for the West with the Greeks. This project has been finished, completed at least in its possibilities, since Hegel. But the ending or accomplishment of this project has naturally taken post-Hegelian forms: two in particular — the Marxist form and the Nietzschean form, which have at least this much in common — they present themselves as overturnings. If one accepts this presentation of things, then one can understand that the modern can signify this finishing, and the beginning of what Heidegger thematised with the name — taken from Nietzsche — of nihilism. The modern is not only to do with the discourse of emancipation, or with the discourse of speculation, if only because Nietzsche is to be

* Translated by Geoff Bennington

found in it. The modern is, rather, the unfolding in all its forms of a finishing philosophy of the subject. And this is the case even with techno-science, to use Lyotard's term, which is autonomous in the sense that it is its own subject. And with the postmodern, which is a retrenchment onto the little subject after the failure of the great Subject (Subject of history, or Subject of humanity).

Secondly, in this unfolding of the modern, either art has been in complicity, or else it has been an obscure, dampened form of resistance. By this I mean simply that art has resisted without having any criteria or ground onto which to articulate this resistance theoretically. What I call complicity (for simplicity's sake) is essentially marked in the ideologies of art. Essentially in aesthetics, but also in the discourses which have accompanied and carried the various artistic movements. In their structure, these were inaugurated by German Romanticism. The avant-gardes, right up to the present day, have regularly repeated that structure. What I call, for want of a better term, resistance — that is, in the invention of another relationship with art, another relationship with the real — happens in certain works of art or certain discourses (sometimes the same discourses which are in complicity), but at their limits. For example, two readings of the Romanticism of Iena are possible. In these works and discourses, it is aesthetics, the aesthetic project itself, strictly defined, which is called into question.

I'd like to add to this second point, for fear of forgetting something important: and that is that the alliance of the avant-gardes with the ideology of emancipation is not an accident, but an essential foundation of aesthetics itself. As I see it, the discourse of emancipation was, to a great extent, born *within* the discourse of aesthetics.

Third point: by calling into question the aesthetic project, I mean any interpretation and practice of art which aims to unsettle art in its aesthetic (i.e. philosophical) concept from itself, and to remove it from its own closure. Both on the side of reception (i.e. taste or *aesthetics*) and on that of creation, in order to give it over to a destination which exceeds it. At the end of the 18th century, this would have been called a metaphysical destination. This is what happened (and I think that Lyotard is partly in agreement with this) with the notion of the sublime, and the irruption of a sublime art in the modern, or the irruption of the sublime in so-called modern art. The sublime is probably (and we share this analysis) the generalization to the whole of art of the Greek (Aristotelian) conception of tragedy. This is grounded in a schema of contradiction and in a logic one could qualify as oxymoronic. I refer to the double tragic stage, or the division of the tragic stage into stage and 'orchestra' (two irreconcilable spaces), and also to the tragic conflict, the contradiction which inhabits the tragic hero (the oxymoron par excellence being that of Oedipus, both guilty and innocent), and thirdly to the double tragic effect — itself contradictory — of pity and terror, to use Aristotle's terms, i.e. of pleasure and unpleasure. Finally, I refer to the properly modern idea that in the tragic there occurs for the first time (and I'll use Lyotard's formulation) the 'presentation' that there is (the) 'unpresentable'. This is what Hölderlin was trying to get at when he said that God is present in tragedy in the figure of death.

Since the Renaissance, that is to say in its modern definition, art has never stopped defining itself with respect to the ancient (this is especially, but not uniquely, true in aesthetics). There is something like an *anamnesis*, a permanent *anamnesis*, in so-called modern art. This anamnesis can take two forms or figures. On the one hand, the utopia (which is more or less clear, but sometimes very clear) of the possibility of a repetition and even a going-beyond of ancient art, and in particular of Greek art. This first figure took its hardest form, and the most catastrophic in its consequences, in post-Romantic German art, which was first of all concerned to re-mythologise itself, to find a modern myth, and secondly concerned to restore the forms of Greek art — I'm referring here to Wagner and to his political successors, to the political aesthetics or aesthetic politics of National Socialism. On the other hand this anemnesis can take a quite different figure: it struggles with the *impossibility* of any repetition or going-beyond of ancient art. It seems to me that this is where resistance in the modern begins. By this I mean that either, by repeating itself, art does no more than confirm the ultimate decree of Western aesthetics, which is to be found in Hegel and which says that art is a thing of the past; or else, in what I'm calling resistance, at the place where art and thinking about art find it hard to accept the question of the sublime, there takes place a ruin of the presuppositions of aesthetics itself. This is the case, for a start, with Kant, and also, in various ways, with a certain Nietzsche, with Diderot (or so Lyotard would say) or, closer to us, with Walter Benjamin, Heidegger or Adorno. (A lot of people will be surprised by this last *rapprochement*, but I think it's possible to argue it up to a certain point.) Given all this, I define the postmodern quite simply as the *failure* of this movement of resistance.

A Response to Philippe Lacoue-Labarthe
Jean-François Lyotard

I'm very impressed by the way Lacoue-Labarthe's thought is dominated by the horizon of an *end* of something. I don't know why all the problems he talks about are presented in the form of an end of something. For example: the end of philosophy — I don't understand that. He can only say that because first of all he identifies philosophy and the philosophy of the subject. But I recall that it is impossible to consider classical Greek philosophy as a philosophy of the subject. You know perfectly well that there is an important trend in the history of philosophy of anti-, or, better, of non-subject philosophy. Not only in Greek philosophy but in modern philosophy too. The idea that the postmodern is just the retreat of the big Subject into the small subject — an idea I hear as an allusion to the micrologies of Adorno — seems to me to be false. In the same mood, you seem to continue with the pretension — the Hegelian pretension — of presenting the situation of art today (that's to say, since the 19th century) as the end of art: art is whole and we are at the time of commentary and of reflecting on art; but art itself is over because it is impossible to overcome the ideal of Classical art, even in its pre-Romantic form.

This mood of decay, of the end of something, reappears

in the alternatives you propose for the current situation of artists: either they repeat (in which case art is over) or they resist, and if the artist resists (in my view, the model of resistance in art is Duchamp), according to you the point is that of destroying aesthetics itself. I think that's the case, but the conclusion is not at all that the task of producing art-works is over: quite the contrary. We are confronted with the following important problem: can we continue to think art in terms of aesthetics?

My point of view is that the frame of aesthetics, of aesthetic commentary, built by pre-romanticism and Romanticism, is completely dominated by (and subordinate to) the idea of the sublime: I agree with you on that. When the question of art is posed in terms of 'what is the right rule for producing a work of art?' we are in the classical approach, and the name of this approach was poetics. When the question of rules for producing art-works dissolved, that is to say when the question of the sublime began at the end of the 17th century, the classical approach was over. Baumgarten, in a sense Burke, and certainly Kant tried to build a new approach, and this new approach is called Aesthetics. This new approach was closely linked to the question of the sublime because it was necessary to conceive a perception of art-works without rules. I think that today we are, *mutatis mutandis*, in a similar situation, after the terrific work of avant-gardism over the last century; and aesthetics is irrelevant because it deals in terms of taste, of genius, and terms like that. When we consider ways of approaching the main works of modern art, we see that such criteria are totally irrelevant. If you read for example the texts written by Barnett Newman (though in general they're unpublished), the question Newman asks is the question of the sublime. Explicitly. And he not only refers to the tradition of the sublime (he read Edmund Burke, for example); in asking the question of the sublime he is also posing the question of what he is doing in painting. And he's aware of the impossibility of commenting on his work in terms of a traditional (that is to say, modern) aesthetic. So we're confronted with this problem, which is a real one: I agree that it is the end of aesthetics, but it is not the end of the question of art. That is the very definition of our task.

Philippe Lacoue-Labarthe Responds

I should like to reply very briefly to two of the reproaches
levelled at me by Jean-François Lyotard. It is true that in
order to keep things simple I talked a lot about ends: it
would take me a long time to explain this. But I'd like to
put something right on one point: I do not think that one
can confuse philosophy in general with the philosophy of
the subject: I simply identified philosophy of the subject
with the phase of ending or accomplishing of philosophy.
The second point — and here we are truly in disagreement
— has to do with Hegel and the decree contained in the
opening pages of the Introduction to his *Aesthetics*, to the
effect that art is a thing which is past. I agree that the end
of aesthetics does not mean the end of art: but what Hegel
means is that art no longer answers to what he calls its
supreme destination. It seems to me that for this reason
essentially, the problem of the possibility or impossibility
of resistance by art to the domination of aesthetics is the
problem which is, as I see it, bequeathed by modernity, or
modernism, or the modern age, I'm not sure what to call it.

*(J.G. Merquior had raised three points in response to Philippe
Lacoue-Labarthe's paper. He felt the conception of the sublime as
generalized tragedy might be too simple and that Lacoue-Labarthe
had suggested too psychologistic a view of Aristotle. He also
questioned the identification of Wagner as the principal 'culprit' in
the attempt of German post-romanticism to get beyond the Greek
ideal: in France and England there was an important and
specifically 'left' reception of Wagner which Merquior identified
with the proper names of Baudelaire, Mallarmé, Lévi-Strauss and
G.B. Shaw. Finally, in Lacoue-Labarthe's closing list of 'heroes
of resistance', Merquior questioned the position of Adorno, who
could be criticized for producing merely a hyper-tragic exacerbation
of the aesthetic tradition, rather than real resistance to it.)*

On the question of the link between Aristotle's doctrine of
tragedy and the aesthetics of the sublime: I concede the fact
that I went over this very quickly. Simply, and this is a
point of agreement with Lyotard, I was thinking that

aesthetics in the modern age takes over from the ancient poetics, and that there is a condensation around the notion of the sublime of a certain number of problems and questions which for Aristotle and the Greeks were questions which concerned tragedy. Having said that, I do not think that there was *aesthetics* properly speaking in antiquity, (unless one calls all philosophy of art by the name aesthetics), although I don't think modern aesthetics would be possible without the philosophy of art inaugurated by, let's say, Plato. Possibly I misunderstood your question about psychologism, but I don't think that in the few things I said about the contradictory structure or the oxymoronic logic of the tragic, I made any reference at all to the psychological. Even when Aristotle talks about the tragic effect, I think one would have to begin to analyse this as a *political* effect. 'Terror' and 'pity' are essentially political notions. They are absolutely not psychological. Pity refers to what the modern age, under the name of compassion, thinks of as the origin of the social bond (in Rousseau and Burke, for example): terror refers to the risk of dissolution of the social bond, and the pre-eminent place of that first social bond which is the relation with the other.

Then there was a question about Wagner. I took Wagner as a symptom, a symbol or example of a certain modern tradition which I think one can say is complicitous with a certain type of triumph of the philosophical. I entirely agree that one would have to nuance this if one were treating Wagner as other than a symptom, symbol, example or figure. But I'll add a few remarks: first, with respect to the political question. You say that one must be attentive to the reception of Wagner: to my mind, what is most important is not the *reception* of Wagner but the Wagnerian *project*. And I think that if one examines the Wagnerian project, one sees that it contains the seeds, and does more than contain the seeds, of something fundamental to National-Socialist politics — a confusion of an aesthetic project and a political project, for the use of a mass society. This is absolutely clear in the project of Bayreuth.

You say that there was a 'left' reception of Wagner in France and England. I think that's true for George Bernard Shaw, whose reading is a left-wing reading and quite interesting in this respect. But I don't think it's quite true of the French reception. On the one hand because two of the three names you mentioned, Baudelaire and Lévi-Strauss, don't seem to me particularly to represent the thought or tradition of the left in France, and on the other hand because the third name, Mallarmé, represents, if one reads the two great texts devoted to Wagner, a great admiration, certainly, but also a very real resistance to Wagner, and specifically to the imperialism of music in Wagner with respect to the other arts. What's very clear in Mallarmé is a defence of poetry against the music drama. Finally, on this question of the left, I think, and this follows a suggestion of Jean-François Lyotard's, who's passed me a note about it, I don't believe that the distinction between left and right has always entirely resisted the political and social explosion or implosion of Nazism. In his note, Lyotard has written: 'In Nazism there were plenty of lefts'. I think that's right, and the revolutionary aspect of Wagner was quite easily mixed in with a *Realpolitik* which we would qualify as being extreme-right — and this is true in many cases in the German tradition.

COMPLEXITY AND THE SUBLIME
Jean-François Lyotard

A large number of questions were raised by panel respondents and by participants from the floor. It will be clear enough from Lyotard's remarks transcribed here what sorts of questions were raised. More specificaclly, Lyotard is here concerned to reply to Terry Eagleton who, among other remarks, expressed doubts about Lyotard's apparent celebration of fragmentation in the name of 'complexification'. Surely late capitalism was doing that for us anyway, and wasn't there a strategic reason to hold onto a traditional view of the subject as a means of providing a critical vantage point on the actual experience of fragmentation in late capitalism? Eagleton also questioned the political implications of Lyotard's exploitation of the notion of the sublime in Burke, recalling that Burke was a reactionary thinker; and later he suggested that by 'sublime' Lyotard meant quite simply 'anti-Leninism'.

In the remark to which Lyotard responds last, Eagleton was suspicious of the apparent ease with which a notion such as that of the class struggle was being passed over, arguing that if it is indeed increasingly difficult to describe events in our late capitalist society in these terms, it would nonetheless be culpably ethnocentric and politically quietist to assume that such notions were obsolete, as could be seen by considering the Third World.

I'd just like to focus what I say around two points. First, the question of complexity, and second, the question of the sublime. I hope that this will allow me to answer, if not the question directly asked, but the question latent in what you were saying: that is, the political question.

Three or four remarks about complexity. What is remarkable (to me, at any rate) in the so-called 'new technologies' is that the machines involved are not substitutes for mechanical operations, but for certain mental and/or linguistic operations. For example: calculation; storage and consultation of information; storage and availability of rules, or literary compositions, and so on. These sorts of machines presuppose a high level of analysis, not only of the mind, but also of matter: that is to say a merging of hard sciences (or sciences of matter generally), and soft sciences. An effect of this merging is that the principle that mind and matter are two different substances (as conceived in Descartes's philosophy, for instance) is less and less convincing. I remember discussing this point with a famous Portuguese epistemologist, Fernando Gil, who told me that contemporary epistemologists are re-reading the philosophy of Leibniz, precisely because in Leibniz there is no substantial difference between mind and matter. This is a sort of anticipation of an idea of complexity. The difference between mind and matter in Leibniz's philosophy is in a sense only a difference of complexity. There are many things to say about this, but I don't have the time now.

The overlapping of mind and matter in contemporary techno-science is the aspect we were particularly concerned to emphasize in the exhibition *Les Immatériaux*. We were trying to exhibit, not the unpresentable, and to that extent it is not a sublime exhibition, but the retreat of the traditional division between mind and matter; what is important now is this sort of continuity between mind and matter. Maybe the human mind is simply the most complex combination of matter in the universe. We're all very eager to meet somebody else in the universe who achieves the same level of complexity. Maybe our task is just that of complexifying the complexity we are in charge of. Perhaps this is a materialist point of view, but only if we see matter not as a substance, but as a series of invisible and ungraspable elements organized by abstract structures. So we can be materialists today and in a sense maybe we must be. But within this horizon, the development of techno-science induces a slow but profound transformation of our conception of the relationship between man and nature.

I have no time to discuss this further. Are you aware of how lack of time — in general and in particular — is characteristic of postmodern man (quite different in this respect from modern man): becauase we have, in every situation, to challenge time: and why? The answer Terry

Eagleton would give is that it's the fault of capitalism. Particularly of late capitalism. I've something to say about the new technologies and late capitalism.

I have a long past as a Marxist militant (not just academic and formal Marxism), and I do not forget the problems posed by suffering, by working-conditions, by contradictions within capitalism, and by unemployment. I would add, by the increasing discrepancy between North and South or, if you prefer, between the Third World and our world. Let me simply make three observations.

First, the complexification due to new technologies in both everyday life and the work-process (and working conditions) makes this traditional province of Marxism more and more important and serious. It is obvious for example that the level of unemployment foreseen by Marx — and created not by the crisis of capitalism but by the development of capitalism — is today a reality. And we have no solution to that. I think this will be the main problem for the next century because it's impossible to consider a mankind in which only one person in ten is working. It's perfectly possible to elaborate this problem in Marxist terms.

But the major question is the second one, and that's my question: is capitalism as such responsible for the development of techno-sciences? At first glance it seems obvious, because it's obvious that the funds are given to research by capitalists or official institutions. But the reality is quite different, because these institutions are obliged to provide that funding if they are to survive. And the result of research in techniques and sciences is destabilizing not only our everyday life but even the traditional institutions (be they political or economic). So — this is just a hypothesis — isn't it more something of an obscure desire which produces this development of techno-science: an obscure desire towards extra sophistication? And isn't it desire (and I could produce many texts of Marx to ground this hypothesis) which seizes hold of the capitalist organization of current society (and maybe minds), to assume the task of complexification? We can perhaps consider human history as a series of attempts at organizing human society and minds, *not* in order to achieve freedom or happiness or anything like that (human aims), but just to achieve the infinite task of complexification. This is just a hypothesis, and a metaphysical one, at that.

As for the sublime, there are a lot of questions about this, but I think it's necessary first of all to fix what we mean by 'sublime'. The most important factor in the conception of the sublime is not whether it comes from Aristotle or anybody else — that doesn't matter — but with the importance given to this term and the whole problematic philosophical cluster of words around this term. With the idea of the sublime, the feeling when faced with a work of art is no longer the feeling of pleasure, or not simply one of pleasure. It is a contradictory feeling, because it is a feeling of both pleasure and displeasure, together. When you read Burke, for example, the importance Burke gives to the question of terror as a necessary component of the feeling of the sublime is remarkable. This aspect presupposes the necessity of rebuilding the idea of the mind, and of rethinking the importance of death in life, because terror (through many expressions — lack of light, lack of words, lack of sounds) is a feeling of the imminence of death.

With the sublime, the question of death enters the aesthetic question. Certainly this was the case with Aristotle's poetics of tragedy, no problem with that; but it wasn't the major aspect of the total Greek practice of art. With this idea of death in the feelings of the spectator or listener of romantic or pre-romantic works, the idea of the sublime comes to the fore in the work of Kant, even more than in the work of Burke. This question, with its component of death or terror, also poses the problem of what is a human community. With the sublime, there is no criterion for assessing the role of taste, and so everybody is alone when it comes to judging. The question then becomes: how can we share with others a feeling which is so deep and unexchangeable?

In Kant's philosophy, for example, the answer is very important. He says that an aesthetic feeling is something different from an individual feeling: it's quite different to say 'that painting is beautiful', and to say 'this steak is beautiful'. It's not the same to say 'I like Cézanne' and 'I like rice'. The difference resides in the fact that in the first case there is a sort of pretension to universalise the feeling.

When we say 'That's beautiful', it signifies, necessarily, that the beauty is to be recognized by every human being. But, says Kant, we know (and it seems to me he's quite right) it is impossible to obtain a consensus about a painting, for example, in the same terms and with the same procedure as in the sciences, for example. So we are obliged to say, concludes Kant, that this feeling demands, and in a sense promises, community. But this community is yet to be. It is not realized. For the first time, maybe, communities begin to conceive themselves in terms of promise, in terms of obligation, and in so doing they are conscious of not being real.

By this means, I would like to point to the very important question which commands the political questions asked in the discussion: 'Is it possible to continue to say what society is in a conceptual way?' as though we were ever going to be able to show anything experiential to correspond to this term, to prove what we are talking about. Nobody has ever *seen* a society. Nobody has ever *seen* a beginning. An end. Nobody has ever *seen* a world. In this case, can we have a sensory intuition of what these questions are about? The answer implied in the critical approach (in Kant's sense) is, no, it's impossible, they are Ideas of Reason (of *Reason*, they're not fantasms). We must consider these Ideas *as* Ideas if we are to avoid illusion: they are like guiding threads, and this is, in particular, the case for the Idea of freedom.

I would say to Terry Eagleton that the same goes for the idea of the proletariat. Nobody has ever seen a proletariat (Marx said this): you can observe working-classes, certainly, but they are only part of the observable society. It's impossible to argue that this part of society is the incarnation of a proletariat, because an Idea in general has no presentation, and *that is the question of the sublime.* How must we read Marx today? That's the question. I'm sure we have to read and re-read Marx, but in a critical way: that is, we must say that the question of the proletariat is the question of knowing whether this word is to be understood in terms of the Hegelian dialectic (that is to say, in the end, in terms of science), expecting to find something experiential to correspond to the concept, and maybe to be the concept itself; or is the term 'proletariat' the name of an

Idea of Reason, the name of a subject to be emancipated? In the second case we give up the pretension of presenting something in experience which corresponds to this term.

Terry Eagleton objects because I use Burke even though Burke was a reactionary. It's true. But remember that Burke is a very strange case: he both opened the new romantic aesthetics, and he is also one of the most important reactionary philosophers of modern times. How is it possible to pursue these two positions? I think he was perfectly aware of this, and although I don't share Burke's view of the French Revolution, nevertheless, and I'm guided in this direction by Kant's analysis of the same question, I think he was aware (and Kant certainly was) of the danger of practising a politics of the sublime. That is to say, to make the terrible mistake of trying to present in political practice an Idea of Reason. To be able to say, 'We are the proletariat', or 'We are the incarnation of free humanity', and so on. Kant understood perfectly that that's what had happened to the French Revolution. Maybe Burke too was aware of this danger.

This is precisely what has happened during the last two centuries. So I think the right position from which to criticize modernity, as a sort of paranoia (the pretension of presenting an Idea of Reason is something like paranoia) is not to use something like phenomenology, hermeneutics, and so on, because they are in the same frame. I think the right position is to carry out an *anamnesis* of criticism itself (in Kant's sense). This doesn't mean a return to an academic reading of Kant. But a real anamnesis of the idea of criticism, and that is what we have to build.

I also have something to say to the questioner who said that the sublime in Kant is always limited and absorbed by the idea of a law-governed universe. Certainly not. Not at all. In Burke as well as in Kant, the sublime emerges when there is no longer a beautiful form. Kant himself said that the feeling of the sublime is the feeling of something monstrous. *Das Unform.* Formless. The retreat of regulation and rules is the cause of the feeling of the sublime. That's what I was trying to say with the idea of death. It is also the death of God (I don't suppose Philippe Lacoue-Labarthe would agree with me, because this is of course exactly Nietzsche's position).

. . . What is the sublime in Marx? Very precisely it is to be found at the point he calls labour force. In the correspondence with Engels, Marx says: I've just re-read Aristotle, and I've found that the concept of *dynamis* is going to be very useful to me. And in fact he starts off by calling labour force 'labour power' (*puissance*). This is a metaphysical notion. And within metaphysics, it is a notion which designates what is not determinate. What is not present and supports presence. You know the importance of this notion in the Marxist theory of value and of exploitation. If there is exploitation, this is because the labour force of the worker allows him to produce more value than he costs his employer during his time of work. The whole theory of exploitation rests on this idea, which is sublime.

This has a lot to do with the question of political quietism. The question is that of ethnocentrism. I understood from what Terry Eagleton said that he thinks that it is indeed difficult to talk about class struggle in our societies, but that it continues in the Third World. I'm simplifying, but that's what I understood him to be saying. I think this is completely false, and that this is part of the question we have to confront. For Marxism, the class struggle has never been the struggle of the poor against the rich. Marx saw very clearly that the poor can very well produce reactionary institutions, as well as revolutionary institutions. For Marx, the class struggle was the struggle of the exploited in industrial conditions: in the situation I've just recalled. When labour-force is exploited in conditions of wage-labour. I don't have to restate that theory: Marx is quite clear on this point. Basically, according to Marx, the condition of wage-labour is a condition of univeralization of struggles. Poverty and the struggles of the poor are not conditions of universalization: to the contrary, rather. They're conditions of localisation and of return to traditional identities. Today we know that a large number of Third World struggles do indeed give rise to reactionary governments and sometimes bloody regimes. I protest against the idea that political progressivism consists in referring to the poor of the Third World the revolutionary task. I think that if the intellectuals of developed countries carry out this operation, then they are behaving in an absolutely irresponsible manner. Their task is that of confronting this question head on, and of elaborating it, not of passing it on to others untouched.

This does not mean that we don't have to concern ourselves with Third World struggles. But we can only help them on an *ethical* basis, not a political one. As a long-standing militant, I helped, for example, the struggle of the Algerians, but knowing very well that nothing revolutionary would come out of that struggle. I mean in terms of a revolutionary government or in terms of an expansion of that struggle. We knew — I say we because I wasn't alone — we knew very well that this government would give Algeria its identity, but no more, and that we couldn't expect a socialist revolution to come from that struggle. So one can contribute and help on an ethical basis. But that basis must not be confused with a political line. I think that the intellectuals should carry out this work of distinction between discursive genres (here the ethical and the political): that's part of the complexification of our situation.

. . . All of this forms a continuity for me. The difficulty I've just pointed out with respect to the question of a political line, and in particular of an intellectual politics, weighs on the failure of the universal, as Marx conceived of it in the figure of the proletariat, the industrial waged worker. We must recognize that Marxism is one of the versions of the Enlightenment. What *we* don't have is that universalization. I think that this underlies everything Kenneth Frampton says and particularly his idea of a critical regionalism. The very notion of region (which is ambiguous — even in Kenneth Frampton's thought — because it is both phenomenological and geo-political) is the mark of the fact that even when it comes to building we don't have a universal idea.

FROM POST-STRUCTURALISM TO POSTMODERNITY: HABERMAS'S COUNTER-PERSPECTIVE*
Peter Dews

In recent years some intriguing — and occasionally startling — realignments have taken place between the major language-based traditions of European and North American philosophy. Analytical philosophy, whose origins stretch back to the logical enquiries into language initiated by Frege, Russell and Wittgenstein at the beginning of the century, continues to predominate in the English-speaking world — but it is difficult to escape the impression that the somewhat myopic self-confidence which sustained analytical philosophy throughout the immediate post-war period and into the 1970s has begun to falter. This shift of climate has been reflected in the international success of works such as Richard Rorty's *Philosophy and the Mirror of Nature* and Hilary Putnam's *Reason, Truth and History*, in which respected analytical philosophers have taken a certain distance from their tradition — in the first case by tracing the process of internal critique through which analytical philosophy has come to challenge and undermine even its own most central assumptions, and in the second by opening out analytical arguments towards the hermeneutic and historically-informed perspectives of continental thought. Rorty and Putnam, however, are merely among the most prominent of those — particularly younger — analytical philosophers

* Parts of this article are extracted from the Introduction to Jürgen Habermas, *Autonomy and Solidarity: Interviews*, published by Verso Editions. Reproduced by kind permission of the publisher.

who have begun, if not to abandon their tradition, at least to acquire a stronger sense of its relativity, and to take an interest in the illumination which the writings of a Foucault or Derrida, a Gadamer or Apel, can bring to their concerns.

In France a similar crisis of confidence can be detected in relation to the remarkable flourishing of thought which spanned the 1960s and 1970s, and which has come to be known by the overlapping labels of 'structuralism' and 'post-structuralism'. In the mid seventies the febrile and journalistic — but nevertheless culturally symptomatic — phenomenon of the 'New Philosophers' forced onto the agenda questions of moral and political principle which had been evaded during the heady years of theoretical experimentation. The result was a shattering of the cohesiveness of the avant-garde ethos of post-structuralism, making possible the re-appraisal and reappropriation of a variety of neglected and marginalized traditions. There has been, for example, a revival of sympathy for phenomenological and existential thought, exemplified by a new interest in the work of Merleau-Ponty, while the current preoccupation with questions of ethics and political rights has been reflected in the rising prestige of Emmanuel Levinas, and in widespread discussion of the philosophy of Kant, who has returned to fashion for the first time since the French Hegel-renaissance of the 1930s. On the foreign front, the appearance of translations of the major texts of Critical Theory during the 1970s has made it possible for the Frankfurt School to evoke a wider resonance in France, particularly the work of Adorno, whose affinities with post-structuralist themes have become increasingly apparent; analytical philosophy, too, has begun to find a broader following, and in some cases to be integrated with more specifically French concerns. In general, French philosophy has become more conscious of its own former subjection to fashion, and more permeable to those major currents of post-war European thought which its vanguardist insularity had previously excluded.

Finally, West Germany also currently presents a similar picture of cross-fertilization. Analytical philosophy has long been part of the intellectual scene in the Federal Republic, but it is only comparatively recently that post-structuralist styles of thought have been taken up to any significant effect. Structuralism met with comparatively little success in Germany; its anti-historical and positivist features inevitably appeared naïve to a culture so imbued with the outlook of historicism and idealism. Gradually, however, it became apparent that post-structuralism was no mere continuation of structuralism, but could be more appropriately considered as an imaginative reworking of the thought of Nietzsche and Heidegger, and a contemporary restatement of their critique of the Enlightenment heritage. The appreciation of these connections and affinities with German traditions has produced some of the most penetrating commentary on recent French thought so far written,[1] while the characteristic attitudes of post-structuralism have penetrated into the wider culture, as they already have in other European countries, intersecting with more indigenous concerns, such as the revival of interest in the relation of myth and reason, a topic which dates back to the early German Romantics. This complex international situation of shifting interactions and alliances has recently been summarized by one observer in the following way: 'A peculiar syncretism is also becoming widespread in philosophy. Everywhere things are being taken up which had been repressed up till now, often hastily and with an undiscriminating simultaneity: in Paris Leo Strauss and Hannah Arendt, Popper and Adorno; in Berkeley and in Frankfurt Levi-Strauss, Foucault and Derrida — and everywhere Feyerabend and Rorty, seasoned with a pinch of Quine and Putnam.'[2]

Perhaps more than any other single thinker, Jürgen Habermas, the author of this snapshot of the *Zeitgeist*, could be said to stand at the crossroads of these developments. Habermas is well-known as the leading contemporary representative of the Frankfurt School tradition, and as such he stands at the centre of debates — which have been intense in recent years — concerning the continued viability of a distinctively Western Marxism. However, in contrast to the founders of Critical Theory, who tended to operate with a comparatively narrow set of canonical texts, Habermas has opened up the tradition to a productive interchange with the major currents of contemporary Western philosophy and sociology. In a series of theoretical

encounters, Habermas has sought to defend the central
insights and emphases of Critical Theory, while nevertheless always learning something of permanent value from his
opponents. Thus, in the early 1960s, he was involved with
Theodor Adorno in the 'positivist dispute', a debate with
Karl Popper and his adherents over the philosophical
foundations of the social sciences. Yet, while firmly
defending a dialectical conception of social science against
the technocratic thrust of Popperian 'critical rationalism',
Habermas did acquire from Popper an enduring awareness
of the fallibility of all knowledge claims, which marks him
off both from earlier Critical Theory and — as we shall see
— from the leading post-structuralists. Similarly, Gadamer's powerful restatement of the tradition of hermeneutic
thought in *Truth and Method* aided Habermas to formulate
his critique of Wittgenstein, and to specify his objections
to a positivist conception of the social sciences. Yet
Habermas has also been a leading critic of the universal
claims which Gadamer has made for hermeneutics, arguing
that such an approach cannot decipher the power-relations
which stand behind 'systematically distorted communication'. During the 1970s Habermas's reading of systems-
theory, in particular the work of Talcott Parsons and Niklas
Luhmann, enabled him to establish a distinction between
social complexity and class-domination, whose absence in
the work of Marx — he now believes — has generated a
damaging ambiguity in much Marxist thought. Nevertheless he has continued to criticize systems theory for its
inadequate equation of social evolution with an increasing
capacity for adaptation. Finally, and most recently,
Habermas has addressed himself to the antecedents and
implications of post-structuralist thought in a book of
lectures entitled '*The Philosophical Discourse of Modernity*'. In
this last case however, despite his genuine tributes to
Foucault, Habermas leaves the impression of having far less
to learn from his opponents — more than any other of his
major writings, *Der Philosophische Diskurs der Moderne* is a
combative work. The reason for this difference of tone is
readily apparent. For whereas the insights of other thinkers
with whom he has engaged — however different their
explicit political intentions — could be incorporated
within the overall project of a defence and continuation of

the radical traditions of the Enlightenment, albeit a late twentieth-century defence which takes full account of the Enlightenment's darker side, post-structuralist modes of thought imply a direct assault on the central concepts of the Enlightenment heritage. It is here, where the very viability of modernity is put into question, that Habermas — in opposition to the dominant mood — is obliged to stand his ground.

The clash with post-structuralism

With hindsight, it is apparent that there is a sense in which this clash with post-structuralism — however long in arriving — was inscribed in the respective origins of Habermas's work, and of the dominant currents of French philosophy in the 1960s and 1970s. Habermas began from a sense of the desirability and necessity of a continuation of the Western Marxist tradition, derived from an early reading of Lukács' *History and Class-Consciousness*, combined with a strong awareness that the Hegelian structures of this form of the philosophy of praxis, the reliance on an objective dialectics of class consciousness and — ultimately — on a philosophy of history, were no longer viable. In fact, as Habermas suggests, by the early 1940s classical Critical Theory had already been forced to confront these problems, and subsequently expended much energy in the search for a solution. The basic dilemma is clear in a text such as Horkheimer's *Eclipse of Reason*, whose argument hangs suspended between a critique of the restriction of reason to its subjective or instrumental aspect, and an attack on attempts to revive a conception of reason as objective, as embodied in the order of the world. In the work of Marcuse, the most affirmative and politically robust of the first generation of Critical Theorists, an escape-route is eventually found in the form of a Freudian-inspired theory of human instincts which lie below the level of historical revolutions, and which can therefore safeguard the promise of a repeatedly betrayed utopia. At the other extreme, Adorno developed a position, during the latter part of his career, which strips the philosophy of history of any optimistic residue, and which paradoxically suggests that it is the very experience of the extinction of critique which alone preserves its possibility. When Habermas began to formulate his own version of Critical Theory in the late 1950s, therefore, he was affiliating to a tradition in which — as recent French enthusiasm for Adorno's 'critique of Marxism' makes clear — the central assumptions of Hegelian–Marxist theory had already been subjected to a searching re-evaluation. Far from involving any return to orthodoxy, his continuation of this tradition has to a large extent been concerned with the problem of restoring, by new philosophical means, the normative basis of critique, which was demolished when the original Frankfurt School abandoned the 'historico-philosophical' conception of reason.

France, in the 1950s and early 1960s, was also home to a strong current of the Marxist philosophy of praxis, although one more phenomenologically and existentially coloured than its German counterpart — more indebted to Alexandre Kojève than to Georg Lukács. In this milieu, too, there was opposition to 'Eastern' Marxism, in the form of the dialectical materialism of an influential Communist Party, combined with attempts to grapple with the problems of a materialist philosophy of history. Maurice Merleau-Ponty struggled to define the status of a 'meaning' of history which would be neither arbitrarily subjective nor remorselessly objective, but was ultimately driven to the conclusion that the fatal flaw of Marxism consisted in its belief that the negativity of social critique could be embodied in a concrete historical agency — breaking off, in fact, where the later Adorno began. Sartre, in the *Critique of Dialectical Reason*, made a heroically over-ambitious attempt to overcome the speculative character of the Marxist philosophy of history by showing how the overall movement of history could be assembled step by step from its smallest, phenomenologically translucent component, the praxis of the human individual. In a similarly experimental vein, the *Arguments* group, which published an influential review from 1956 to 1962, developed an open Marxism capable of integrating existential, psychoanalytical and anthropological perspectives, and indeed were among the first thinkers in France to take an active interest in, and to publish work by, the Frankfurt School.

Even as these philosophical explorations and revisions of Marxism were taking place, however, a handful of younger French thinkers had already become convinced that the Gordian knot must be cut — that Marxism was inescapably burdened with an unjustifiable belief in the rationality of the historical process, and that only Nietzsche could provide the tools with which to break out of the entire modern problematic of teleological subjectivity. Michel Foucault has recalled how, in the mid 1950s, an encounter with Nietzsche enabled him to escape from what he refers to as 'Hegelianism and historicism', and in fact — it could be argued — set the basic co-ordinates of his entire subsequent intellectual development. Gilles Deleuze's suspicion of phenomenology and dialectics can be traced back even further, to his post-graduate days in the 1940s, although it was not until 1962, with the publication of *Nietzsche and Philosophy*, that he produced a book which explicitly mobilized Nietzschean motifs against any form of dialectical thought, including that of Marxism. For most of the 1960s these anticipatory developments underwent a kind of 'latency period', while the temporary enthusiasm for a positivistic structuralism waxed and waned. But they irrupted with full force in the wake of May '68, leading to the generalized post-structuralist assault on the 'repressive' character of philosophical conceptions of reason and truth, and eventually to an explicit repudiation of Marxism. Thus, during the two decades in which Habermas, through a wide-ranging series of enquiries and debates, was attempting to renew the project of Critical Theory, as the most advanced and self-critical outpost of the Enlightenment heritage, French thought turned against any such reconstruction, and moved towards a denunciation of the 'totalitarianism' of Enlightenment, indeed of the 'Western metaphysical tradition' as a whole.

For nearly twenty years these two contrasting philosophical projects pursued their very different directions in isolation. By the end of the 1970s, however, objective pressures had built up, of both a theoretical and a political nature, which were pressing towards a confrontation. During the 1970s post-structuralist thought, both at home and abroad, had been the vehicle for generic radical sentiment, with an emphasis on the 'liberatory' breaking-down of academic compartmentalizations, and on the fictionalizing release of an expressive subjectivity. However, a host of unresolved tensions were implicit in this attempt to employ Nietzsche for critical and libertarian purposes. For, as the 'New Philosophers' were among the first to point out, there was little to separate this 'left Nietzscheanism' from an amoral individualism; and the unmasking of all truths as effects of power could all too easily be reversed — as it is in Nietzsche himself — into an elevation of power as the only criterion of truth. It is this situation which helps to explain the appearance in 1979 of two books by Jean-François Lyotard, whose history of activism on the far-left had always marked him out as the most politically alert and concerned of recent French philosophers. In one of these texts, *Au Juste*, which is cast in discussion format, Lyotard introduces the concept of justice and struggles with the problem of how a political account of this concept can be developed on an anti-universalist and anti-rationalist basis. In the second book, *The Postmodern Conditon*,[3] Lyotard attempts to connect this conception of justice to a broad characterisation of the present age and its political possibilities, which is nevertheless organised around a post-structuralist suspicion of comprehensive and unifying perspectives. In this respect *The Postmodern Condition* formed a kind of turn-of-the-decade bridge between the self-consciously fragmented critique of reason of the 1970s, and the return to larger-scale considerations of modernity, and of the conceptual foundations of post-Enlightenment politics, which have become an important strand of French thought in the 1980s.[3] This attempt to provide a general account of the demise of modernity also obliged Lyotard to engage directly with Habermas's work. Indeed, *The Postmodern Condition* can in large part be read as an attempt to steer a third course between technocratic consciousness and its supposedly outdated opponent, Critical Theory, and in particular as an attack on the Habermasian linkage of justice and consensus.

On the opposite front, it was again not until the late 1970s that Habermas became aware of the need to take an explicit stand on the question of post-structuralism. During the 1960s Habermas had engaged with Nietzsche's thought — *Knowledge and Human Interests* contains a

discussion of Nietzsche, and in 1968 he had appended a
critically sympathetic postscript to a volume of Nietzsche's
writings on the theory of knowledge, which he edited.[4]
During most of the following decade however, Habermas
— as the director of a research institute — was absorbed in
an ambitious collaborative programme to reformulate
historical materialism as a theory of social evolution, and
did not pay a great deal of attention to developments in
French philosophy. But it gradually became clear that the
spread of post-structuralist styles of thought was an integral
part of the *Tendenzwende*, the major shift of political and
intellectual climate in West Germany which began during
the second half of the 1970s, and that the arguments of the
post-structuralists demanded a considered reply. In 1980
Habermas delivered a lecture in which he suggested that
the post-structuralists could be viewed as 'Young Conservatives', who 'on the basis of modernistic attitudes . . .
justify an irreconcileable anti-modernism',[5] and this somewhat casual aside evoked an unexpectedly widespread and
vehement response, including a broadside from Lyotard in
the essay on postmodernism which concludes *The Postmodern Condition*. In proposing that the radical credentials of
post-structuralism should not be taken so readily for
granted, Habermas undoubtedly touched a raw point of
contemporary intellectual life. Since then, a widespread
international debate has developed around these questions,
including most recently an exchange between Lyotard and
Rorty, Habermas own book on the discourse of modernity,
and contributions by other defenders of the Critical Theory
position.[6] Indeed much of the contemporary shifting of
philosophical fronts, which was evoked at the beginning of
this article, can be seen as taking place around a single
central preoccupation: the question of whether we are
currently experiencing the final exhaustion of the project of
the Enlightenment, or whether our present discontents and
disillusionments stem from the fact that this project has
only been onesidedly and inadequately realized. The
question, in other words, of modernity and postmodernity.

Postmodernist Thought and Critical Theory

In the space available here, it would be impossible to explore the many ramifications of this debate. Instead, I would like to concentrate briefly on one of the key areas of disagreement between postmodernist thought and Critical Theory: the relation between the problem of systematicity and universality in philosophy, and the social and epistemological fragmentation which is taken to be characteristic of postmodernity. It is clear, from *The Postmodern Condition*, that the concept of a 'language-game' borrowed from Wittgenstein, performs a dual function in Lyotard's thought, both aspects of which can be traced back to Nietzsche's critique of traditional philosophy. On the one hand, Lyotard employs the concept ontologically, in order to describe an unstable, heteromorphous, dispersed social reality which cannot be captured within the totalizing format of a 'grand narrative' — this strategy derives from Nietzsche's contention that no comprehensive system can exhaust a world of endless becoming. On the other hand, Lyotard also employs the concept of a language-game epistemologically, in order to bolster a Nietzsche-inspired assault on any putatively universal truth. It is evident, however, that there is a tension — not to say contradiction — between these two usages, which parallels the tension in Nietzsche's work between the doctrine of the 'eternal return' and that of the 'will to power'. For, if his account of postmodernity is to be sustained, then Lyotard cannot admit that his own language-game pluralism is itself merely perspectival. This difficulty emerges clearly when Lyotard remarks that 'One can occasionally add together or even combine efforts and effects, mix particular narratives and their enactments, but it is contrary to realism, which is pagan, to totalize them on a long-term basis.'[7] The invocation of 'realism' in this context appears bizarre.

For Habermas, by contrast, it is not systematicity as such which poses the problem, but the fact that philosophical systems — interpretations of the world as a whole — were based upon a fundamental principle immunized against critical probing, that philosophy traditionally conceived itself as a discourse operating at a level entirely distinct from that of empirical confirmation or disconfirmation. Habermas shares with the post-structuralists a sense of the crisis of philosophy after Hegel, of its struggle to step over into another medium. But he continues the materialist argument of the original Frankfurt School in suggesting that this medium must be constituted by a collaboration between philosophy and empirical social science. Through such a co-operation, philosophy preserves the social and human sciences from empiricist and elementarist myopia, while the sciences lend philosophy a substantive, but non-dogmatic, content. For Habermas, in other words, it is not the *universality* of philosophical truth-claims which is to be abandoned, but rather their non-fallibilist aspect. Post-structuralism, however, is driven into an abandonment of systematic cognitive claims, indeed, because of its hostility to the universal, frequently into a quasi-aesthetic suspension of truth claims as such. The result of this manoeuvre, however, is that genuine attempts at social and cultural analysis become vulnerable to anecdotal and inadequately theorized evidence, a fact which explains the constitutive vagueness and portentousness of general accounts of postmodernity. Indeed, this vulnerability can be seen in the diffusion of the term postmodernism itself. In the domains of architecture and the visual arts, the word possesses a more or less determinate meaning, referring to a renunciation and critique of distinct traditions, of a levelling technocratic functionalism in architecture, and of a programme of negation in modernist art which led from abstract expressionism, through minimalism, to conceptual art. It is certainly the case that these localized crises are symptomatic of more fundamental problems of modernity, problems of technology, of aesthetic experience and commodification, of environmentalism and democratic control. But this in itself does not justify the inflation of the term 'postmodernity' into the diagnosis of an epoch, an announcement of the collapse of the 'Enlightenment project' as a whole.

One cannot, in other words, provide a coherent account of postmodernity without a determinate concept of modernity; and such a concept cannot be developed a priori, but is necessarily dependent on the theorization of long-term historical processes, of the kind which Habermas attempts in his reconstruction of historical materialism. Lyotard and other contemporary thinkers often seem to ignore this basic requirement, assuming that it is sufficient to recite the disasters of the twentieth century in order to blacken the entire Enlightenment heritage. At the crudest level, this position appears to imply a denial of the meaningfulness of any counterfactual history, the belief that no epoch can contain possibilities other than those which have been actually realized. Thus Lyotard affirms — in explicit opposition to Habermas — that 'Modernity . . . is not "incomplete", rather it has been liquidated. After Auschwitz and Stalinism it is certain that no-one can maintain that the hopes which were bound up with modernity have been fulfilled. To be sure, they have not been forgotten, but rather destroyed.'[8] The implausibility of this argument is intensified by the fact that it is only in the light of the democratic and humanitarian aspirations of the Enlightenment that fascism and Stalinism appear in their full horror. In general, the discourse of postmodernity, in its constant oscillations between depression and exhilaration, its bitter-sweet ambivalence, provides evidence in favour of Habermas's contention that modern consciousness is essentially constituted by an intersection of historical and utopian perspectives, the one — for example, in the form of the memory of political disasters which Lyotard evokes — providing a necessary ballast for the other. For Habermas, what has been exhausted is not utopian energies as such, but a particular model of utopia based on the notion of self-realization through labour, which is dubious both in its philosophico–anthropological origins, and in its lack of purchase on contemporary industrial processes. However, whether the decline of this particular model of self-realizing subjectivity signals a collapse of belief in the possibility of progress as such, depends on one's theoretical conception of the potentials of modernity.

In the case of post-structuralist thought, the rational principle of modernity is equated — although more often implicitly than explicitly — with cognitive-instrumental thought. This then permits post-structuralist theorists to invoke the characteristic experiences of aesthetic modernism — of a subjectivity freed from the demands of utility and morality — as the radical other of Enlightenment reason and societal modernization. In viewing cultural modernity as a disruptive intruder, post-structuralism curiously coincides with neo-conservatism, although the polarity of values is reversed from one position to the other. For the neo-conservatives the spread of life-styles and attitudes inspired by aesthetic modernism poses a threat to the ideology of achievement and obedience which is essential to the continuing process of capitalist modernization. For post-structuralism, by contrast, the celebration of the untamed energies of mind and body — of madness, intensity; desire — is the only means of opposing a modernity conceptualized exclusively in terms of economic and administrative rationalization. It is important to note that Habermas by no means underestimates the emancipatory potential of modern culture, although he would argue — against the one-sidedness of post-structuralism — that a concern for human and civil rights, and for democratic self-determination, is no less central to cultural modernity than the values of expressive subjectivity. Habermas even accepts that the contemporary 'cult of immediacy, the deflation of noble forms, anarchism of the soul, the celebration of the concrete all along the line, relativism even in the theory of science' must be respected as expressions of 'the need for concretion, the wish for engagement, the attempt to test the critical content of ideas here and now, to take ideas seriously in the way one lives one's life.'[9] What he refuses to accept, however, is that the immediacy and experiential adequacy which has enabled post-structuralist thought to hold up a mirror to contemporary processes of fragmentation, loss of identity, and libidinal release, to provide something like the 'natural' descriptive vocabulary for the culture of advanced consumer capitalism, can provide an adequate substitute for a theoretical understanding of the present. His work is a testimony to the fact that systematic ambitions can be combined with empirical flexibility, that a 'grand narrative' can be developed which is neither 'metaphysical', nor authoritarian, nor insensitive to the complexities of contemporary societies.

Notes

1. An outstanding example is Manfred Frank, *Was ist Neostrukturalismus?*, Frankfurt 1983.

2. Jürgen Habermas, 'Untiefen der Rationalitätskritik', in *Die Neue Unübersichtlichkeit*, Frankfurt 1985, p. 113.

3. For a brief overview of developments in French thought in the 1980s, see Olivier Mongin, 'Dégénérescence Intellectuelle où Régénération?', in *Esprit* 8–9, August–September 1985, pp. 109–118.

4. Reprinted as 'Zu Nietzsches Erkenntnistheorie', in Jürgen Habermas, *Kultur und Kritik*, Frankfurt 1973, pp. 239–263.

5. Jürgen Habermas, 'Modernity — An Incomplete Project', in Hal Foster, ed., *Postmodern Culture*, London 1985, p. 14.

6. See Jean-François Lyotard, 'Histoire Universelle et Differences Culturelles', and Richard Rorty, 'Le Cosmopolitisme sans Emancipation', followed by an exchange between Lyotard and Rorty, in *Critique*, no. 456, 1985. For the Critical Theory position see Axel Honneth, 'Der Affekt gegen das Allgemeine: Zu Lyotards Konzept der Postmoderne', in *Merkur*, December 1984, pp. 893–902; and, most notably, Albrecht Wellmer, *Zur Dialektik von Moderne und Postmoderne*, Frankfurt 1985. The title essay of this collection has been translated as 'On the Dialectic of Modernism and Postmodernism', *Praxis International*, Vol. 4, no. 4, pp. 337–362.

7. Jean-François Lyotard, *Instructions Paiennes*, Paris 1977, pp. 83–4.

8. Jean-François Lyotard, 'Sprache, Zeit, Arbeit', in Lyotard et al., *Immaterialität und Postmoderne*, Berlin 1985, pp. 37–38.

9. Jürgen Habermas, 'Einleitung zum Band 1000 der edition suhrkamp', in *Kleine Politische Schriften I–IV*, Frankfurt 1981, p. 436.

SPIDER AND BEE: TOWARDS A CRITIQUE OF THE POSTMODERN IDEOLOGY
J.G. Merquior

The postmodern label has been attached to at least three things:

(a) a style or a mood born of the exhaustion of, and dissatisfaction with, modernism in art and literature;
(b) a trend in French philosophy, or, more specifically, in poststructuralist theory;
(c) the latest cultural age in the West.

Central to (b) seems to be the assertion of (c). But the more one shifts from sense (a) to senses (b) and (c), the more conceptual problems arise: lots of questions tend to be begged in both the description and the evaluation of postmodern art and thought. Let's try and spell out some of them.

The concept of a postmodern trend in art history — where the label was first lodged, chiefly in connection with architecture — is obviously predicated on the claim of decisive differences between several contemporary works and movements and the intentions and achievements of the modernist avant-garde in the earlier part of the century. Yet postmodern art is anything but uniform. Christopher Butler rightly discerned in it a dialectic between over-organisation and deliberate disorder: in literature, it would correspond to the scions of *Finnegans Wake* as against the descendants of Pound's *Cantos*.

I can see their opposition rather than their dialectic mediation. Actually there seem to be *two main programmes in postmodern aesthetics*. On the one hand, there is a stress on structure. Octavio Paz, for one, sees structuralist poetics as dropping one of the two great principles animating western art from romanticism on, the first of such principles being the language of *analogy* (directed against *analysis*, the spirit of science and mainstream modern thought); and the second being the constant exercise of *irony*, a relentless self-deprecation dictated by the restlessness of a transcendental consciousnes — the Faustian cast of mind of modern man. According to Paz, structuralist art keeps analogy but ditches irony: it offers endless transformations of form and meaning unrelated to a transcendental viewpoint or the authority of the self. The 'death of the author' literature is its best-known illustration, starting from the *nouveau roman*.

On the other hand, there are many postmodern currents which stress randomness rather than structure, as in the music of Cage, the texts of Burroughs, the living theatre, etc. Here the relevant opposition would be one between the modernist search for the *new form* and the postmodern lust for the *antiform*. It is now almost fifteen years since Ihab Hassan wrote a masterpiece of conceptual fog on 'the vanishing form' of the 'literature of dismemberment', lumping together Broch and Céline, Iris Murdoch and Günter Grass, Edward Albee and Jerzy Grotowski, and the then new American absurdist novel (Pynchon, Heller, Brautigan and Barthelme) — without forgetting to invoke the holy name of Duchamp. We might summarise the overall difference by saying that postmodern aesthetics allows two self-definitions, one structuralist and the other neo-dadaist.

However, *is postmodern art really so different from modern art?* . . . Some critics hold that it marks a move away from the modernist mix of high seriousness coupled with ideals of formal coherence. Yet modern masters such as Gide and Picasso, Joyce, Klee or Musil desacralised art and defetishised form long ago. Much modern literature substituted a grotesque outlook and a will to parody for the pathos and high-mindedness of romantic and Victorian works: just think of Svevo, Bulgakov or Gombrowicz as compared to Tolstoy, Hardy or Fontane. As noticed by one of the shrewdest analysts of the modernist ethos, Ortega y Gasset (1925), the primacy of the ludic was a watershed between modern and 19th century aesthetic culture (romantic and decadent).

To take another key aspect: postmodernism, at least in its neo-dada dispensation, dotes on a 'beyond the image' horizon. It disembodies the aesthetic from the artistic. Happenings, not works, are the thing. Conceptual art needs no artwork: 'the catalogue is the exhibition'. As mentioned, the ghost of Duchamp haunts postmodernism. But was Duchamp such an odd man out among the modern avant-garde? At any rate, the art-in-the-mind idea was no dadaist monopoly. Worringer — an expressionist theorist if ever there was one — claimed it as part and parcel of modern visual arts as a whole. Again, the borderline between modern and postmodern gets blurred.

There is, therefore, a great deal of continuity between modern and postmodern attitudes towards art. What about their respective worldviews? The modernist mind, wrote Cyril Connolly (*The Modern Movement*, 1965), was a blend of Enlightenment and romantic traits: it combined the scepticism of the former with the passionate intensity and the deep uneasiness about the present age of romanticism. Art criticism as well as literary criticism have long acknowledged that the modernist outlook exacerbated the contestatory animus, the counterculture drive of the romantic tradition: they saw modernism as an art of protest (Herbert Read) given to an utter, primitivistic break with social culture (Lionel Trilling). Modernism was in this sense romanticism with a vengeance. While the first stylistic waves since romanticism were more relaxed in their refusal of modern culture, *modernism declared war on modernity*. It committed the arts to the function of the novel according to Lukács: the pursuit of a quest for values in an (allegedly) valueless society.

It was the intransigence of this cultural rejectionism that goaded the avant-garde into a purist view of the arts. When Loos deprived architecture of ornament, Schoenberg purged music of Wagnerian chromatism, Kandinsky freed painting from sculptural values, Brancusi sought a sculpture shorn of Rodin's pictorialism and the *poésie pure* movement dramatised the difference between verse and statement, underneath all this purism there lurked a puritanism: the fervour of a moral indignation against bourgeois culture. But the point is, throughout two centuries, the gist of advanced aesthetic production has been 'adversary' art. This decisively qualifies Eliot's famous antithesis between modern and romantic on the grounds of impersonality versus subjectivism. Between Edmund Wilson's *Axel's Castle* and Frank Kermode's *Romantic Image*, essential affinities between the romantic and modern aesthetics and poetics have been laid bare.

High Modernism and Social Progress

Now in the case of high modernism, this strong element of *Kulturkritik* became specified in *a code or values often at odds with social progress*. Unlike romantics from Shelley to Heine and Hugo or post-romantics like Ibsen and Zola, most modernists were libertarians in art but outright social reactionaries. One can hardly disagree with John Gross (in his book on Joyce): the democratic temper of *Ulysses* was by no means characteristic of high modernist fiction. But politics apart, the illiberal component was also conspicuous in other, more general aspects of the modernist worldview. For instance, modernism in general intensified romantic claims about art as a vessel of higher truths — something far beyond the sheer vindication of the cognitive relevance of art, denied by scientism. Progressive Victorian intellectuals, e.g., John Mill, detected the epistemological imperialism of German aesthetic theory, the doctrine of Art as Vision. But humanist sages like Matthew Arnold, warned that poetry was about to replace religion as a source of belief and morality. It was no longer enough to learn poetry: it was necessary to learn *from* poetry. Small wonder if, from Mallarmé to Yeats, as from Hermann Hesse to Ernesto Sábato, highbrow literature became a gnostic forge, churning lofty arcane truths to blind mankind. The priestly literati proffered profound verities well above the social creeds. Graphocracy — the rule of the literary elite — became a widespread fantasy of the humanist clerisy, and the avant-garde sect was the perfect graphocratic institution. Surrealism, which initially appeared to be a revolution against all aestheticisms, was in fact the utmost literary gnosis: it promised to put an end to the divorce of art and life by forcibly subjecting the whole of life to radically poetical values. Significantly, whenever leading avant-garde writers eventually accepted social, i.e., extra-literary, creeds, their modernist form mellowed into less harsh techniques: thus, with Eliot turned Christian, or with Brecht turned communist.

Besides being often anti-democratic and prone to graphocracy, the moderns evinced what may be reckoned a structural illiberalism in their very artistic praxis. For modernism generally meant obscurity, 'difficult' art and literature. More often than not, the modern style turned out to be at once *highly impersonal and irretrievably subjectivist*, since the meaning of so many modern works remained out of the reach of most readers and spectators. This threw the modern artist, willy-nilly, into a strongly authoritarian position: modern art was experienced as *a tyranny of the creative imagination* over the public, even the cultivated one. Increasingly, the most advanced among aesthetic humanists, disgruntled as they were at the course of civilisation, proved also embattled against the mind of common man.

Now has postmodernism, in general, deviated from such a pattern? Has it avoided the modernist war against modernity? Has it shunned the illiberal drives of the avant-garde? In literature the situation is somewhat ambiguous. To take the problem of wilful obscurity, one might say that the Borges paradigm cherished by much recent narrative is far less obscure than the Kafka paradigm; but what about the dense progeny of the other model of postmodern prose, Beckett? Equally, poetry from Auden to Enzensberger is at times almost didactically clear; but what of Paul Celan or René Char?

The truth is that *postmodern virtues often aggravate modernist vices*. Consider the postmodern acceleration of ludic experiments. Using Kierkegaard to unmask and debunk Picasso's protean art, Hans Sedlmayr once suggested that instead of seeing the metamorphic binge of the echt modern painter as a joyous outcome of Dionysian vitality, we should see it as the nihilistic result of an empty egotism: the shallow soul of 'aesthetic man' according to the Dane. Fever and Angst instead of bounteous energy — can we say that the frantic experimentalism of the postmodern scene got rid of it?

Then there is the contradiction between self-referring

form and its thorough dependence on interpretation. Are
we any better with the postmodern insistence on metafic-
tional devices? At most, what the postmodern propaganda
has done is to flaunt something just hinted at by the
modernist utopia, namely, that the freedom of arch-
experimental art is a metaphor of social liberation.
Insistence on such a metaphor was at the heart of *Tel Quel*
theory in its strident Maoist stage, by the mid- and late
sixties. Today, however, no one seems eager to buy the
fallacy of mistaking a dubious analogy for a real way of
shaping history. To begin with, we look much more
soberly at revolutionism and the hope for radical, wholesale
change. And we have grown particularly disillusioned by
revolution as a kind of *art pour l'art*, by revolt as ritual, as it
were.

All these queries suggest two conclusions. First, *postmodernism is still largely a sequel to, rather than a denial of,
modernism* — without any visible improvement of it. The
postmodern is at most an ultramodernism — an extremist
remake of avant-garde tics. Epigones are often ultras, and
that is what most postmodern stuff is: hopelessly epigonic,
in both art and theory. Hence the exaltation of marginal,
minor, obsessional lesser gods in the modern pantheon:
Artaud, Roussel, Bataille, Webern, Mondrian, Duchamp.
An art of exhaustion (to quote John Barth) looks for a
pedigree of maniacs and eccentrics, establishing 'alternative' modern traditions in the process. But no matter how
extremist, epigonic art is bound to remain largely
derivative. Therefore, like other premature or misleading
uses of the same prefix (e.g., in 'postindustrial society',
roughly corresponding to postmodernism in my (c) sense),
'postmodern' is to a great extent a bogus concept. Second,
it works as a cultural *ideology* whose function is to conceal
much of what is most debatable in the crooked humanisms
of our time.

I now turn, briefly closing these remarks, to the
relationship between postmodern (a) to (b), that is to say,
to postmodernism as theory, in thinkers as dissimilar as
Foucault, Deleuze, Derrida or Lyotard.

To Habermas, as we have seen, the glory of modern
culture lies in its stubborn Kantian distinction of different,
autonomous value spheres: science, art and morality; and

the danger of modern culture is the recurrent spell of reductionisms: scientism, politism, aestheticism. By the same token, Lenin or Baudelaire and Nietzsche were as reductionist, in their different ways, as the positivists, old and new. Consequently postmodern thought, Nietzschean to the marrow, is a betrayal of what is worthiest in modern culture.

Let me take off from this Habermasian ground. We can, I submit, go further along this line and see the postmodern *skepsis* — the typical deletion or suspension of notions like objective truth or universality of meaning — as *a modernist invasion of theory by aesthetic concepts*; or, if you prefer, as a surrender of 'ideas' to the ethos of 'form'. Postmodern thought is the habitat of metamorphic Wittgensteinians, for whom truth and meaning are just *ad hoc* functions of infinitely transformable language games.

Perhaps you care to recall that in *The Battle of the Books* (1704), his satirical contribution to the quarrel of the ancients nad the moderns, Swift has Aesop compare the moderns to spiders, spinning their scholastics out of their own bellies, whereas the ancients, like bees, went to nature for their honey. Possibly Swift was wrong about his moderns — but our postmoderns are spiders all right. Theirs is a narcissistic, Byzantine acrobatics incensed against all referentiality, because wanting to make a virtue of the dire necessity of impotence. All is done, of course, in the name of a big underlying assumption: that modern civilisation is just rubbish. Yet one feels tempted to carry the ban on the mimetic — that first commandment of postmodern theory — into the camp of their own Kulturkritik. What *if the idea of a crisis of modern culture, far from mirroring historical reality, were a figment of the humanist imagination?*

After all, it is only to be expected that we, humanist intellectuals, declare and deplore the range and depth of the cultural rot — even if our techno-liberal civilisation is indeed intrinsically sick, then who are its 'natural' doctors, both as diagnosticians and as self-appointed healers? Why, the humanist intellectuals, of course. Thus our vested interest as crisis-theory-mongers is painfully conspicuous; and the crisis-consciousness itself may well be, to a large extent, an 'iatrogenic' effect.

Postmodernism, be it art or theory, means either frozen modernism or the avant-garde gone wild — but in both cases, its deep meaning reenacts the modernist indictment of the modern age. Therefore it stands or falls with whatever cogency such an indictment may have. I must confess I am not impressed. And before anyone calls this too philistine a stance, let me just remind you that no apocalyptic superstition was ever required for genuine art to go on with 'the imaginative recreation of moral perplexities', as Hilary Putnam wisely put it. We can do better than to leave our thought and sensibility in thrall to a worn-out, groundless ideology of refusal and despair.

IN THE EMPIRE OF THE GAZE: FOUCAULT AND THE DENIGRATION OF VISION IN 20TH CENTURY FRENCH THOUGHT*
Martin Jay

If, as Michel Foucault has taught us, authorial originality pales before the constraints of epistemic or discursive determination, then the proper contextualizing of his own seemingly idiosyncratic work becomes a particularly intriguing task. Unfortunately, it has proved to be a no less troublesome one. For when the initial efforts to categorize Foucault as a structuralist or semiotician foundered, alternative candidates quickly proliferated. As a result, he has been variously described as a latter-day Nietzschean, a heterodox Heideggerian, a wayward Western Marxist, a postmodernist and, most frequently, a post-structuralist. With all the difficulties attending each and any of these categorizations, it may seem most prudent to accept the advice of two of his recent commentators and conclude that 'whoever wants to understand Foucault should not make him something he is not. Take him on his own, difficult terms'.

And yet, to do so risks ignoring Foucault's own lesson of the power of discursive formations to undermine the alleged sovereignty of the creator subject. For his 'own terms' ironically imply that the terms can never be 'his

* This article will appear in *Foucault: A Critical Reader*, edited by David Couzens Hoy (Basil Blackwell, 1986). In this latter edition, it contains its full complement of notes.

unifying function of *a* subject, the various enunciative modalities manifest his dispersion. To the various statuses, the various sites, the various positions that he can occupy or be given when making a discourse. To the discontinuity of the planes from which he speaks.' The partial truth of each of the rubrics under which he has been subsumed may thus be admitted without necessarily trying to force a reconciliation among them. Foucault instead should be seen as occupying the dynamic nodal point of a force-field of discursive impulses, which resist totalization into a coherent whole.

It is therefore with no intention of providing a master key to unlock the mysteries of his heterogeneous *oeuvre* that I offer the following analysis. Rather, I hope to draw attention to only one of the intersecting planes, hitherto unexamined, which can help us make sense of his remarkable work, in particular the source of its puzzling critical impulse. The plane in question can be called the anti-visual discourse of 20th century French thought, or more modestly, the interrogation of sight carried out by a wide and otherwise disparate number of French intellectuals beginning perhaps with Bergson.

Although I hope to explore its full ramifications at a later date, a few schematic remarks are necessary now to make clear the importance of the anti-ocular discourse in which Foucault can be situated. Long accounted the 'noblest' of the senses, sight traditionally enjoyed a privileged role as the most discriminating and trustworthy of the sensual mediators between man and world. Whether in terms of own'. Foucault, to be sure, never argued that individuals could be reduced to mere instances of a larger unified field. 'In the proposed analysis,' he wrote in *The Archaeology of Knowledge*, 'instead of referring back to *the* synthesis of *the* actual observation with the two eyes (often understood monocularly rather than in their true stereoscopic operations) or in those of internal mental speculation, vision has been accorded a special role in Western epistemology since the Greeks. Although at times more metaphorical than literal, the visual contribution to knowledge has been credited with far more importance than that of any other sense. A cursory and impressionistic 'glance' at such common English words and phrases as insight, perspective, overview, far-sighted, survey, point of view, demonstration, and synopsis reveal that there is more than an arbitrary choice of images in the question, do you see what I mean? As Richard Rorty has recently emphasized, modern thought at least since Descartes has generally privileged mental representations in 'the mind's eye' as mirror reflections of an external reality.

The role of vision in the imaginative history of Western man is no less important, as students of religious and mythical symbols have convincingly demonstrated. The visionary search for illumination, whether through mystical or mundane means, has generated a rich tradition of what Carlyle called 'spiritual optics'. Here the resonance of related clusters of images surrounding the sun, the moon, the stars, fire, mirrors, and day and night show how basic visual experience has been in structuring our attempts to make sense of the sacred as well as the profane. In negative terms, the fear of being watched by an omniscient God or followed by the evil eye shows how highly ambiguous the role of sight has been, especially when it includes the experience of being the object instead of the subject of the look. The complicated scopophilic-scopophobic dialectic of exhibitionism and paranoia that is evident in such figures as Rousseau shows the intimate linkages between vision and psychological phenomena. Indeed, thinkers from the time of Augustine have recognized a fundamental relationship between ocular experience and desire, especially in its unfulfilled form.

To detail the history of attitudes towards vision, including such anti-ocular moments as the Jewish prohibition of graven images, the iconoclastic controversy of the 8th century or the Protestant Reformation, is impossible here. Suffice it to say that with the rise of modern science, the Gutenberg revolution in printing and the Albertian emphasis on perspective in painting, vision was given an especially powerful role in the modern era. In France in particular, the domination of visual experience and the discourse of sight seems to have been especially strong. Whether in the theatrical spectacle of Louis XIV's court, the emphasis on clear and distinct ideas in Cartesian philosophy, the enlightening project of the *philosophes*, or the visual phantasmagoria of the 'city of light', the ocularcentric character of French culture has been vividly apparent. So too has the French fascination with technical improvements in the capacity to see, evident from the time of Descartes' paean to the telescope in *La Dioptrique*, through Baudelaire's critique of photography, all the way to Barthes' ruminations on the camera and Deleuze's recent writings on the cinema. Not surprisingly, one of the most striking aspects of 20th-century French thought is the almost obligatory consideration of painting on the part of a wide variety of thinkers, such as Merleau-Ponty, Sartre, Derrida, Lyotard, Kofman, Lefort, Marin, Deleuze, Starobinski and, of course, Foucault himself. And as a recent commentator on the poet Jean Tardieu's visual preoccupations remarks, 'a list of poet-art critics of the late nineteenth and twentieth centuries would be almost identical to a list of great poets of the era: Baudelaire, Valéry, Apollinaire, Reverdy, all the Surrealists, Ponge and Bonnefoy'. One might add novelists like Robbe-Grillet, Tournier and Simon to hammer the point home even more firmly.

If the French obsession with vision has continued unabated to our own day, it has, however, taken a very different turn from its earlier direction. Beginning with Bergson's critique of the spatialization of time, the French interrogation of sight has tended increasingly to emphasize its more problematic implications. The link between privileging vision and the traditional humanist subject, capable of rational enlightenment, has been opened to widespread attack. The illusions of imagistic representation and the allegedly disinterested scientific gaze have been subjected to hostile scrutiny. The mystifications of the social imaginary and the spectacle of late capitalist culture have been the target of fierce criticism. And the psychological dependence of the ideological 'I' on the totalizing gaze of the 'eye' has been ruthlessly exposed.

Thinkers as different as Bataille and Sartre, Metz and Irigaray, Althusser and Levinas have all called into question the time-honoured nobility of sight. Even Merleau-Ponty, whose phenomenological exploration of perception can be seen in part as a celebration of embodied vision, was deeply suspicious of what he called *pensée au survol*, the high-altitude thinking which maintained the Cartesian split between a distant, spectatorial subject and the object of his sight. In short, although the reasons are still uncertain, it is legitimate to talk of a discursive or paradigm shift in 20th-century French thought in which the denigration of vision supplanted its previous celebration.

The degree of hostility has varied from thinker to thinker, as has the precise dimension of vision under attack; indeed, in certain cases, what is disliked by one critic is defended by another, and on occasion, ambiguities arise within an author's *oeuvre*. How complicated the story actually is can, in fact, be discerned if we now turn to the special role played by Foucault in the anti-visual discourse. For although it is immediately evident that Foucault recognized important links between *voir* and both *savoir* and *pouvoir*, the nature of his fascination with the ocular is uncertain. One recent commentator, Allan Megill, has contended that in his earlier, more structuralist moments, Foucault was himself intent on portraying 'a lucent, Apollonian world' within which ocular-centrism was neutrally accepted, although he abandoned this attempt in his later writings. Another, Michel de Certeau, has argued that throughout Foucault's work a tension can be discerned between his substantive critiques of the power of the gaze and his own 'optical style', which drew on visual astonishment to subvert that power. There may in fact, be justification for both these analyses in the labyrinthine, often highly ambiguous corpus of Foucault's writings. But the story is more complicated still, as a systematic consideration of his many references to aspects of vision will help us to understand.

The Fascination of Vision

That Foucault was fascinated with vision from the beginning of his career is not surprising in view of his early interest in Merleau-Ponty's phenomenology of perception, Ludwig Binswanger's existential psychoanalysis and Heidegger's phenomenological ontology. For in these thinkers, the traditional Cartesian privileging of a detached, contemplative subject was decisively repudiated, as was Husserl's notion of an eidetic consciousness capable of intuiting essences through a *Wesensschau*. The humanist notion of a centered, rational subject, so Heidegger insisted in his influential essay on 'The Age of the World View' was rooted in scientific, pictorial subjectivism; indeed, the very notion of *theoria* introduced by the Greeks was grounded in a technological appropriation of the world dependent on the same spectatorial split between subject and object. For Merleau-Ponty and Binswanger, the problematic distinction between consciousness and body was closely linked to the elevation of perspectival vision with its single point of view. More unmediated senses like touch were thus necessary to remedy the hypertrophied role of vision in Western experience.

In all of these cases, however, another, more attractive visual mode was also possible. Heidegger spoke of a type of circumscribed vision (*Umsicht*) in which the mediated distance of representation was abandoned in favour of a more primordial encounter with ontological reality. His celebrated if somewhat fuzzy, evocation of a 'clearing' (*Lichtung*) in which Being might manifest itself, expressed this hope for a more revelatory visual experience. For Binswanger and especially Merleau-Ponty, embodied vision, the reversible, chiasmic intertwining of the visible and invisible, the viewer and the viewed, in the 'flesh' of the world, could be the locus of positive meaning.

From the beginning, Foucault seems to have been less confident of the viability of their alternatives, even as he absorbed the phenomenological critique of Cartesian ocularcentrism. Although it may appear in hindsight that he overemphasized his own distance from phenomenology, it is nonetheless striking that he would condemn the phenomenology of perception as a final variant of the very 'transcendental narcissism' that it claimed to overcome. Unlike Merleau-Ponty, he never placed his faith in an ontology of vision that would replace the discredited epistemology derived from Descartes. Instead, he drew on earlier manifestations of the anti-visual discourse, most notably those evident in Bataille and Sartre, and combined them with others coming apparently from Nietzsche, to probe far more thoroughly than the phenomenologists the dark side of the primacy of sight. Even in his most 'structuralist' moments, Foucault never endorsed the possibility of a transparent, fully visible and meaningful reality. Well before his celebrated and influential critique of panopticism in *Discipline and Punish*, he was aware of the costs of visual primacy. The writings of the early 1960's — *Madness and Civilization* (1961), *The Birth of the Clinic* (1963), *Raymond Roussel* (1963), and 'A Preface to Transgression' (1963) — demonstrate this awareness in numerous ways.

Foucault's emphasis on the sinister implications of ocularcentrism is strikingly apparent in his analysis of the history of madness in 'the age of reason' or what he called 'the classical age' (roughly 1650 to 1800). The modern category of insanity, he contends, was predicated on the dissolution of the medieval and Renaissance unity of word and image, which liberated a multitude of images of madness deprived of any eschatological significance. As a result, madness became a pure spectacle, a theatre of unreason:

> During the classical period, madness was shown, but on the other side of bars; if present, it was at a distance, under the eyes of reason that no longer felt any relation to it and that would not compromise itself by too close a resemblance. Madness had become a thing to look at.

For the 'classical' mind, the essence of madness was either blindness, a term which 'refers to that night of quasi-sleep which surrounds the images of madness, giving them, in their solitude, an invisible sovereignty,' or dazzlement, which means that 'the madman sees the daylight, the same daylight as the man of reason (both live in the same brightness); but seeing this same daylight, and nothing but this daylight, he sees it as void, as night, as nothing'. For Foucault, the Cartesian distrust of the actual senses nonetheless betrayed an ocular bias that worked to exclude the insane:

> Descartes closes his eyes and plugs up his ears the better to see the true brightness of essential daylight; thus he is secured against the dazzlement of the madman who, opening his eyes, sees only the night, and not seeing at all, believes he sees when he imagines . . . Unreason is in the

same relation to reason as dazzlement to the brightness of daylight itself. And this is not a metaphor. We are at the centre of the great cosmology which animates all classical culture.

There was, as well, an institutional expression of the visual definition of insanity in the birth of the asylum, where 'madness no longer exists except as *seen* . . . The science of mental disease, as it would develop in the asylum, would always be only of the order of observation and classification. It would not be a dialogue'. For the main psychiatrist of the post-classical era, Pinel, the patient was not merely the object of another's scrutiny; he was turned instead into a self-reflective mirror so that 'madness would see itself, would be seen by itself — pure spectacle and absolute subject'. And even though Freud introduced a linguistic moment into his psychoanalytic practice, he never abandoned entirely the specular bias of the psychiatric tradition. 'It would be fairer to say,' Foucault contended, 'that psychoanalysis doubled the absolute observation of the watcher with the endless monologue of the person watched — thus preserving the old asylum structure of non-reciprocal observation but balancing it, in a non-symmetrical reciprocity, by the new structure of language without response.' In fact, only in the non-psychiatric discourse of artists like Goya and de Sade were the marginalized claims of darkness and the night allowed to reassert themselves in the modern world, thus providing a prototype for the recovery of 'unreason' in art, the reverse side of madness.

The Birth of the Clinic

The Birth of the Clinic has been called an 'extended postscript' to *Madness and Civilization*, which is an especially apt description if its concentration on the complicity of visual domination with the rise of modern medicine is acknowledged. In this work, Foucault more explicitly underlines the disciplinary power of '*le regard*' (the gaze or the look), a word with powerfully negative connotations in French thought since the celebrated chapter devoted to it in Sartre's *Being and Nothingness*. Here as elsewhere, a subterranean affinity between two thinkers normally understood as opposed can be discerned, insofar as both express variations of the anti-visual paradigm of recent French thought.

Sartre, to be sure, is never mentioned in the work, but it is difficult to avoid hearing echoes of his chilling description of the alienating and objectifying power of the Other's gaze in Foucault's historical account of the rise of a specific medical practice in the classical age. Less conjectural is the role of another student of the power of sight in Western theory and practice, the distinguished historian of science, Georges Canguilhem, who commissioned *The Birth of the Clinic* for a series of studies he edited in the history and philosophy of biology and medicine. Canguilhem, who had also been the official supervisor of *Madness and Civilization* for Foucault's *doctorat d'état*, had given a course at the Sorbonne in 1957 on the role of vision as the model of cognition in Western thought. Although Foucault, who was still teaching in Upsalla, Sweden at the time, could not have attended the lectures, it is highly probable that he learned something of their content when he returned to Paris. Later, he would acknowledge Canguilhem's influence as a methodological model, but it is no less likely that Foucault also became sensitized to the importance of sight in constituting medical 'knowledge' in the 18th-century through the example of his mentor.

The Birth of the Clinic, in fact, describes the medical innovation of the classical age in terms of an intensified faith in visual evidence. 'The breadth of the experiment,' he argues, 'seems to be identified with the domain of the careful gaze, and of an empirical vigilance receptive only to the evidence of visible contents. The eye bcomes the depository and source of clarity.' The new medical gaze differs, however, from the Cartesian privileging of internal vision at the cost of the actual senses. Instead, it emphasizes 'the sovereign power of the empirical gaze', which plays over the solid and opaque surfaces of the body. 'No light could now dissolve them in ideal truths; but the gaze directed upon them would, in turn, awaken them and make them stand out against a background of objectivity. The gaze is no longer reductive, it is, rather, that which establishes the individual in his irreducible quality.' But what is in fact 'seen' is not a given, objective reality open to an innocent eye. Rather, it is an epistemic field, constructed as much linguistically as visually, which is no more or less close to the 'truth' than what it replaced. 'In its sovereign exercise, the gaze took up once again the structures of visibility that it had itself deposited in its field of perception.'

Although the initial focus on visible surfaces and symptoms gave way in 'the age of Bichat' to a more penetrating gaze into the internal organic landscape, the search was still for an 'invisible visibility'. The unexpected result of the ever more curious visual penetration of the body, Foucault suggests, is a focus not on the vitality of a patient, but rather his mortality:

> That which hides and envelops, the curtain of night over truth, is, paradoxically, life; and death, on the contrary, opens up to the light of day the black coffer of the body: obscure life, limpid death, the oldest imaginary values of the Western world are crossed here in a strange misconstruction that is the very meaning of pathological anatomy . . . Nineteenth-century medicine was haunted by that absolute eye that cadaverizes life and rediscovers in the corpse the frail, broken nervure of life.

What makes this development in the seemingly limited field of medicine so fateful for Foucault was its function as a model for future investigations in all of the 'sciences of man'. 'It will no doubt remain a decisive fact about our culture,' he concludes, 'that its first scientific discourse concerning the individual had to pass through this stage of death.' And because the importance of perception, sight in particular, in this cadaverization of life was so great, it is impossible, Foucault suggests, to turn to it for an antidote to positivist reification, as the phenomenologists had hoped. In a passage covertly directed against Merleau-Ponty, he wrote,

> when one carries out a vertical investigation of this positivism, one sees the emergence of a whole series of figures — hidden by it, but also indispensable to its birth — that will be released later, and, paradoxically, used

against it. In particular, that with which phenomenology was to oppose it so tenaciously was already present in its underlying structures: the original powers of the perceived and its correlation with language in the original form of experience . . .

The surprising convergence of positivism and phenomenology on the level of their common privileging of ocular perception, with its penchant for death over life, did not, however, exhaust the importance of vision in the modern experience, as Foucault interpreted it. The complicated interlacing of language and vision was also apparent in the literary experiments of the writer to whom he devoted a very different kind of study at the same time as he was writing the history of the clinical gaze, Raymond Roussel. Often neglected because of its seeming irrelevance to Foucault's more central concerns, the book demonstrates the complexity of his fascination with vision. That he thought it fundamental to Roussel's work is witnessed by his publishing a short piece specifically on saying and seeing in Roussel a year before its publication. In the longer book, he expanded his analysis to cover the entire *oeuvre* of a writer whose experimental prose intrigued French intellectuals from the Surrealists to Robbe-Grillet. Roussel is perhaps best known for his game of beginning a novel with a sentence which was phonetically repeated at its end, with only one element changed to make the meaning of the two sentences utterly different. Roussel's blithe disdain for the representative or referential function of language made him an obvious candidate for praise on the part of those who wanted to privilege the complete self-referentiality of language.

But significantly, in developing his unique style, Roussel revealed as well a preoccupation with vision, expressed even in the titles of certain of his works, such as *La Vue* and *La Poussière de Soleils*. According to Robbe-Grillet, '*sight*, the privileged sense in Roussel, rapidly achieves an obsessive acuity, tending to infinity'. Foucault, whose interest in the catachrestic dimensions of Roussel's language had been remarked, was also very sensitive to the role of vision in his work. Like Robbe-Grillet, he emphasized its function as an impediment to meaningfulness in the novels. Contrary to the Surrealists, who were

bent on seeking a hidden significance beneath the surface of
Roussel's mysterious prose, Foucault insisted that his work
'systematically imposes an unformed, divergent, centrifug-
al uneasiness, oriented not towards the most reticent of
secrets, but towards the redoubling and the transmutation
of the most visible forms'. Roussel's repetitive linguistic
play was 'like the redoubling of the mask above the face; it
would open on the same eclipse of being', thus revealing an
infinite reflection of mirrors without a privileged point of
origin.

In places, Foucault seemed to appropriate Merleau-
Ponty's terms in describing the 'interlacing' of the visible
and the invisible in 'exactly the same tissue, the same
indissoluble substance', or in claiming *La Vue* presented a
universe without perspective, or more precisely, 'combin-
ing the vertical point of view (which permits everything to
be embraced as in a circle) and the horizontal point of view
(which places the eye at ground level and gives to sight only
the first dimension) so well that everything is seen in
perspective and yet each thing is envisaged in its complete
context'. But rejecting Merleau-Ponty's optimism,
Foucault emphasized the meaninglessness of Roussel's
visual universe, where light was cast on a world which only
reabsorbed it in the 'mutism of objects'. Roussel's writing,
he argued, invoked 'images visibly invisible, perceptible
but not decipherable, given in a lightning flash and
without possible reading, present in a radiance that
repelled the gaze'. Although Foucault noted a shift between
the early and late Roussel — the works up to *La Vue* were
illuminated by a dazzling, homogeneous light, the light of
a sun too bright to permit any nuanced shadows, whereas
everything written after, most notably the *Nouvelles
Impressions de l'Afrique*, were cloaked in the darkness of a
'closed-in sun' (*soleil enfermé*) — the implication was the
same: the visual in Roussel provided only 'an empty lens'
(*lentille vide*) incapable of focussing on a clear and distinct
world. Genuine transparency, in the sense of a medium
which completely dissolved to reveal an unequivocal truth
or unambivalent meaning, was thus denied to both
language and perception.

It was, in fact, Foucault's awareness of the visually
opaque dimension within language itself, which he called

its perpetually rebus-like character, that makes it problematic to characterize him as primarily structuralist, even
of a heterodox kind. There is no enigma to be decoded, no
spatial coherence to be mapped out in two-dimensional
terms. Roussel was not the only figure to whom Foucault
was drawn because of his debunking of this hope; the
Belgian Surrealist painter, René Magritte, was another. In
an essay written in 1968 and then expanded into a little
book five years later, Foucault explored a more explicitly
visual version of the phenomenon he had discerned in
Roussel. Describing Magritte's canvases as the opposite of
trompe l'oeil because of their undermining of the mimetic
conventions of realistic painting, he also referred to them as
'unraveled calligrams' because they refused to close the gap
between image and word. In the terms he had introduced
in *The Order of Things*, written between the Roussel and
Magritte studies, the Surrealist had discarded art's claim to
provide representative 'resemblances' of the external world
in favor of repetitive 'similitudes', which circulate a series
of visual and linguistic signs without an external referent.
Whereas resemblances always affirmatively assert the
irreducible sameness of image and object, similitude,
Foucault argued, 'multiples different affirmations, which
dance together, tilting and tumbling over one another'.

Foucault's celebration of difference, heterogeneity and
the dance of otherness in *This is Not a Pipe* clearly
demonstrates his affinity with one of the most seductive
voices in the anti-visual discourse of twentieth-century
French thought, that of Georges Bataille. His contribution
to *Critique*'s 1963 homage to Bataille shows how drawn
Foucault was to Bataille's attempt to valorize a transgressive experience, 'where the subject who speaks has just
vanished, where the spectacle topples over before an
upturned eye'. The upturned, unseeing eye referred to
Bataille's celebrated pornographic novel, *The Story of the
Eye*, with its metaphoric exchange of ocular symbols —
eggs, testicles, the sun, etc. — all pierced, bleeding,
enucleated, overflowing and blind. Foucault recognized
Bataille's fundamental challenge to the hierarchical privileging of vision in the Western tradition, its fateful
linkage, as Freud points out, with man's vertical posture,
the repression of his sexual and anal erotic urges and the rise

of 'civilization'. He also noted its challenge to the visually derived constitution of the reflective, Cartesian subject:

> Bataille reverses this entire direction: sight, crossing the globular limit of the eye, constitutes the eye in its instantaneous being, sight carries it away in this luminous stream (an outpouring fountain, streaming tears and, shortly, blood), hurls the eye outside of itself, conducts it to the limit where it bursts out in the immediately extinguished flash of its being. Only a small white ball, veined with blood, is left behind, only an exorbitated eye to which all sight is now denied . . . In the distance created by this violence and uprooting, the eye is seen absolutely, but denied the possibility of sight: the philosophizing subject has been dispossessed and pursued to its limit.

As in Roussel, the ultimate blindness of sight, the opacity of the seemingly transparent, also suggested the limits of linguistic meaningfulness. For 'the upturned eye has no meaning in Bataille's language, can have no meaning since it marks its limit'. Instead, it signals the point at which language explodes 'in laughter, tears, the overturned eyes of ecstasy, the mute and exorbitated horror of sacrifice'. As such it shows the link between language, human finitude and the death of God, 'a sun that rotates and the great eyelid that closes upon the world'.

The Order of Things

The eclipse of the solar divinity was linked for Foucault with the decline of his secular analogue, the humanist concept of Man. Hostility to visual primacy and the critique of humanism were intricated linked in the work which most vividly established Foucault's credentials as an anti-humanist, *The Order of Things*. Significantly, the work begins with a now celebrated description of a visual scene, Velásquez's *Las Meninas*, and ends with a no less frequently cited visual metaphor of man's face etched in the sand being erased by the waves at the edge of the sea.

Rather than focusing on these now widely discussed framing moments in the text, I want to explore instead the arguments in between insofar as they bear on the question of vision. Whether or not the spatial preoccupations of the book betokened an affinity for Apollonian structuralism, as Megill, following Derrida, has claimed, or merely reflected Foucault's subject matter, as he himself later argued, *The Order of Things* does not seem quite as obsessively fixed on '*le regard*' as does his earlier work. Or rather it seems to be so only in Foucault's account of the classical age. As in *Madness and Civilization*, he describes the onset of that period in terms of the breakdown of an assumed unity of word and image before the end of the 16th century. In a culture based on semantic resemblances, images were understood to be decipherable hieroglyphs of meaning. The result was 'a non-distinction between what is seen and what is read, between observation and relation, which results in the constitution of a single, unbroken surface in which observation and language intersect to infinity'.

For reasons that are not clear and which Foucault unfortunately never deemed worthy of explication, the classical age emerges when this unity is undone and images no longer resemble readable texts. Both Bacon and Descartes, if for different reasons, denounce thinking through resemblances or similitudes and warn against the illusions to which it is prone. One implication of the breakdown of this unity, first evident in Cervantes, is the growing awareness of the binary and representative nature of the sign, which frees it from the assumption that it bears an intrinsic figural resemblance to what it signifies. As an arbitrary human tool, language is understood as a neutral medium of communication. Inclined towards nominalism, language in the classical age also privileged the most neutral verb possible: the verb 'to be'.

Another implication of the breakdown is the compensatory unleashing of perception in general, and vision in particular, as the sole means of ascertaining reliable knowledge about the external world. According to Foucault, 'the manifestations and sign of truth are to be found in evident and distinct perception. It is the task of words to translate the truth if they can; but they no longer have the right to be considered a mark of it. Language has withdrawn from the midst of beings themselves and has entered a period of transparency and neutrality'. The

classical age is thus dominated by a new faith in the power
of direct and technologically improved observation and by a
concomitant taxonomic ordering of its findings in the
visible space of the table. Although such tables are
necessarily linguistic, the names they arrange in spatial
relations are assumed to be utterly without density of their
own. The triumph of natural history is thus the triumph of
the visual:

> One has the impression that with Tournefort, with
> Linnaeus or Buffon, someone has at last taken on the task of
> stating something that had been visible from the begin-
> ning of time, but had remained mute before a sort of
> invincible distraction of men's eyes. In fact, it was not an
> age-old inattentiveness being suddenly dissipated, but a
> new field of visibility being constituted in all its density.

Other senses like touch or hearing are denigrated, as
scientific language struggles to turn itself as much as
possible into a transparent record of the observing gaze.

Moreover, to the extent that visual knowledge is
dominant in the classical age, there is assumed an observing
eye capable of seeing the visible tables, but from a position
outside of them. It is in this sense that *Las Meninas*, as
Foucault interprets it, is itself a representation of classical
representation. For it is the absent sovereigns, there only in
their reflections in the small mirror on the back wall of the
painter's studio, who 'see' the picture in front of us. We are
thus not yet in a fully humanist age characterized by the
positive appearance of Man:

> In Classical thought, the personage for whom the repre-
> sentation exists, and who represents himself within it,
> recognizing himself therein as an image or reflection, he
> who ties together all the interlacing threads of the
> 'representation in the form of a picture or a table' — he is
> never to be found in that table himself. Before the end of
> the eighteenth century, *man* does not exist . . .

If, then, it is only with the end of the visual primacy of
the classical age that full-fledged humanism emerges, what
is the connection between ocular-centrism and the rise of
man? At first, there does not seem to be any, which would

call into question the importance of the anti-visual discourse in Foucault's work, at least at this stage of it. For when he comes to describe the end of natural history and its replacement by biology at the time of Cuvier, he explicitly stresses the new emphasis on invisible, anatomic and organic structures which supplant the empirical classifications of the classical table. 'The visible order, with its permanent grid of distinctions,' he writes, 'is now only a superficial glitter above an abyss.' With the concomitant emergence of historical consciousness, functional analogy and succession — temporal rather than spatial values — replace the static order of the classical age. Life, labour and language all break free from the domination of the taxonomic gaze. The putative transparency of language gives way to a growing opacity, which culminates in the appearance of pure 'literature' in Mallarmé.

And yet, in a subtle way, the post-classical, humanist episteme, as Foucault describes it, is still hostage to the primacy of sight. We can become sensitive to this continuity across the seemingly abrupt rupture in discursive formations if we remember Foucault's argument about Bichat, Pinel and Freud in *Madness and Civilization* and his highly speculative claim about the link between the later sciences of man and the medical gaze in *The Birth of the Clinic*. In those works, he insisted that even as the surface of the body was penetrated to let the hitherto invisible become the object of inquiry, even as language was introduced to supplement the psychiatric gaze, vision did not falter as the dominant cognitive sense. It is for this reason that at the same time modern biology was positing 'life' as its object, it paradoxically discovered 'death' at its heart.

But in an even more fundamental sense, the primacy of the visual was preserved in Foucault's account of the rise of the human sciences. For with the eclipse of the classical age,

man appears in his ambiguous position as an object of knowledge and as subject that knows; enslaved sovereign, *observed spectator*, he appears in the place belonging to the king, which was assigned to him in advance by *Las Meninas*, but from which his real presence has for so long been excluded. As if, in that vacant space towards which Velazquez's whole painting was directed, but which it was nevertheless reflecting only in the chance presence of a mirror, and as though by stealth, all the figures whose alternation, reciprocal exclusion, interweaving, and fluttering one imagined (the model, the painter, the king, the spectator) suddenly stopped their imperceptible dance, immobilized into one substantial figure, and demanded that the entire space of the representation should at last be related to one corporeal gaze.

In this extremely important paragraph, Foucault reveals the extent to which humanism is based in his view on the replacement of the absent spectator, the king, by the 'observed spectator', man in a still visually constituted epistemological field. Thus, the arrival of this 'strange empirico-transcendental doublet' means that 'man' functions both as an allegedly neutral metasubject of knowledge and as its proper object, viewed from afar. Even phenomenology, Foucault insists once again, falls prey to this way of perceiving the world, showing its 'insidious kinship, its simultaneously promising and threatening proximity, to empirical analyses of man'.

Only with the triumph of an opaque and self-referential concept of language does the visually determined humanist episteme begin to be effaced enough for Foucault to claim that 'man had been a figure occurring between two modes of language'. Perhaps with writers like Roussel and Bataille — as well as others Foucault mentions, like Artaud and Blanchot — the crisis of the primacy of sight has reached a point at which an epistemic shift is on the horizon. Now those hitherto forbidden elements that had been consigned to the realm of darkness ever since the onset of the classical age, such as madness, difference and transgressive eroticism, can be rescued from the domination of light, transparency and the Same. For with the weakening of ocular primacy goes a concomitant questioning of the translucency of language, which had been its handmaiden ever since the breakdown of the pre-classical unity of word and image. But rather than a return to that prelapsarian state in which latent meaning was available to be deciphered, the post-humanist condition will be characte-

rized more by the mutual opacity we have seen Foucault
celebrate in his study of Roussel.

The Order of Things marked the last great instance of what
has become known as Foucault's archaeological period,
which was brought to a close by his summary, if somewhat
cryptic, methodological statement, *The Archaeology of
Knowledge*. In a footnote in that work, he noted that 'the
term "*regard medical*" used in my *Naissance de la clinique* was
not a very happy one', which may suggest a certain
weakening of his earlier visual preoccupations. But in fact,
all it implied was a more heightened awareness of the
anthropocentric fallacies involved in positing a synthetic,
unified subject doing the looking. For it was precisely this
apparently transcendental subject that *The Order of Things*
claimed was a function of ocularcentrism rather than a
precondition for it. Vision he now seemed to suggest, could
help constitute an episteme without the implied presence of
an absent sovereign or his humanist surrogate, whose gaze
totalized the discursive field. Here, interestingly, he
showed a continued filiation to Sartre, whose paranoid
ontology of '*le regard*' in *Being and Nothingness* did not
require an actual subject looking at an objectified other.
According to Sartre, 'the look will be given just as well on
occasion when there is a rustling of branches, or the sound
of a footstep followed by silence, or the slight opening of a
shutter, or a light movement of a curtain'. This generaliz-
able experience of being observed by an unknown and
omnipresent 'eye' is, of course, precisely what Foucault
next described in his powerful investigation of panopticism
in his next major work, *Discipline and Punish*.

Foucault had been sensitive to the relations between
social and political constraint and the objectifying power of
the gaze as early as *The Birth of the Clinic*, where he linked
the rise of modern medicine to the reforms of the French
Revolution:

> This medical field, restored to its pristine truth, pervaded
> wholly by the gaze, without obstacle and without
> alteration, is strangely similar, in its implicit geometry, to
> the social space dreamt of by the Revolution . . . The
> ideological theme that guides all structural reforms from
> 1789 to Thermidor Year II is that of the sovereign liberty

of truth: the majestic violence of light, which is in itself supreme, brings to an end the bounded, dark kingdom of privileged knowledge and establishes the unimpeded empire of the gaze.

Discipline and Punish

But it was only in *Discipline and Punish*, the first major fruit of his so-called genealogical method, that he discovered the more subtle social mechanism which allowed ocular domination to extend beyond the boundaries of an all-seeing sovereign or a despotic revolutionary state.

Foucault's analysis, to be sure, begins with an evocation of the spectacle of sovereign power in the classical age. With characteristic visual *éclat*, he describes the torture and execution of the failed regicide Damiens in 1757 as a 'theatrical representation of pain' in which the power of the monarch was literally inscribed in the visible flesh of the condemned man. As in his earlier accounts of the constitution of madness, the medical gaze in the clinic, and the taxonomic system of natural history, the privileging of vision is evident. Not only does it appear in the 'spectacle of the scaffold' of the ancien regime, it continues as well through the 'great theatrical ritual' of the Revolutionary guillotine.

But as in his earlier analysis, Foucault notes the decay of the classical mode in favour of a more complicated, but still visually determined alternative in the 19th century. Although he acknowledges its prototype in the military schools, military camps, and clinics of the 18th century — and he might have added the court society at the end of Louis XIV's reign — he chooses Bentham's model prison as the most explicit version of the new ocular technology of power. For it was here that the disciplining and normalizing function of the gaze was at its most blatant. Reversing the principle of the dungeon, the Panopticon, with its hidden supervisor watching from a central tower like an omniscient, but invisible God, is an architectural embodiment of the most paranoid of Sartrean fantasies about the 'absolute look'. The object of power is everywhere penetrated by the benevolently sadistic gaze of a diffuse and anonymous power, whose actual existence soon becomes superfluous to the process of discipline. The Panopticon is a 'machinery that assures dissymmetry, disequilibrium, difference. Consequently, it does not matter who exercises power. Any individual, taken almost at random, can operate the machine'.

Complementing the role of the gaze — or rather the sensation of always being its target — in the control and rehabilitation of criminals is the prophylactic power of surveillance, which is designed to prevent potential transgressions of the law. Here the external look becomes an internalized and self-regulating mechanism, which extends the old religious preoccupation with the smallest detail, whose importance 'in the sight of God' was immense. The normalizing function of the institutions and practices of surveillance was successful enough, according to Foucault, to dispense with the more heavy-handed displays of sovereign power needed earlier to render the population docile. Napoleon was the transitional moment, as he

> combined in a single symbolic, ultimate figure the whole of the long process by which the pomp of sovereignty, the necessarily spectacular manifestations of power, were extinguished one by one in the daily exercise of surveillance, in a panopticism in which the vigilance of intersecting gazes was soon to render useless both the eagle and the sun.

Thus, implicitly taking issue with Marxists like Guy Debord, who castigated the consumer-oriented 'society of the spectacle', Foucault concluded that 'our society is one not of spectacle, but of surveillance . . . We are neither in the amphitheatre, nor on the stage, but in the panoptic machine'.

That our imprisonment in this machine owed much to the well-intentioned goals of the Enlightenment and the Revolution it helped spawn Foucault did not doubt. 'The "Enlightenment", which discovered the liberties,' he contended, 'also invented the disciplines.' Unlike more sympathetic defenders of the *siècle des lumières*, like Jürgen Habermas, who emphasized its contribution to a public sphere centered on talking and listening, Foucault tended to privilege its visual dimension instead. And although he

protested near the end of his life against 'the intellectual
blackmail of "being for or against the Enlightenment" ', it
is difficult to miss a certain hostility in such observations as
the following remarks in an interview called 'The Eye of
Power':

> I would say Bentham was the complement to Rousseau.
> What in fact was the Rousseauist dream that motivated
> many of the revolutionaries? It was the dream of a
> transparent society, visible and legible in each of its parts,
> the dream of there no longer existing any zones of darkness
> . . . Bentham is both that and the opposite. He poses the
> problem of visibility, but thinks of a visibility organized
> entirely around a dominating, overseeing gaze. He effects
> the project of a universal visibility which exists to serve a
> rigorous, meticulous power. Thus Bentham's obsession,
> the technical idea of the exercise of an 'all-seeing' power, is
> grafted on to the great Rousseauist theme which is in some
> sense the lyrical note of the Revolution.

Here, significantly, he explicitly drew on the important
analyses of Jean Starobinski, which were influential on
other exemplars of the anti-visual discourse, such as Jacques
Derrida and Sarah Kofman. Rousseau's vain search for
perfect transparency, both personal and political, could
easily be turned into a target of reproach for those who
detected in it a nostalgia for unmediated presence or a
license for coerced unanimity. Relying on a penetrating
gaze which would pierce the surface of reality, it was no less
illusory than the theatrical perusal of 'mere' appearances in
the spectacles of the classical age.

Although Foucault took pains to avoid the implication
that all modern technologies of power derived from the
Rousseauist–Benthamite principle of perfect visibility, he
nonetheless acknowledged its importance in constituting
and then controlling the next phenomenon he investigated,
that of sexuality. 'With these themes of surveillance, and
especially in the schools,' he claimed, 'it seems that control
over sexuality becomes inscribed in architecture. In the
Military Schools, the very walls speak the struggle against
homosexuality and masturbation.' The sciences of man,
intended to help in the macrological control of populations
as well as the micrological normalizing of individuals, drew

on that mixture of the gaze and discourse which Foucault had identified with psychoanalysis as early as *The Birth of the Clinic*. Although he now stressed the power of discourse, such as that of the confession, in creating the very notion of sexuality, he insisted on the importance of spatial, visual controls in policing it. Nowhere was this function as evident as in the ostracism of the sexual 'pervert' whose very deviance was 'written immodestly on his face and body because it was a secret that always gave itself away'.

In so arguing, Foucault demonstrated his implicit debt to yet another central text in the anti-visual discourse of 20th-century French thought, Sartre's *Saint Genet*. For according to that work, not only was Genet compelled to label himself a 'thief' because he was observed by the 'other' in the act of stealing, he was also forced into assuming the character of the homosexual by the same gaze. As Sartre put it,

> Sexually, Genet is first of all a raped child. This first rape was the gaze of the other, who took him by surprise, penetrated him, transformed him forever into an object . . . Undressed by the eyes of decent folk as women are by those of males, he carries his fault as they do their breasts and behind . . . Having been caught stealing *from behind*, his back opens when he steals; it is with his back that he awaits human gazes and catastrophe.

Although Foucault never wrote about Genet and would have likely rejected Sartre's existentialist insistence on the victim heroically choosing to identify with his labels, his more general account of the ocular objectification of the deviant fits well with the analysis of '*le regard*' in *Saint Genet*.

To mention Genet is to reopen the question of possible resistance to the process of visual objectification. For certain of his works, such as the film he made with Jean Cocteau, *Un Chant d'Amour*, have been interpreted as visual challenges to the voyeuristic sadism of modern culture. Can Foucault himself be said to have offered a visual antidote to the disciplinary power of the gaze? How strong a weapon was that 'optic of astonishment' noted by de Certeau in Foucault's struggle against the policing of space? Or perhaps did he implicitly draw on other senses in his evocation of 'bodies and pleasures' as a counterweight to the domination of sexuality and desire?

At times, Foucault did explicitly call on the disruptive power of images, especially against the claims of language to represent a perfectly self-contained and self-sufficient system. Thus, for example, in his introduction to Binswanger, he criticized psychoanalysis in general and Lacan in particular for failing to credit the visual dimension of dreams, which they reduced instead to merely linguistic phenomena. And, as we have seen, his analyses of Roussel and Magritte emphasized the power of sight to subvert the homogenizing drive towards the 'same' implicit in naïve linguistic versions of representation. What in *The Order of Things* he called 'heterotopias' were disturbingly inconsistent spatial configurations which undermined the alleged coherence of linguistic systems. Indeed, one might say that against both linguistic and visual *trompe l'oeil*, he preferred a kind of catechresis, which preserved ambiguity, otherness and chiasmic intersection.

And yet, in all of these cases, the role of vision remained essentially negative. Like Jean-François Lyotard in *Discours/ Figure*, he pitted vision against language, especially in its structuralist incarnations, but did so only in order to emphasize its viewing a world of opaque meaninglessness. As we have seen in his frequent criticisms of Merleau-Ponty, Foucault never felt attracted towards an ontology of embodied vision in which a different kind of perception might provide answers to the unresolved problems raised in philosophies of consciousness. Unlike many non-French commentators on the implications of vision, he resisted exploring its reciprocal, intersubjective, communicative function, that of the mutual glance. '*Le regard*' never assumed its alternate meaning in English of caring or esteeming. As de Certeau has pointed out, Foucault focused so insistently on the dangers of panopticism that he remained blind to other micro-practices of everyday life that subvert its power. In short, despite his obvious delight in visual phenomena, he remained very much in thrall to the anti-visual discourse so pervasive in French thought in this century. For Foucault, the upturned eye was always preferable to the empire of the gaze.

Nor is it likely that he held out much hope for another sense as the antidote to ocularcentrism, as is the case with other critics of visual primacy such as Luce Irigaray. Feminists may choose to turn to touch or smell as more consonant with female than male sexuality, but Foucault was always too sceptical of any search for essentializing immediacy — and also, too unconcerned with female sexual experience — to feel that this choice provided an answer. Indeed, as he emphasized in one of his last interviews,

> I am not looking for an alternative . . . what I want to do is not the history of solutions, and that's the reason why I don't accept the word *alternative*. I would like to do the genealogy of problems, of *problématiques*. My point is not that everything is bad, but that everything is dangerous.

Which dangers one chooses to stress are, of course, more than an arbitrary decision. It has been the purpose of this paper to demonstrate that Foucault was particularly sensitive to the putative dangers of ocularcentrism because of his embeddedness in a larger discourse, which he never himself problematized. It is only by understanding his debt to that discourse, I would argue in conclusion, that we can make sense of one of the most perplexing dimensions of his work: the source of its undefended, but deeply felt critical impulse. Foucault's failure or unwillingness to probe the normative basis for his 'history of the present' has frequently troubled commentators eager to uncover the roots of his outrage. When pressed, as he often was, to defend himself, Foucault would fall back at times on a weak separation of facts and values that echoed Weber at his most neo-Kantian. But his practice was very different from Weber's because of the current of ethical commitment that ran throughout virtually all of his writings. Although in his last years, Foucault began to reflect on the ethical impulse of his work, he never developed a fully satisfactory account of it. Perhaps the explanation can be found in his unavoidable inability to 'see' beyond the horizon of his own episteme and question the premises and implications of the anti-visual discourse itself.

The generative power of that discourse in revealing

hitherto unproblematized dimensions of our culture cannot be denied; Foucault's own work shows how fecund its influence can be. And yet for those not completely caught in its gravitational field, it may be time to begin probing the costs as well as benefits of the anti-ocular counter-enlightenment. Its own genealogy needs to be demystified, not in order to restore a naïve faith in the nobility of sight, but rather to cast a little light on the manifold implications of its new ignobility.

SOME REFLECTIONS ON POSTMODERNISM AND ARCHITECTURE
Kenneth Frampton

I find it necessary to provide you with something of a context in which to situate this presentation, a hypothesis which, from the outset, will suffer from the ambiguity of being in part critical and in part postulative. That is to say that in part, I wish to mount a critique of the reduction of contemporary environmental culture to a proliferation of images. In part, I wish to postulate a ground from which to attempt to resist the current commodification of building, that is, the reduction of buildings to consumable goods — including even the larger and apparently more important object of the fabric, which hitherto as a class has tended to resist the rapid amortisation of industrial society, by virtue of a literal anchorage into the ground. What I shall present today will be a reworking of the hypothesis I attempted to describe in my essay 'Towards a Critical Regionalism', included in the volume *Postmodern Culture*, edited by Hal Foster.

Before proceeding with the main substance of this piece, however, something needs to be said about how I came to write this essay, since only then will you have some idea of the circumstances under which I formulated my position.

My interest in that which I was to perceive as sporadic, marginal, regionally-based pockets of resistance in the field of architectural culture arose out of the recognition of the power of Anglo-American hegemony in the field of so-called postmodern architecture, ideologically recognized and polemicized as such in Charles Jencks' highly influential book, *The Language of Post-Modern Architecture* (1977), a book which interestingly enough, from my point of view, had some 400 illustrations, most of which were photographs distributed at the rate of one shot per building. A few years later, Arthur Drexler, curator of architecture at the Museum of Modern Art, staged an exhibition entitled

'Transformations' which, in effect, repeated the same
operation, namely purporting to be a critical survey of the
transformation suffered by modern architecture over the
previous fifteen to twenty years, that is to say, since the
mid-60s. This featured some 500 photographic images,
also distributed at the rate of one shot per building. Clearly
the method was a popular success with the public . . .

Finally, and this is the last formative event which I shall
mention, 1980 was the year of the Venice Biennale in
which an architectural section curated by Paolo Portoghesi
was mounted under the singularly demagogic, if ironic,
title 'The Presence of the Past, the End of Prohibition', an
event whose then unstated ideological *parti pris* caused me
to resign from the advisory commission at the planning
stage. The commission incidentally included three American architectural critics, that is, if you consider Robert
Stern as an architectural critic, apart from myself, if I am to
be considered as an American . . . This exhibition, as you
will no doubt recall, later provoked Habermas to formulate
his Adorno prize address of that year under the title
'Modernity — An Incomplete Project', which actually
begins the collection, *Postmodern Culture*.

By the early 80s, it was clear to me that, as far as the
American architectural establishment was concerned, a
reactionary cultural operation was consciously under way
and had been in the offing, ever since Robert Venturi's
Complexity and Contradiction in Architecture (1963) which, I
might remind you, in the first edition, contained the
somewhat embarrassing and I suppose ironic passage in
which he asserts that Americans do not need *piazzas*, since
they should be at home watching television.

Just in case you think that this reaction is now losing its
hold, permit me to inform you that the next exhibition at
the Royal Institute of British Architects in London will
feature the work of Kohn Pedersen Fox, who are today the
number one American architectural firm, replacing Skid-
more, Owings and Merrill, and engaged in wholesale
commercial developments, featuring cannibalised historicist skin-deep masks drawn over the normative skeleton of
optimised production.

I felt the need, then, as a critic and as a teacher to mark
some alternative theoretical base with which to continue,

however, marginally, the cultured practice of an
architecture which is not exactly avant-garde in a positive
sense; but which somehow reconstitutes and develops the
emancipatory, liberative, if you like even hedonistic,
features of modern architecture, as this has been postulated
and to some extent realised by that movement in its prime,
prior to the tragedy of the Spanish Civil War, and in a more
muted and possibly more subtle way, to the destruction of
the New Deal, as far as American social urban planning was
concerned, in the debacle of the McCarthy era. (This is the
moment in which they sell back all of the greenbelt,
Roosevelt new towns to private ownership; apart from
bringing the Los Angeles planning authority up before the
Committee of Unamerican Activities.)

It seemed to me in the early 80s — and I have to admit I
had already had intimations of this in the 60s — that the
more sensitive, liberative and even critical architectural
works of our time could be found in the peripheries, rather
than in the so-called centres of late capitalist development,
be these New York, London, Paris, Frankfurt or Tokyo.
And these peripheral centres of architectural energy were
able to sustain the multi-layered elaborate quality of their
work for a number of reasons, ranging from local prosperity
to a kind of assumed cantonal identity and even power, to a
desire and willingness on the part of a group of architects
and, more importantly, their clients, to attempt to
cultivate and attain an inflected, modern expression, which
— whilst still bearing the modernising thrust of contemporary development — would nonetheless mediate and
qualify this universal civilisation by virtue of a consciously
cultivated local culture. The phenomena by which this
culture made itself manifest varied over a wide range, such
as topography, climate, light, construction materials,
vestigial craft methods and local mores to transmuted
traditional architectonic tropes and even the myths,
self-consciously cultivated, of a particular place.

It is important to remember in this regard, and in all
that I will say here, that architecture, unlike the other arts
is embedded in the life world. It is for this reason that one
may talk in terms of architecture being experienced by the
body, or rather by the whole being, beyond that dualism of
body and mind to which Jean-François Lyotard alluded.

Hence, it is critically possible to address the field of architecture in terms of its tactile potential rather than in terms of the primacy increasingly given to the visual from the Renaissance onwards. Of course, this does not in any way imply that one can transcend the biological privilege given to sight.

Critical Regionalism

I have broached this theme of critical regionalism two times already, firstly in an article in *Perspecta 20*, 1982 and secondly in the article bearing the same title in *Postmodern Culture*. What I am going to do here is to attempt a brief re-reading of this second version. But before I do so let me say a little about where I seem to find myself in both a philosophical and a political sense.

The term Critical Regionalism is not my invention and derives from the writings of Alex Tzonis and Liliane Lefaivre, who significantly enough happen to be of Greek and French–Canadian origin, and to be teaching in Delft. So much for critical regionalism . . . In an essay entitled, 'The Grid and the Pathway' (1981), they proceed, after coining the term, to caution against the ambiguous, not to say reactionary nature of regional reformism, as this has manifested itself at various times from the last quarter of the 19th century in Greece, and certainly, of course, in the Germany of the Third Reich.

At the risk of being redundant, I feel compelled to add that by critical regionalism I do not mean any kind of specific style, nor of course do I have in mind any form of hypothetical vernacular revival, nor any kind of unreflected so-called spontaneous grass roots culture. Instead, I wish to employ this term in order to evoke a real and hypothetical condition in which a critical culture of architecture is consciously cultivated in a particular place, in express opposition to the cultural domination of hegemonic power. It is, in theory at least, the critical culture, which while it does not reject the thrust of modernisation, nonetheless resists being totally absorbed and consumed by it.

This brings me not only to the subtitle of my second essay, 'Six Points for an Architecture of Resistance', but also to Philippe Lacoue-Labarthe's concept of pushing the aesthetic project to the limit so that it passes from a condition of complicity to a condition of resistance. It also brings me to caution you and myself with regard to the form that the rest of this presentation will take: namely, that while I will often present these points as dialectical pairs or diads, I do not wish to suggest that they can necessarily be raised to a higher level of synthesis or that they are to be seen idealistically as being manipulated by me so as to favour the triumph of one over the other.

This leads me, by way of caveats, to declare the obvious, namely that I find myself in a thoroughly postmodern split position from both the philosophical and political points of view. Anyone who is familiar with my writing will at once detect the influence of two different lines of critical thought which in the main are German in origin — lines stemming from Hegel and Marx and culminating in Gramsci and the Frankfurt School; and another line, stemming from Nietzsche and Husserl, the school which encompasses in its range both phenomenology and existentialism and stretches to the writings of Heidegger and Hannah Arendt.

Following some of this conference's exchanges, one can readily anticipate that current critical Marxist thought will find such a conjunction uncomfortable, not to say a scandal, although, naturally, for my part, I feel somewhat reassured by Lacoue-Labarthe's association of Adorno and Heidegger within the tradition of resistance. I can find further comfort in the following remarkable formulation advanced by Donald M. Lowe in his book, *History of Bourgeois Perception*:

> Both phenomenology and Marxism are anti-positivist. Both derive their concepts of reason from the world. However each proposes a different 'reason' for a different world configuration. What the life world is to phenomenology, totality is to Marxism. Phenomenologists use the concept of intentionality to describe the life world, whereas Marxists use the concept of dialectic to analyse totality. If dialectic is the structure of totality in transformation, intentionality is the subjectisation of that dialectical structure.

Here then, very briefly, six points for an architecture of resistance. You should take them as models about which I feel critical cultural thought, as far as architecture is concerned, should revolve if we are to generate a post-modern expression.

Culture and Civilisation

For this point I am doubly indebted, firstly to Dalapor Vesley, because it was he who introduced me to a particular text by Paul Ricoeur by which I have been, I suppose, unduly influenced. The text, written in 1961, is entitled 'Universal Civilisation and National Cultures'. I shall cite it briefly here and leave it at that, since its purpose to my general position about culture and civilisation will be relevant to some of my later points.

> The phenomenon of universalisation, while being an advancement of mankind, at the same time constitutes a sort of subtle destruction, not only of traditional cultures, which might not be an irreparable wrong, but also of what I shall call for the time being the creative nucleus of great cultures, that nucleus on the basis of which we interpret life, what I shall call in advance the ethical and mythical nucleus of mankind . . . It seems as if mankind, by approaching *en masse* a basic consumer culture, were also stopped *en masse* at a subcultural level. Thus we come to the crucial problem confronting nations just rising from underdevelopment. In order to get on to the road towards modernisation, is it necessary to jettison the old cultural past, which has been the *raison d'être* of a nation? . . . Whence the paradox: on the one hand, it has to root itself in the soil of its past, forge a national spirit and unfurl this spiritual and cultural revindication before the colonialist's personality.

Ricoeur was writing at the time that France was divesting itself of Algeria, I believe. He goes on:

> But in order to take part in modern civilisation, it is necessary at the same time to take part in scientific, technical, and political rationality, something which often requires the pure and simple abandon of a whole cultural past. It is a fact: Every culture cannot sustain and absorb the shock of modern civilisation. There is the paradox: how to become modern and to return to sources; how to revive

an old, dormant civilisation and take part in universal civilisation. (*History and Teuth*)

Ricoeur is very interesting in as much as he makes the case that no developing country can refuse the benefits of universal civilisation — such as modern medicine, modern communication techniques, etc.

There is also, in Ricoeur, although he never makes it specific, the idea of a world culture — a reference to the history of tradition as a kind of treason, to the possibility of revitalisation through a potential real critique of the Occident by the Orient. He ends his essay by saying:

> No one can say what will become of our civilisation when it has really met different civilisations by means other than the shock of conflict and domination; but we have to admit that this encounter has not taken place at the level of an authentic dialogue. That is why we are in a kind of long inter-regnum in which we can no longer practice the dogmatism of a single truth and in which we are not yet capable of conquering the scepticism into which we have stepped.

The Metamorphosis of the Avant-Garde

My second point, after culture and civilisation, has to do with the metamorphosis of the avant-garde, or what I have called the rise and fall of the avant-garde. While I have very little sympathy for the transavant-garde, as Achille Bonita Oliva has characterised it in his book, *Transavantgarde*, (which tends in considerable measure to be avant-gardist in posture, structure and gesture, but somewhat reactionary in content), I nevertheless now feel that we should analyse this whole issue in a more discriminatory and appropriate way. While the avant-garde as we know it may well be dead, critical culture affords a position which may well be regarded as a transmutation of the avant-garde. I am thinking at this juncture of Peter Wollen and his useful distinction between positive and negative avant-garde, a distinction in which we may think of the positive avant-garde as conceiving of themselves and of their work as being totally compatible with the modern project of the

Enlightenment and with modernisation; and of the negative avant-garde as being passionately involved with the dissolution of all bourgeois culture, including the positive project of the Enlightenment.

There are instances in the twenties when these positive and negative impulses tend to fuse with each other, as say in Tatlin's Monument to the Third International, although even here the project is ultimately negative. Examples can be given in the history of 20th century architecture and applied arts, where both the positive and negative avant-garde arrive at a dissolution of classical aesthetics, and I suppose this can even be construed as a metamorphosis of the sublime, as in say Duchamp's anti-painting painting or Adolf Loos's anti-architecture architecture.

I would like to suggest that we may perhaps think of the positive and negative avant-garde as being transformed into two similar positive and negative aspects in current critical culture and manifest in the phenomena of postmodernism. For me, the mediation of the visual by the tactile, the prospects for an anti-phallocentric, anti-Eurocentric reflexive culture, the possibility for an architecture of place creation versus space endlessness — these all point to an affirmative critical culture. As for the other line, the prospect for a dissenting, but also exuberantly theatrical, allegorical and, I suppose, *visual* proliferation of dialectically scintillating images, always revealing the void beneath — as indeed we find it in certain aspects of current Japanese critical architecture, or for that matter in the post-situationist critique of Jean Baudrillard — say, a critical posture which favours art rather than architecture, may we not think of this as a metamorphosis of the negative avant-garde?

Here, of course, the categories of complicity and resistance once again suggest themselves, particularly when one reflects on the complicity of today's superannuated avant-gardists who are in a sense neither positive nor negative, but merely consumptive or complicit in consumption. I am thinking of Andreas Huyssens' remark that the American postmodernist avant-garde is not only the end game of the avant-garde. It also represents the fragmentation and decline of critical adversary culture.

Development vs Place-Forms

My present views on development versus place-forms has also changed slightly from the position taken in *Postmodern Culture*. When I speak of development, I suppose I am thinking of optimised applied science. I have previously treated this issue under the title, 'The Resistance of the Place-Form'. Here I feel it is necessary to stress how modern development, together with the autonomous nature of the techno-scientific world, the one focusing with the other and vice versa, has indeed brought into being a more or less universal, highly privatised, megalopolis, celebrated as a modernising triumph by postivistic urban planners, such as Melvin Webber, whose ideological concept of 'community without propinquity' and 'the non-place urban realm', are nothing if not slogans devised to rationalise the disappearance of the public realm in the modern motopia. It was Webber, by the way, who was the ideologue behind the plan of the last English new town of Milton Keynes. So much for imperial domination . . .

For the concept of the place-form, my own coinage, as far as I know, I am of course indebted to Heidegger. In his essay 'Building, Dwelling, Thinking' (1954), he opposes the Latin and Teutonic terms for space, namely *spatium* and *extensio* with the German *Raum*, the latter having the connotations of a phenomenologically concrete and bounded place. As he puts it, 'a boundary is not that at which something stops, but as the Greeks recognised, the boundary is that from which something begins its presencing'.

I am also indebted to Hannah Arendt who, in her book, *The Human Condition*, (1958) stressed the *res publica* as the political space for public appearance and made her categoric critique of the universalisation of the suburbs: 'The only indispensible material factor in the generation of power is the living together of people. Only where men live so close together that the potentialities for action are always present will power remain with them'. Here, there is a certain perceivable affinity between Arendt and Jürgen Habermas, particularly in Habermas' essay 'Technology and Science as Ideology' where he talks about the necessity for undistorted communication mediating the autonomy of the techno-science field, at least as applied techno-science.

Against this thesis of resistance we have to set the increasingly privatised universal reality of the megalopolis where there is quite literally no more 'there, there', to paraphrase Gertrude Stein, above all where 'there' is the public institution and the space of public appearance. You have to remember, in my making these remarks, that I am perhaps unduly influenced by the experience of the United States — and I don't mean New York. Moreover, here we are witness to an apocalyptic consumption of resources of energy, not to mention ecological destruction on a vast scale and an essentially violent relationship with nature. Perhaps with the exception of China this is universal. With our subtle, rationalised perceptions of technology as a new and augmented nature, the manifest waste of megalopolitan privatised development is so self-evident as to need no emphasis, and yet it continues to expand its domain unremittingly. Indeed, it seems just as autonomous as the techno-scientific autonomy recognized by Lyotard and in which he seems to place, in my view, too much faith — in terms of its structurally liberative, open-ended creativity, the 'space or time in which something can happen'. (Although I suppose his remarks are really directed more towards pure science rather than to applied science.) The whole predicament reminds me of Thomas Maldonado's aphorism that while it is not possible to create anything without waste, this is distinguishable from an ideology of waste. Once again one thinks of China. Moreover, it is easy to see how the privatisation of the megalopolis perpetuates the domestic enslavement of women; how it maintains the atomised nuclear family in a state of alienated isolation, a condition of private somnambulism through the psychological facility of television — which is not without certain ambiguities.

The critical, but necessarily marginal potential of the place-form in this regard, not only as a physically bounded form, but also as a potentially liberative programmatic institution, should be self-evident from what I have already said: for example, the possible social condensation to be achieved by a nursery school in the suburbs if that were a universal provision . . . which it isn't.

Culture vs Nature

In *Postmodern Culture*, I tried to combine in a much too condensed way, topography, climate, light and tectonic form. These are issues I won't over-elaborate here, because there simply isn't time, but I just want to say that perhaps there are three aspects for this. One, the question of building the site, that is, inscribing the built work into the ground, rather than building free-standing objects, which are obviously potentially consumable objects.

The second point is the regional inflection of buildings, or rather their potential for regional inflection by the impact of climate, light and so on, above all as this affects the perception of place-time. I'd like to give two examples which might help explain where a resistance to universalisation might lie, an opposition to the rule of optimised applied science.

One example would be air conditioning, which as you know is fairly frequent in this country, but practically ubiquitous in the United States, to such an extent that in many large institutional buildings one cannot open a window and one is stuck with the air conditioning forever. This ubiquitous air conditioning is a main antagonist of a rooted culture. To work out a particular form of relationship with local nature would be far better.

Another example is the optimised curatorial drive of certain American curators, who are very anxious about the preservation of their stock certificates and would like their works to be kept in windowless, perfectly climatised boxes, and thereby protected from the potentially injurious effects of natural light. This is also, in my view, optimised applied science and is equally destructive of an idea of place and also, by the way, the *place* of an art work, because in fact the art work is *nowhere* under such conditions.

Finally, the question of the limits of architecture and the distinction between architecture and art come into this sphere of culture vs nature. I am thinking of the essentially tectonic aspects of architecture in terms of its construction and its resistance to gravity and climate. Here I just want to mention briefly in passing a number of figures. First of all the Italian Giorgio Grassi, who in an essay 'Avant-Garde and Continuity' was to point out that a great deal of

modern architectural development was subject, or overin-
fluenced, let us say, by the avant-gardist art deconstruction
of the perspectival inheritance of the Renaissance. He is
alluding to neoplasticism or purism, I suppose in this
regard, and how by being over-influenced, architecture
departed, so to speak, from its own intrinsic tradition as a
cultural field. One thinks of Greenberg's comment about
the arts being deprived by the Enlightenment of all tasks
they could take seriously and seeking to re-establish
themselves through redefining their discipline. I suppose
there is something of this in the whole of this presentation.
The Viennese architect, Adolf Loos, makes a distinction
between architecture and art in an essay entitled
'Architecture' (1910), where he oscillates between describing the house as conservative and the art work, art, as
subversive. He ends with this beautiful ironic passage, 'and
so the man loves his house and hates art'.

Visual vs Tactile

My fifth point concerns the visual vs the tactile and
information vs experience. This is not spelled out in my
earlier essay. Here, I suppose of course, I am really
departing from my caveat that I do not imply a pattern of
opposition between pairs — although I think any kind of
resolution of this proposition, a victory of either one over
the others is unthinkable and undesirable. But I do think
that much of what passes for postmodern architectural
culture today is, in fact, simply a proliferation of images, or
if not, the reduction of architecture to pure information, in
the same way that television is really a machine of
information rather than experience. I am opposing here the
split between body and mind, this semiotic, communicational manipulation that television represents in dividing
body from mind; conditions in which the liberative,
emancipatory heritage of modern architecture vis a vis the
body, is deliberately neglected. There is a marked
tendency, in American postmodernist architecture in
particular, to reduce architecture to surface images — to a
kind of gratuitous and supposedly reassuring *mise en scène*, to
a scenography oriented towards marketability, social

control and towards an optimisation of building production and consumption.

I would like, by way of conclusion, simply to read the passage that occurs at the very end of my essay in *Postmodern Culture*.

> In this way, Critical Regionalism seeks to complement our normative visual experience by readdressing the tactile range of human perceptions. In so doing it endeavours to balance the priority accorded to the image and to counter the Western tendency to interpret the environment in exclusively perspectival terms. According to its etymology, perspective means rationalised sight or clear seeing, and as such it presupposes a conscious suppression of the senses of smell, hearing and taste, and a consequent distancing from a more direct experience of the environment. This self-imposed limitation relates to that which Heidegger has called a 'loss of nearness'. In attempting to counter this loss, the tactile opposes itself to the scenographic and the drawing of veils over the surface of reality. Its capacity to arouse the impulse to touch returns the architect to the poetics of construction and to the erection of works in which the tectonic value of each component depends upon the density of its objecthood. The tactile and the tectonic jointly have the capacity to transcend the mere appearance of the technical in much the same way as the place-form has the potential to withstand the relentless onslaught of global modernisation.

ARCHITECTURE AND THE POSTMODERN CONDITION
Demetri Porphyrios

Of the many preoccupations which describe the cultural values of postmodern architecture today, I would like to identify a few which may be claimed to comprise the core of its postmodern condition.

First, there is an emphasis on fragmentation; an emphasis on the disintegration of the compositional and stylistic systems that lived on from earlier years, including the modern avant-gardes. Buildings are de-composed, exploded or attacked by foreign bodies until they disintegrate. There is an emphasis, therefore, on fastidious syntax that decentralises both composition and iconography.

The second preoccupation of postmodern architecture relates to the use of ironic commentary and parody. The postmodern architect no longer is the celebrant of human or technological order, but instead reaches for a redeeming image in the world of parody, mockery or nostalgia. When applied to architecture parody may involve exaggeration, distortion, pastiche, etc.

Thirdly, there exists an emphasis on phantasmagoria at the expense of material quality or significant meaning. Architecture (which traditionally has been the 'art of building' — *baukunst* — deriving its authority from tectonic reason) in its postmodern version effaces the very traces of its production and becomes a mere decorated shed. By means of the illusion of phantasmagoria the postmodern architect buries himself in the voluptuous surfaces of historical styles and the modern avant-gardes, as if to re-assure himself of their reality.

Lastly, postmodern architecture is marked by the demise of the public realm. Questions of public/private and of the meaning of *res publica* are silenced since they are considered anachronistic and irrelevant in a world dominated by mass-media. The public realm — and by extension the city

— is debunked. All continuity of life, of tradition, of history, of culture and of practical reason is undermined by the industrial and real-estate markets which, in the name of the Spirit of the Age, win over both client and architect.

These preoccupations with fragmentation, parody, phantasmagoria and the demise of the public realm converge under the general umbrella of the postmodern ideology of pluralism. Under the pretexts of democratic toleration, relativism and conciliatory culture, the postmodern ideology of pluralism presents itself as the only means by which to recuperate a philosophy of the subject and by extension freedom. But once tradition and culture are no longer animated by an ethical force, they disintegrate into spurious and vacuous imagery.

In connection with Kenneth Frampton's paper, therefore, I would like to think that it is possible for regionalism to play a critical role today, provided that it safeguards against the cooption of tradition by the strategies of pluralism. This means that the architect must be in a position to understand the technical, economic and social process that guarantees the authenticity of a regional culture. Unless such constant vigilance is observed, regional culture is quickly reduced to the phantasmagoria of the *homme sauvage* and tradition converges with barbarism.

RESPONSE TO KENNETH FRAMPTON
Jean-François Lyotard

Listening to Kenneth Frampton, it seems to me that there is a tragedy of architecture, for a precise reason. People don't build simply in order to put a roof over their heads, they build in order to render homage. The act of building is an act of honour rendered, and the tragedy is that of knowing who or what is the addressee of this gift. The great architectures of the past knew to whom buildings should be addressed. It could be a divinity, in all forms; it could be a prince; it could be an Idea of Reason, such as the Republic, or the People, or the Proletariat, as in certain aspects of the Modern movement. But it was always the universal addressee. Today we don't know the destination of building, and this too is an aspect of the failure of the universal. And clearly it's this failing that postmodern architecture tries to scar over with parody, denounced both by Kenneth Frampton and by Demetri Porphyrios. Parody, irony, quotation: this is indeed 'political quietism' (if one understands by 'political' much more than 'professional' politics) because it means 'don't talk to me about the addressee of architecture': that's what's apolitical. Let's have a good time. It's like the last waltz of the passengers on the Titanic.

The other aspect of architectural tragedy has been pointed out several times. The same building which is addressed to something must *also* meet the demands of human life, of humans as living beings. If the architect *only* answers this demand, then architecture is necessarily conservative, insofar as its function is that of conserving human beings, of putting into conservation.

The tragedy of architecture is also the question of the body. Kenneth Frampton stressed the need to pay attention to the body, and several questioners from the floor also insisted on this. The words accompanying this emphasis are 'tectonic' and 'tactile', and there's a real problem here. In a sense, and in a sense only, architecture is constructed for the body insofar as the body occupies a space. How are we to conceive of this space? If we think of it as a functional space, this means that we think of the body as a set of functions, and this is already a presupposition as to the nature of the body. A scientific, technoscientific or pseudo-technoscientific presupposition.

You'll have noticed that, against this, Kenneth Frampton links his thinking to a phenomenological and even Heideggerian tradition. This means he introduces the idea of a body space which is not functional. What is this non-functional space, and what is a non-functional body? When Heidegger reflects on this question he gives it an ontological scope. It's a space in which the body is not the centre, but rather an instance of *gathering*: something gathers itself. It's a space in the sense of *Raum*, a space — and here I'm obliged to use metaphors — in which meaning *breathes*. It's a space which is empty or, rather, blank. That's what I'm trying to get at with this notion of gathering. One can say that the first model of this space is the mother's womb, as first dwelling.

In the current situation, the body is a technological object. An object of technical operations the number and scope of which will increase in the years ahead. Think of bio-medicine, bio-engineering, all imaginable prostheses, genetic surgery. Ten days ago I was involved in a discussion with a bio-medic who was saying among other things that in 15 years it will not be necessary for women to bear their children: the whole period of gestation could take place *in vitro*. Whence the disappearance of the first dwelling.

In a sense, what characterises the modern dwelling is that it no longer has walls. Not in the physical sense, but in the sense that the separation between the outside and the inside is increasingly problematical. The inside is becoming filled with instruments for the sending and receiving of messages, communicating with the outside. Here too the dwelling is affected. My question is the following: the body is to my mind an essential site of resistance, because with the body there is love, a certain presence of the past, a capacity to reflect, *singularity* — if this body is attacked, by techno-science, then that site of resistance can be attacked. What is the unconscious of a child engendered *in vitro*? What is it's relationship with the mother, and with the father? The mediatisation of the body makes me ask the following question of Kenneth Frampton: can we still base ourselves on a phenomenology or an ontology of the body to designate one of the principal functions or destinations of architecture today? I believe that Kenneth Frampton is very aware of all this, and that it's part of his concern.

REVISING MODERNISM, REPRESENTING POSTMODERNISM: CRITICAL DISCOURSES OF THE VISUAL ARTS
Michael Newman

The subject of our discussion[1] is not new, even in the visual arts where the term 'postmodernism' achieved currency slightly later than in literature and architecture. In 1971 Brian O'Doherty published an article in *Art in America* entitled 'What is postmodernism' which began 'Now that the modernist era (1948–1969?) is over . . .'. He complained that although postmodernism 'is our diagnosis for what surrounds us, one never hears it defined' and suggested that 'there is an unconscious agreement to withhold a definition, partly because everyone's definition will expose the confusion the word is designed to cover'.[2] Fourteen years on we are no longer short of definitions of postmodernism, though perhaps no less confused.

It is not my intention to offer here yet another definition of postmodernism. Rather, I'd like to take this opportunity to attempt an analysis of some of the underlying assumptions as well as the implications of a few of the terms and assertions prominent in the art criticism of the past years which has had postmodernism as its theme. A critical lexicon of such terms will form the second part of my paper.

How postmodernism is understood will be dependent upon two interrelated assumptions: the definition of modernism and a theory of history, which may be implicit in a theory of art. Confusion arises because 'modernism' and 'postmodernism' are used as both aesthetic categories and terms for cultural phenomena which coincide with epochs of history. Modernity has been understood as the period of modernization; and post-modernity as the period of consumer society within corporate capitalism; the period of fundamental technological changes; or as the period of the loss of legitimation by the great narratives of Enlightenment.[3] Some theory of history, even if it is that of the failure of theories of history, is always involved. As Fredric Jameson has written, 'to grant some historical originality to a postmodernist culture is also implicitly to affirm some radical structural difference between what is sometimes called consumer society and earlier moments of capitalism from which it emerged'.[4]

As an aesthetic category for the visual arts, modernism might be interpreted in, broadly, two ways. Arguments around postmodernism become confused if it is not made clear which version of modernism is being referred to. The formalist account is that associated with Clement Greenberg's theory that the work of art should be rendered 'pure' by being confined to the effects specific to its own medium.[5] Another interpretation of modernism would identify a critically rather than formally reflexive tendency which might include Cubism, Dada, photomontage, the readymade and conceptual art, together with the utopian attitudes of Futurism and Constructivism which embrace social modernity.[6]

Many of the arguments which assume Greenberg's theory of modernism and assert a postmodernism using post-structuralist categories may in effect be retheorizing a pre-Greenbergian modernism. This is an attempt to maintain a reflexive radicality, a questioning of the institution of art, and an emancipatory ethic — art as a contribution to knowledge and social self-awareness; but without a utopian conception of historical development and, in most but not all cases, without any commitment to a specific political project. Looked at critically, this might be seen as an attempt to maintain the stance of a modernist avant-garde in conditions where this is no longer possible or appropriate, and to do so through critical discourse. It is hardly surprising, therefore, that such discourse tends to become increasingly Byzantine in its convolutions around such terms as 'allegory' and 'desire'.

To prepare for my critical lexicon, I will consider both modernism and postmodernism, and the divergent critical positions of affirmation and negation within the problem of the 'aesthetic' as a category, or rather, the way in which the category of the aesthetic points to a problem. Modernism is then interpreted as a set of responses to the autonomy of the aesthetic (which is to be understood socially as well as philosophically). I will then discuss the recent history of art, focussing in particular on Pop, Minimalism and Conceptualism, as preparing the way for the practices which are currently described as postmodernist (this history being understood as only *relatively* autonomous).

I The Autonomy and the Death of Art
The Aesthetic as Problem

Two thinkers, both influential in discussions of post-modernism and associated with contrasting political positions, take as fundamental to their consideration of aesthetics Hegel's notion of a 'withering away' or 'death' of art conceived as a moment of becoming in the dialectic of Absolute Spirit. And even if the consequences they draw from it are different, they agree that the formulation of the aesthetic by Hegel's predecessor Kant — as the fundamentally subjective realm of judgements of taste indicating the freedom of the autonomous individual — is a part of the emergence of modernity and an indication of a crisis. Heidegger writes of Hegel's *Lectures on Aesthetics* (1828–29), 'At the historical moment when aesthetics achieves its greatest possible height, breadth, and rigor of form, great art comes to an end. The achievement of aesthetics derives its greatness from the fact that it recognizes and gives utterance to the end of great art as such'.[7] Adorno extrapolates from Hegel the thought that the absolute aspect of art, its non-identity with the dimension of life and death, as content, 'might precisely be arts' mortality'; so that, from Adorno's modernist point of view, 'The revolt of art which programmatically defined itself in terms of a new stance towards the objective, historical world has become a revolt against art' such that 'Aesthetics today is powerless to avert its becoming a necrologue of art'.[8]

We need not accept that great art ceased to be produced

after the treatises on Aesthetics of Kant and Hegel, but rather that, with the loss of what Walter Benjamin calls its cultic function in a world which is ever more disenchanted, the *status* of art becomes a problem. Whereas previously aesthetics took as its subject how to make art, as in poetics, and the effect of art, from Kant and Hegel the first question is 'What is art?'. This problem continues to be the problem for postmodernism, but now it is considered with a greater understanding, perhaps even the understanding of the failure of the two solutions associated with the lineages of Kant and Hegel respectively: the *autonomy* of art, and the *withering away* of art into social practice or theoretical discourse.

Towards the end of the 19th century the aesthetic as a realm of subjective judgement, the basis of Romanticism, had been constituted by a group of writers and artists centered on Paris, as an autonomous 'life-world', a minority culture opposed to the levelling and technologizing effects of bourgeois modernity. The logic of the latter was both exemplified and negated by Symbolist art which was at once progressive (a negation of tradition in, for example, *vers libre*), autonomous (in that art was to pursue its own aims and not those of positivist science or the means-end rationality of society) and synthetic (synesthesia to express a state of the soul; the Wagnerian ideal of the total work of art; and, by extension the aesthetic as a model for the whole of life, which was to have consequences for utopian modernism).

A central problem for Kant was to demonstrate how subjective judgements of taste could manifest a universal standard of value. The problem was posed, as D. Vasely has argued, by the split interposed, since Descartes' thought experiment of radical doubt, 'between traditional symbolic, cosmologically based representation and modern instrumental thinking'.[9] It was also manifested during the 17th century by Claude Perrault's distinction in architecture between 'positive beauty', mechanical and inevitable, and 'arbitrary beauty' which depends on inclination;[10] and in the 19th century in Baudelaire's distinction between the eternal and the transitory elements in art. For Baudelaire, who begins his essay *The Painter of Modern Life* (published 1863) by contemplating fashion engravings dating from the Revolution to the Consulate, modernity and *mode* were deeply intertwined, the forward thrust of the New leading to the melancholy cycle of obsolescence, and requiring redemption by an 'eternal and immutable' — indeed a Classical — element which is itself subject to the possibility of sterility. If the content of art was mutable, where was its transcendant value to be found? For Symbolist theory, which tended to make a categorical distinction between content and form, it was in the latter that 'aesthetic' value resided, entirely separate from what Mallarmé described as the 'journalistic' and what Clement Greenberg was later to call kitsch.

Three aspects of modernism and their closure

Many discussions of postmodernism are vitiated by too narrow a definition of modernism, specifically according to Greenberg's neo-Kantian formalism, based on the Symbolist influenced interpretation of French art by Roger Fry and Clive Bell. It would be closer to the truth to see Symbolism as the horizon out of and against which 20th century modernism emerged. I propose to distinguish three tendencies within modernism all of which are towards heteronomy rather than autonomy,[11] and all of which were closed off in Greenberg's revisionist theory.

The first is that of art conceived as an expression of Modernity through a mode of representation or abstraction which is considered to be historically privileged because its form most appropriately manifests the *Zeitgeist*. Cubism, Futurism, Suprematism and De Stijl could be taken as examples. Such a mode is always threatened with the loss of privilege: with becoming a 'style' which is just one option among others. This already begins to occur with Cubism around 1914, and by 1917–18 Picasso is using an eclectic range of cubist, rococo and classical styles.[12] This kind of eclecticism, which could be described as an arbitrary historicism, is also manifested in the late work of de Chirico, Picabia and *vache* period Magritte, all of which have enjoyed revaluation by postmodernist criticism. It appears to be almost a cyclical inevitability within modernism itself that an historically privileged mode will collapse into stylistic pastiche. This raises the possibility that current pastiche is the outcome of the collapse of the privileged Minimal and Conceptual modes within a modernist historical logic.

The second aspect of modernism is that of the avant-garde critique of the aesthetic as an autonomous realm — against the horizon, as I have suggested, of the Symbolists. Rooted in 19th century Realism, against the positivism of which the Symbolists set themselves, it emerges in the ontological tension of the Cubist collage, because, as Peter Bürger argues, it is only after Symbolism that autonomous art becomes perceivable as a social institution or form of life. Constructivism and Dada stand as the positive and negative sides of a total and utopian critique, in terms of order and chance, of art within social modernity. Photomontage was used during the 1930s as an instrument of agitprop. Surrealist heteronomy involved the break-up, under the influence of Freud and Jung, of the univocal, rationally self-conscious subject, even if its more politically revolutionary aspirations for a total transformation of life were easily recouped — as were those of the Surrealist-inspired student revolutionaries of the Paris of 1968. From Duchamp's presentation of a urinal as *Fountain* signed by R. Mutt to Conceptual art, the avant-garde has been concerned with bringing art into consciousness as a social institution and breaking its autonomy. While the modernist avant-garde may be seen as a part of the project of the Enlightenment, the 'death' of the avant-garde in postmodernism doesn't necessarily exclude the possibility of a critical and socially emancipatory role for art, which needs to be considered in less total, more limited and more specific terms.

A third heteronomous aspect of modernism would be its repeated absorbtion of that which is extrinsic to the Western high-art tradition, largely in the pursuit of renewal and reinvigoration. This would include material from a very wide range of sources and the adoption of a variety of different models for the artist's practice: for example primitive art and the art of the insane and of children, commercial and mass media imagery, and subcultural forms such as graffiti. These sources assume particular meanings within different contexts, ranging from a critique of bourgeois modernity to an attempt to assimilate it, from assertions of primal expressive authenticity to 'appropriation' of the Other.

To an extent the heteronomy of modernism can be understood as a variety of responses, whether positive or negative, to the *urban* condition of social modernity. The theme of the city, and its effects of displacement and alienation coupled with an infinite extension of possibilities and roles, is a repeated motif of both modernism and what we have come to call postmodernism.[13] This needs to be interpreted in terms of the nexus of the city and Capital pointed out by Walter Benjamin's study of Baudelaire.[14] The question for any study of postmodernism is whether the two terms have undergone or are undergoing a decisive shift, and the ways in which this might be mediated through art which is, after all, mostly circulated and experienced in urban settings.

A turning point is marked by Rauschenberg, Johns and Warhol who step into the void opened up by the failure of perhaps the last credibly 'expressionist' art movement, American Abstract Expressionism; a failure insofar as the purportedly 'tragic and timeless' inwardness of the art did not prevent its exploitation as ideology. Johns uses old-masterly patina, economically produced with encaustic and sculpmetal, to neutralize banal signs and objects, turning them into elements in a Duchampian game. Rauschenberg re-opens art to the detritus and imagery of the sinful city in a negation of puritan exclusion and Barnett Newman's Jewish iconoclasm. Warhol exploits the mechanisms towards the creation of the artist's public image which had been unleashed on Pollock. The question of whether Warhol's strategy is a continuation of a modernist concern with urban modernity, or a break towards the postmodernist assertion of the loss of a model in the real and a generalized state of equivalence or simulation is obviously an important one. There is certainly a failure to realize the emancipatory potential of the loss of aura through photographic reproduction which Walter Benjamin asserted. Indeed Thomas Crow has argued, taking a position closer to the more pessimistic one of Adorno, that in its 'appropriation from fringe mass culture', 'the avant-garde serves as a kind of research and development arm of the culture industry', setting in motion a one-way cycle of exchange: 'oppositional practices upward, the return of cultural goods downward' such that 'modernist negation becomes, paradoxically, an instrument of cultural domination'.[15] Crow's argument, which he applies from Impressionism onwards, is limited by an over-monolithic conception of the 'culture industry' and the failure to theorize intermediate and potentially resistant institutions, a civil society', between the individual and the state, problems from which many Frankfurt School based analyses suffer.

Nevertheless, Crow's argument does have some validity if applied specifically to U.S. postmodernist art, insofar as we take Rauschenberg and Warhol to represent a turning point where modernity is associated with mass-consumerism. Both establish an equation between 'aesthetic' appreciation and the 'consumption' of commodities and images — or, more precisely, commodities which have become primarily image in the emphasis, through advertising and packaging, on connotational value. Thus art participated in the constitution of the 'consumer' required by post-war capital to function as a passive receiver. Rauschenberg's canvas becomes, like the Lockean consciousness, a *tabula rasa*, a blank screen to receive the imprint of the silkscreened reproduced image;[16] and Warhol reintroduces the dandified aestheticism of the *fin de siècle*, only now brought down from its quasi-aristocratic roots to be 'democratized', made accessible to the fan through the star system. The 'disinterested' aesthetic of subjectivity is eventually refashioned to serve the interests of consumerism. American Pop Art, far from emancipating its public through the use of mechanically reproduced imagery, as Benjamin had hoped, served to reify the image detached from the content of social relations, and mimetically reproduce the attitude required of the postwar consumer. Aura did not cease, but was displaced from the supposed immediacy and authenticity of brushstroke — the artist's gesture as 'signature' — to the media-projected persona. The process which was begun, tragically, with Pollock completes itself with the depthless pose of Warhol.

Autonomy and Kitsch

Greenberg's attitude to kitsch, as a debased popular, commercial art, the product of the industrial revolution which deals in vicarious experience, in a way which 'changes according to style but remains always the same' parallels Adorno and Horkheimer's castigation of the American 'culture industry' after their escape from Nazism to the USA.[17] Kitsch and the culture industry become the Other of autonomous high modernism. While for Adorno the autonomous forms of modernism bore a mimetic relation to the isolated and atomized condition of the individual under high capitalism, for Greenberg the development of his theory of modernism involved the abandonment of a social dialectic for a return to the Kantian ideology of disinterested taste; and a logic of development which was purely internal to each art form towards the manifestation of their conditions of appearance so that, in its 'purity' and 'self sufficiency' painting, for example, should strive towards a non-illusionistic flatness and the 'sheer visibility' of colour.

Thus Greenberg appeared to close off by exclusion the heteronomous tendencies which I have described in a distortion of the history of modernist practice to serve the interest of the international promotion of American Abstract Expressionism. This amounted to a return to a version of the aesthetic of Symbolist art reduced to the autonomy of the object itself. However Greenberg seems not to have realized that his version of modernism left it dependent upon kitsch for its own self-definition, debased kitsch as the Other of an autonomous high modernism which was thereby inevitably infected by it, and could hardly provide the transcendence which he envisaged. By an inadvertant irony, Greenberg's modernism remains heteronomous despite itself. It could even be argued that Greenberg's modernism is not properly modernist at all, since it closes off the critique of the institution of art which Bürger associates with modernism. In this sense, the art of the 60s and early 70s could be understood as an attempt to return to a critical modernism at a time when Greenberg's aesthetic had become an institutional norm. This would apply to Pop Art's attempt at a *rapprochement* with commercial art, Minimalism's theatricality, the embracing of 'low' materials and process by Arte Povera, and Conceptual Art's insistence on discourse: attempts to overcome Greenberg's transformation of social and self-critical reflexivity into formal reflexivity.

Thus we must try to situate any instance or critical theory of postmodernism in relation to these three 'moments' of Modernism: (1) Modernism's heteronomy in relation to social modernity and the institution of art. (2) The institutionalized formalist aesthetic of Clement Greenberg. (3) Attempts to return, given (2), to a practice closer to (1). Over a short span of time this third moment tends to recapitulate the 'problem' of art, either withering away (Fluxus, Conceptual Art), or reverting towards an institutionalized autonomy by the end of the 70s.

The success and failure of Conceptual Art

Conceptual Art was, in part at least, a response to the unrealized potential of Pop and Minimal Art. Pop Artists, while engaging in the 'kitsch' culture of mass media and publicity excluded by Greenberg, turned their images into high art emblems in a way which blocked any insight they might have afforded into the social relations of consumerism and ideological reproduction. An exception to this was Warhol's mimicry of factory production and corporate identity, which became a model for the return to 'insincere' object-production during the later 1970s. The reductiveness of the Minimal object threw the emphasis from the 'purely visual' presentness of the formalist abstract painting to the phenomenological experience of the perceiving subject's body in relation to the modification of gallery space brought about by the objects which were, as Donald Judd suggested, to be perceived as a whole and not in terms of formal part-to-part relationships (a negation of the 'European' tradition of composition).

The then Greenbergian critic Michael Fried criticized Minimal Art for its 'theatricality'. He was prompted to this by the Minimalists' introduction of duration as against modernist instantaneousness which supports a state of timeless absorbtion.[18] Fried had with unwitting accuracy identified that aspect of Minimal Art which was to be important to Conceptual and other post-Minimal approaches. Theatricality was symptomatic of the questioning of subject–object relations as a continuation of sculpture since Cubism. (For Minimalism this was blocked by the empiricist exclusion of language from perceptual experience, but taken up by William Tucker's reintroduction of illusion and developed further by Richard Deacon's object poetics.) Given the factory-finish of the Minimalist artwork, and the division of labour this implied, such questioning of subject–object relations could not avoid the problem of commodification, and more generally of urban modernity. The theatricality of the Minimal installation implied an element of quotation: an isomorphic resemblance to the forms of modernity, such as the glass skyscraper and the corporate logo,[19] and a framing of the experience by the shell of the gallery. Taken together these point to the question of art as a social institution. While it is hard to demarcate between who is a Minimal or Conceptual artist (e.g. which is Sol Lewitt?), on the whole this line of development was blocked for Minimal Art by its construction of the viewer as an experiencing subject to resolve the tension between the empiricism of the specific object and the transcendental claim to universal value which the institution demanded. Thus, for example, the social implications of the corporate technology of fluorescent lighting adapted by Dan Flavin remain undeveloped in the formal experience of a dematerialized abstraction which his installations evoke (these social implications were to be elaborated later by Jeff Wall in his back lit cibachrome photographs). If, as Fried put it, 'presentness is grace', then the theatricality of Minimalism could be taken as a sign of bad faith, since its anti-monumentalism was hardly adequate as a response to the rationalizing corporate technologies which its objects evoked.

Conceptual Art was preceded by the writings of the Situationist International (1957–72) in France and the neo-Dada anti-art activities, including 'happenings', of the artists associated with Fluxus (1961–). Both were concerned to use art as social action, through *détournement*, refunctioning and recontextualizing of elements, and direct

intervention in society — the street, systems of distribution (e.g. mail art), publicity and so on. Exhibitions which
identified Conceptual Art began to be held in 1969, the
year following the Paris 'May 68' and international wave of
student occupations and rebellion. As far as the US context
is concerned, that this was the period of protest against the
Vietnam War is of great importance. However the
problems of extinguishing art into Dada-type social action
(its effects are politically negligible and it looses the
exemplary status dependent upon its identification as art)
and the capacity of the establishment to recuperate the
tokens of protest (posters from the Paris rebellion were
already being shown in New York museums and sold by
galleries as collectors items by 1969) were becoming
apparent. Although the term 'avant-garde' was used to
describe the art and its exhibitions, there seems to have
been little belief, after the turn of the decade, in any
politically vanguardist role, apart from feminism, and the
displacement of activism into the art-politics of the slogan
'painting is dead'. In the USA the writings of the Frankfurt
School — including Adorno and Marcuse who were there,
and translations of some essays by Walter Benjamin —
demonstrated the subjective effects of social forms, and
drew attention to the recuperative power of a totalistically
conceived 'culture industry' which functions as a consumer-
moulding form of propaganda, incorporating and distort-
ing utopian ideals of happiness.

The critical targets of Conceptual Art were: above all the
commodity status of the art object; the aesthetics of the
object (especially Greenberg's version of Modernism) and
the identification of art with the 'traditions' of painting and
sculpture; and the art system as a social institution. To
some extent this was prepared for by Minimalism's
displacement of attention from the object to its physical
context. Resources were provided by Wittgenstein and the
Anglo-Saxon analytical philosophy of language (Art &
Language, Joseph Kossuth, Lawrence Weiner) and by social
anthropology and sociology (Hans Haacke), and to some
degree by ecology (Richard Long). On the whole the
Conceptual theory of art was nominalist and functionalist,
taking an anti-essentialist position — tending, with Art
and Language, towards historical materialism. The attitude

to Duchamp as a source of nominalist aesthetic strategies was ambiguous. Duchamp's unassisted readymades drew attention to art as institution. His social indifference was alien to the constructivist tendency in Conceptual Art. The functionalist emphasis, exemplified by the use of public systems of communication such as advertising (e.g. Victor Burgin) and magazines (Robert Smithson, Dan Graham, Art & Language's journal, Joseph Kossuth), could be understood as a continuation of the productivist tendency of Constructivism, but without the 'withering away' of art since it was preserved as a category: however as a category which did not necessarily have to subsume objects, but could be applied to uses of language, activities and interventions of various kinds. Although certain conceptual artists (e.g. On Kawara, Lawrence Weiner) didn't mind if their products or propositions were identified as art or not, they still maintained careers within art institutions. Steve Willats, the most constructive (and information theory influenced) Conceptual artist in Britain has conducted parallel activities of social intervention and an art-world career. A solution of French Conceptualist Daniel Buren was to reframe, using his characteristic stripes, the architecture of the museum which frames, protects and closes the meaning of the artwork.

The critique of the object was as I have suggested concerned with a refusal of commodity status: as 'idea', art could be common property, so language (disseminated in documentation, magazines and books) became a primary medium. The aim was to restore the early Modernist critical and contextual reflexivity which had been reduced to formal reflexivity by Greenberg. For many of the artists, this involved an extension from language as the work of art to an engagement with a second-order critical discourse, which was presented as a 'higher' form of work (Art & Language) and/or used to re-appropriate the creation of context from administrators and critics.

There were a number of problems with Conceptual Art which are rarely acknowledged by its practitioners who now often see the need to defend it against a 'return to painting'. As an 'avant-garde' it was without an army following along behind: Conceptual Art failed to develop a social constituency outside the art world. It aroused incomprehension

and hostility from the public, stimulated by sections of the
art world with career and financial interests in object art
and by the mass media eager for a scandal. And once
Greenbergian formalist aesthetics declined in credibility,
the meta-language of conceptual art was left without an
articulated theory to oppose. The identification of political
recuperation with the commodification of the object proved
problematic in two ways: first when the tokens of
Conceptual Art activities were themselves recuperated by
art institutions and commodified and exchanged in the
market (which is linked to the problem of the status of
documentation in Conceptual Art); and in more general
terms because the centre of gravity of capitalism had shifted
from the individual enterpreneur, through the phase of
imperialism to the multinational corporation. Just as
Minimal Art mimicked the corporate logo, so Conceptual
Art, perhaps the last truly international art movement,
ended up reproducing the technological rationality of
international corporate and state-capitalist bureaucracy.[20]
As a rationalization of art (in the Weberian-Frankfurt
School sense), Conceptual Art failed to appreciate the
problem of expressiveness (not to be identified with revival,
quasi-ironic versions of expressionism which can be taken as
an ideological answer to the problem, nor with the
formalist aesthetics of the object). To a public whose
expressive possibilities were already reduced and reified,
Conceptual Art offered little in terms of consolation or a
critical reflection on this process. The return to painting
and a purported neo-expressionism during the late 70s and
early 80s was overdetermined both by the revived capita-
lization of the art market and the deep public need which
painting stepped in to fulfill. That it has done so
unsatisfactorily and in bad conscience is due to its
ideological complicity with the conditions which produced
the need — the false resolution of a consolation in art for
social unfulfillment — and to the success of conceptual art
in questioning the social relations of art production and
consumption, and the traditional status and role of the
artist.

The contradiction of a 'clean' vanguardism operating
within the art world necessitated renewed attempts at
interventionist strategies: both within the traditional

domains of the production and circulation of art objects, painting and sculpture (e.g. Art & Language have been showing paintings 'as objects for second order discourse' since 1980); and in the wider social field, particularly in relation to mass media and architecture. Joseph Kossuth identified the problem retrospectively in 1975, 'What began in the mid-sixties as an analysis of the context of specific objects (or propositions) and correspondingly the questions of *function*, has forced us now, ten years later, to focus our attentions on the society and/or culture in which that specific object operates.'[21] Kossuth's 'revelation' was long anticipated by Robert Smithson (in his articles) and Dan Graham who spotted the isomorphism of the Minimal object and productionline product as early as 1966–67 when he published his article 'Homes for America' in *Arts Magazine*, parodying the 'kitsch' journalistic reportage in a picture story on suburban housing. Graham's writings and his own work have been an inspiration to a generation of younger artists who have used Conceptual Art strategies in relation to social forms, content and intervention. A line can be traced from, for example, Lawrence Weiner's hypothetical propositions for sculpture, through Graham, to Jenny Holzer's slogans using public sign systems. The example of Graham is also behind Jeff Wall's 'refunctioning' of the back-lit cibacrome photograph of the advertising display system. More generally, the lessons of Conceptual Art underwrite attempts to re-engage with painting without lapsing into gestural immediacy, whether from the position theorized by Tom Lawson in terms of the Situationist 'Society of the Spectacle' (Guy Debord) and Adorno and Horkheimer's 'Culture Industry' (e.g. Jack Goldstein, David Salle, Robert Longo, Lawson himself — who are also informed by the example of Warhol) or the more politically astute Gramscian perspective of Terry Atkinson, an ex-member of Art & Language whose approach is comparable to that of the recent paintings of the veteran American radical artist Leon Golub. In one way or another, these artists all accept the inevitability of recuperation without allowing that to exclude some kind of critical or subversive potential. However, because such 'subversion' forgoes the utopian social aspirations of the early, heroic Modernist period, its success evades assessment in terms of any identifiable social effects, remaining within the limits of Warholian mimicry or the elicitation of the consciousness of ideological positioning and reproduction.

The critique of the traditional object combined with the need for a renewed social content led to an engagement with the mass media photographic image and to video and performance (an example of the last two would be Martha Rosler). In Britain photowork looked back to the examples of Constructivism and photomontage, while benefiting from avant-garde film, especially Goddard, film theory and structuralism. Text, the Conceptual mode, was combined with image to maintain critical distance (Victor Burgin, John Hilliard, early John Stezaker). This is also the case with the feminist photo-text work of American Barbara Kruger. However, American artists, in line with the emblematic quality of American Pop Art, have tended more towards an up-front surface immediacy (Richard Prince) even where a deconstruction of masquerade might be the point (Cindy Sherman, Laurie Simmons).

That so much of this photographic imagery is concerned with sexuality is an indication of how important feminism became as a political project for Conceptual Art (whether or not particular works are feminist). Mary Kelly's Lacanian documentation of her child's development and acquisition of language, *Post Partum Document*, and Susan Hiller's, Rose Garrard's and Sue Arrowsmith's works in a variety of media (all have recently used painting) would be examples of feminist art deriving from Conceptualism. Along with feminism goes the questioning of authorship (already begun by Conceptual Art, influenced by Barthes and Foucault, and more recently, absorbing Derrida), and the constitution of subjectivity. In terms of discourse, this is characterized by a shift from the Anglo-Saxon philosophy of language typically used by early Conceptual Art, to semiotics and post-structuralism.[22] Politically, it is a part of a move away from class politics based on the relations of production and a base-superstructure model, to an emphasis on ideology and a more fragmented democratic politics not necessarily organized according to traditional class lines (e.g. women, gays, blacks, the old, the unemployed). Many practitioners were involved in the student radicalism

of the 60s and have witnessed its failure in the current
reactionary climate. How far this experience has been
instrumental in driving them into questions of subjectivity
— sexuality, desire, pleasure — in a way which theorizes
alienation and unfulfilment as an inevitable part of
psycho-sexual constitution, is obviously an important
question.

Whether postmodernism is interpreted as a return to
historical sources and traditional media, or a renewed
modernist radicalism, it is clear that in the visual arts at
least, Conceptual Art was the turning point, both in
exemplifying the contradictions of modernism, and in
opening new lines of enquiry and engagement. Although
there were 'post-modernist' precedents during the modernist period, and artists continued painting during the 60s
and 70s to be amply rewarded during the 80s, the *discourse*
of postmodernism, which serves to identify them, devolves
in one way or another, whether pro or anti, from
Conceptual Art. The current resurgence of interest by
younger artists in Conceptual Art based strategies testifies
to its continuing importance.

II A Critical Lexicon of Selected Terms from the Discourse of Post-modernism

The Transavantgarde

For Italian critic Achille Bonito Olivia the transavantgarde
follows from the death of the avant-garde and the failure of
the Conceptual Art which he supported earlier in his career.
He has used this label to promote the work of the Italian
'three Cs', Clemente, Chia and Cucci, as well as Mimmo
Paladino and Nicola de Maria, and it has been extended to
cover the international phenomenon of the revival of
gestural image-painting. Bonito Oliva's theory, if it can be
called that, is premised on the collapse of legitimacy of
what he calls the 'linguistic Darwinism' behind the
Modernist avant-garde. The consequence of this is an art

which eclectically uses material from different historical periods and geographical locations, often in relation to the assertion of some kind of local or national identity. However the theory itself is not strictly speaking a traditional one, as it is strongly influenced by *désirant* post-structuralism.

Against a notion of art history as a linear development, based on an Enlightenment view of history as progress, Bonito Oliva offers a model of discontinuity:

> The initial precept is that of art as the production of a catastrophe, a discontinuity that destroys the tectonic balance of language to favor a precipitation into the subject of the 'immaginario', neither as a nostalgic return, nor a reflux, but a flowing that drags inside itself the sedimentation of many things which exceed a simple return to the private and the symbolic.[23]

Bonito Oliva asserts catastrophe as a 'breaking with social needs' in which art asserts its own value by its irreducibility, 'the irreducibility of every fragment and the impossibility of recreating unity and balance': instead of the work as a fragment which is subsumed into a totality within 'political, psychoanalytic and scientific ideologies', the work succeeds 'in transferring its ends from outside to inside itself in its possibility of establishing a fragment of the work as a totality which recalls no other value outside of the fact of its own appearing'. This bypasses the avant-garde's feature of 'setting itself up as an enquiry', presenting instead an image 'which is simultaneously enigma and solution'.

The concept of subjectivity which underlies this is that of fragmentation — 'This subjectivity is asserted in its very fragmentation' — and fluidity. The characteristic movement of this subjectivity is 'drifting':

> . . . language no longer follows the logic or the mainstream of recent years, characterized by rectilinear and consistent development. New expressiveness instead sinks its roots into an open and drifting nomadism — without getting trapped into geometric and consequent development. The idea propelling this new work is *drifting*: a movement with no preconstituted directions, no departure

and no arrivals, but accompanied by the desire to find a different provisory anchorage each time around in the sensibility's movements.

As opposed to the soldier of the avant-garde, these artists are 'nomads', 'finding in the lightness of nomadism the possibility of an image at the crossroads of repetition and difference'. The nomadic subject is propelled by desire to pass through states of intensity, producing images which 'are symptoms of an inexhaustible store-house which in showing itself off doesn't let a univocal language stop it'. While post-conceptual art takes on board Lacan, Althusser, Foucault and later Derrida in order to formulate a critique of the bourgeois subject, Achille Bonito Oliva adapts to his ends the 'desiring production' of Deleuze and Guattari's book *Anti-Oedipus* (1972) in which they oppose a fluid, amorphous 'desire' to the repressive agencies of Law and institutions (rather than seeing desire and law as mutually dependent, as Lacan does). Bonito Oliva's nomadic artist resembles their 'schizophrenic out for a walk': '. . . the reality of ' matter has abandoned all extension, just as the interior voyage has abandoned all form and quality, henceforth causing pure intensities — coupled together, almost unbearable — to radiate within and without, intensities through which a nomadic subject passes.'[24] That this is a description of the subject in the novels of Samuel Beckett, and that Deleuze and Guattari's notion of the schizophrenic as a 'body without organs' comes from Antonin Artaud, suggests that this postmodernist subject might be a continuation of modernist displacement (which will be discussed in the conclusion to this paper).

Bonito Oliva shrewdly seized on the problems with conceptual avant-gardism: its underestimation of the importance of the (at least relative) autonomy and irreducibility of the work of art, and its exclusion of expressiveness which in itself became repressive. However, in the pursuit of an amorphous affirmation, his somewhat incoherent theorization, which incorporates post-structuralist notions of fragmentation, difference and desire, deprives art of its modernist critical reflexiveness and capacity for negation. Thus the art remains wholly undefended from ideological exploitation by the society to whose instrumental rationality it is supposed to provide some kind of alternative. The subjectivity of the artist which is described as fragmented and nomadic can easily be recomposed as an identity to be marketed: Clemente poses on the cover of *L'Uomo Vogue* and Schnabel is promoted as the new American hero, without even the residue of irony that accompanied Warhol's creation of himself as a brand name for the output of his 'Factory'.

'The Death of the Author'

In 1981 an exhibition of contemporary American art at the Nigel Greenwood gallery, London, selected by painter and critic Tom Lawson, included a work by Sherrie Levine. This comprised a framed reproduction of German Expressionist Franz Marc's painting *Red Roe Deer II* together with a statement. Included were the words, 'we know that a picture is but a space in which a variety of images, none of them original, blend and clash . . . A painting's meaning lies not in its origin but in its destination . . .' Which may well have a familiar ring as these statements are themselves not 'original', but adapted from Roland Barthes' well known essay, 'The Death of the Author': 'We know now that a text is not a line of words releasing a single "theological" meaning (the "message" of the Author–God) but a multidimensional space in which a variety of writings, none of them original, blend and clash'; and 'the reader is the space on which all the quotations that make up a writing are inscribed without any of them being lost; a text's unity lies not in its origin but in its destination.'[25]

Barthes' text, if we can still allow ourselves to name it by its author, is itself an example of what it describes, being compounded of an intertextual tissue of echoes from Foucault, Derrida and Kristeva among others. The idea of the 'death of the author' quickly entered the discourse of conceptual art — it was already implicit in Duchamp's 'unassisted readymades' — and was subsequently taken up by postmodernism to construct the critical space for works using appropriated imagery and stereotypes, largely through photography (see section on Allegory).

It would be a pity, however, if this idea remained confined to the discussion of the media of mechanical reproduction in their polemical opposition to the return to painting. Painting is attacked by the defenders of a practice based on conceptual art as the site of an ideologically regressive phantasma of authenticity. From the other side painting then becomes the repository of humanist values to be defended against the dehumanizing effects of the mechanical media. However, insofar as the slogan of 'the death of the author' marks a stage in the critique of the notion of the autonomous, transcendental subject which has been underway since Hegel's *Phenomenology of Spirit*, it should be understood as involving a general theory of art which would apply as much to painting as to the mechanically reproductive media. While there are problems with the way in which this theory has been applied, concerned in particular with the relinquishing of autonomy, which I will go on to consider, I would like first to discuss its sources and broader implications.

Foucault argues in *The Order of Things* (1966) that the humanist subject 'man' is the product of the discourses of a particular historical moment, 'Before the end of the eighteenth century, *man* did not exist — any more than the potency of life, the fecundity of labour, or the historical density of language',[26] and Foucault ended his book with the 'wager' that, if this were so, and the discourses which secured 'man' were to disappear, 'that man would be erased, like a face drawn in sand at the edge of the sea'. Barthes in the text from which I have quoted extended the implications of Foucault's discussion, as well as Derrida's argument concerning the privileging of speech over writing in the western tradition, into an infectious polemic against the idea of the author which he dissolves, following Derrida, into 'writing' which is 'the destruction of every voice, of every point of origin'. He argues that it is the reader, not the author, who is the point at which the traces of the text attain their unity: the reader is, we might say, constituted *as that point*. An analogy in the visual arts would be perspective representation which organizes the picture so that it attains its unity from the point of view of the spectator.[27]

In 1969, the year following the publication of Barthes'

text, Foucault published a text entitled 'What is an author?' which both developed the implications of *The Order of Things* and took issue with Barthes dissolution of the author into *écriture*. Foucault makes three points which would seem to align him with Barthes and Derrida: freed from the necessity of expression, writing is transformed 'into an interplay of signs, regulated less by the content it signifies than by the very nature of the signifier'; writing is now involved with the death or 'sacrifice' of the author into the text; and the boundaries according to which a 'work' is constituted are thrown into question. Where Foucault locates his disagreement is in what he sees as the substitution of 'writing' for the author, as if the author could be conjured away into a 'transcendental absence'. He argues rather that the disappearance of the author takes place at a particular historical moment, 'since Mallarmé, an event of our time' and that 'we should reexamine the empty space left by the author's disappearance'. The conditions for the discourses of 'man' and the 'author' should be grasped in their historical specificity:

> the subject should not be entirely abandoned. It should be reconsidered, not to restore the theme of an originating subject, but to seize its functions, its intervention in discourse, and its system of dependencies . . . we should ask: under what conditions and through what forms can an entity like the subject appear in the order of discourse; what position does it occupy; what functions does it exhibit; and what rules does it follow in each type of discourse? In short, the subject (and its substitutes) must be stripped of its creative role and analysed as a complex and variable function of discourse. [28]

And he concludes 'We can easily imagine a culture where discourse would circulate without any need for an author'.

A problem with Foucault's theory of discourse is the opposition which is set up between a rigid discourse in which the subject is offered a position, and the amorphousness of subjectivity associated, for instance, with the fluid desires of the body. As a consequence it is difficult from within his theory to account for the process of formation of the subject, and to project a praxis. This is the outcome of the need to historicize the subject as the construct of discourse at a particular moment, and the opposition to psychoanalysis as a universal theory of subject formation follows logically. However it has been an aim of the political theories which inform the branch of postmodernist criticism under discussion here to attempt to reconcile psychoanalysis and politics. A path to psychoanalysis is opened by the passage in Foucault's text which describes how previously writing (or perhaps more properly storytelling) was considered a protection against death, which the narrative deferred, whereas now writing is involved with the sacrifice or murder of the self:

> Writing is now linked to sacrifice and to the sacrifice of life itself; it is a voluntary obliteration of the self that does not require representation in books because it takes place in the everyday existence of the writer. Where a work had the duty of creating immortality, it now attains the right to kill, to become the murderer of its author . . . If we wish to know the writer in our day, it will be through the singularity of his absence and in his link to death, which has transformed him into a victim of his own writing.[29]

While Foucault specifies that this occurs 'in our day', Derrida generalizes this modernist self-erasure into a condition of representation:

> Representation is death itself. Which may be immediately transformed into the following proposition: death is (only) representation. But it is bound to life and the living proposition which repeats it originarily.[30]

And for Lacan this process of birth–death is the entry of the subject into the Symbolic Order:

> The subject is born insofar as the signifier emerges in the field of the Other. But by this very fact, this subject — which was previously nothing if not a subject coming into being — solidifies into a signifier.[31]

A central role in this process of solidification is played by the Oedipus complex through which the subject accepts a position in terms of sexual difference which in patriarchy involves the primacy of the masculine position, the Symbolic phallus and the 'Law of the Father'. Prior to the

Oedipus, comes the 'mirror stage' when the child, previously a polymorphous, uncoordinated being, is invited to identify his or her self with the image in a mirror: identity is constructed as an 'Imaginary' image. Whether this is understood literally or metaphorically, Lacan's re-reading of Freud has had an enormous impact on 'critical' postmodernism which seeks to deal with media representations and ideology.

A way of uniting the psychoanalytic formation of the subject to a materialist conception of discourse and ideology was considered to have been provided by Althusser. Individuals are 'interpellated' into their positions as subjects in society:

> I shall then suggest that ideology 'acts' or 'functions' in such a way that it 'recruits' subjects among the individuals (it recruits them all), or 'transforms' the individuals into subjects (it transforms them all) by the very precise operation which I have called *interpellation* or hailing, and which can be imagined along the lines of the most commonplace everyday police (or other) hailing: 'Hey, you there!'[32]

An example of the application of this theory in the postmodern visual arts is the work of Barbara Kruger. Texts are collaged over photographic images: 'Your gaze hits the side of my face' on an image of an art deco bust of a woman, 'You invest in the divinity of the masterpiece' over Michelangelo's creation of Adam, 'You make history when you do business' with a photo of suited and skirted legs. This juxtaposition enables the deconstruction of both Imaginary and Symbolic interpellation.[33]

Althusser adapts Lacan's theory of the Mirror Stage to the general theory of ideology. The structure of ideology is 'doubly specular' because it both constitutes ideology and ensures its functioning. Using the metaphor of religion, Althusser argues that ideology is centred on a super-Subject (God, or in Lacanian terms the Law of the Father), which interpellates the individuals around it into subjects, '*subjects* the subjects to the Subject', while at the same time offering them an image in which they can recognize each other and themselves:

The duplicate mirror-structure of ideology ensures simultaneously:
1. the interpellation of 'individuals' as subjects;
2. their subjection to the Subject;
3. the mutual recognition of subjects and Subject, the subject's recognition of each other, and finally the subject's recognition of himself;
4. the absolute guarantees that everything really is so, and that on condition that the subjects behave accordingly, everything will be all right: Amen — 'So be it'.[34]

There are a number of problems in Althusser's theory. Ideology is an Imaginary relation, required by Capitalism to position individuals as subjects in the division of labour, but according to Althusser it appears also to be singular and universal, so that there is no position outside ideology (this would be contradictory since positions are constructed by ideology) nor is there a competing ideology (it is on this issue that Gramsci has replaced Althusser as a theoretical model for the left). Secondly, Althusser's theory is not true to Lacan's conception of the subject: Althusser flattens the subject so that it is nothing other than as interpellated. For Lacan, however, the subject-of-the-enunciation and the subject-of-the-enounced are never completely correlated, and the 'suture' or stitching of the subject to the Other, the Symbolic Order, is never final but rather always in process, motivated by desire which is unsatisfiable. It is in this gap and this incompleteness that the unconscious occurs. As Stephen Heath puts it, 'the subject is a category of division, of lack' and 'The unconscious is the fact of the constitution-division of the subject in language'.[35] In other words, there is no place in Althusser's schema for the psychoanalytic concept of the unconscious. The question of the relation between the subject of political ideology and the subject of psychoanalysis remains unresolved. It is this aporia which continues to vitiate art-critical arguments which seek to combine a constitutive theory of ideology with a constitutive theory of the unconscious.

(Lacan's theory could itself be interpreted as having politically reactionary implications, as it was by Deleuze and Guattari in *Anti-Oedipus*, where they argue that Lacanian desire, in binding the subject to the social order, works in the service of repression. They want to argue for a primary desire which can resist and overcome the imposition of repressive discourses and institutions, taking schizophrenia as their model. This repeats the opposition between discourses/technologies of power/institutions and an amorphous subjectivity of resistance and the body and its pleasures in Foucault, and leaves unresolved the problem of the mediation and relation between the two. However their criticism of the implications of Lacanian theory has some justification.)

In order to discuss the kind of argument in art theory which seeks to reconcile discourse-theory with psychoanalysis at its strongest, I will take as my example some texts by Victor Burgin and Mary Kelly. Both are artists who combine theory with practice, and whose theoretical rigour is exemplary. In taking issue with their arguments, I am not constructing a defence of that which they set out to oppose, a gestural, expressionist and commodity-based approach to art. Rather I am questioning the assumptions and implications of the polarity they set up between critical and supposedly collusive practices, a polarity which I see as a legacy of conceptual art in its opposition to Greenbergian modernism, and which is in my view no longer relevant to present conditions. A revision of this polarity will involve a reconsideration of the theory of the subject, in particular as regards the question of autonomy.

None of these texts claims to be arguing a theory of postmodernism. However issue is taken in all of them with Greenberg's paradigm, and so they could be construed, within my schema, as arguing for a continuation of a critically self-conscious modernism. Reference to critical early modernism is made in Burgin's essay 'Photography, Phantasy, Function' (1978–79) which opens with a Soviet debate around photography from the early 1920s concerning the issue of the point-of-view, and it concludes with a plea for the politicization of photography around the identification of 'new questions'. Kelly's 'Re-viewing modernist criticism' (1981) and Burgin's later catalogue essay 'The absence of presence: conceptualism and post-modernisms' (1984) are explicitly interventions in a context where postmodernism had become an issue.[36] They both associate modernism with Greenberg's theory of art, and define postmodernism as a revival of or return to painting.

Thus Greenberg and postmodernism are combined in terms of the ideological centrality of painting in the discourse of modern art. Contesting this are other practices which the centrality of painting marginalizes, practices which question and deconstruct the positioning of the subject, especially in terms of the feminist project within sexual difference. Burgin privileges photography as the medium of mechanical reproduction through which, in its combination with text, such questions are raised since it subverts the investment of authenticity and authority in the aura of the unique gesture. For both Burgin and Kelly painting upholds the status of the artist-creator within the patriarchal ideology of capitalism, and is the primary historical form for the artwork as commodity. And, according to modernism in its Greenbergian version, the primacy of painting reinforces the separation of the ontology of vision from the epistemology of language in a way which blocks any possibility for the centrality of a theoretically informed critical and deconstructive practice.

The following opposition could be extracted from these texts:

Modernist art: painting as art object, self-possessed autonomous subject, phallocentric patriarchy *vs.*

Conceptual-derived practice: photography/discursive intervention, subject as split and positioned in discourse, feminism. Postmodernism is seen as a recuperative move to roll back the critical achievements of conceptual art, a kind of aesthetic Thatcherism. This has a degree of truth so far as certain manifestations of postmodernism, and current critical positions such as that of Peter Fuller, are concerned. The problem, as I see it, arises when the attempt is made to unite the strategic opposition, which relates to the artists' critical position as practitioners, with a theory of the subject which combines discursive and psychoanalytic formation. (As there is not the space for a detailed discussion of and quotation from the texts, I am paraphrasing their implications as I see them. Mary Kelly's essay is more concerned with discourse than with psychoanalysis, so what I am saying applies to a consideration of 'Reviewing modernist criticism' together with her practice in *Post-Partum Document* (1973–79). This extended work, which has been published in book form, uses Lacan as a theoretical basis for a representation of the entry of Mary Kelly's son into the Symbolic Order of language, and her relationship as a mother to that process. It is one of the most important works not only of feminist but of contemporary art in general.)[38]

The aim of both Burgin and Kelly is admirable: to link psychoanalysis and politics in a way which has been extremely important to feminism. As far as theory is concerned, the outcome, however, tends towards a polarization which masks and reinforces the aporia in the theory which I have described. To criticise the theoretical basis of conceptual-derived practice is made to look like taking a reactionary, regressive position; whereas painting is a threat not only because of its ideological and economic centrality, but also because of the theoretical aporia.

The conceptual art opposition to Greenbergian modernism is combined with the structuralist opposition to phenomenology. Thus conceptual-based practice asserts its own textuality while handing 'experience' over to the opposition. Furthermore, 'autonomy' is associated with a Greenbergian modernist conception of 'art for art's sake', and at the same time the theory of discourse disallows any autonomy to the subject: so to argue for a degree of autonomy of the subject appears also to be to imply a defence of the autonomy of painting. The blockage in the theory arises partly because 'experience' and 'autonomy' are irredeemable associated with late modernist phenomenology (the primacy of vision, the art object as commodity, expressionist authenticity) as opposed to structuralist textuality.

Thus the setting up of Greenberg's conception of modernism as the opposition, which is inherited from conceptual art, impedes the further development of an important line of critical thought. In this opposition autonomy is associated both with Greenberg's theory of art and (for Burgin) with liberal humanism. What is forgotten is that even formalist abstract art can, in certain circumstances, have a degree of critical social content which derives from its very claim to autonomy. Also any radical political theory with a program of emancipation must allow some degree of autonomy to the subject. Some advance could be made if a more sophisticated theory of modernism, such as that of Adorno, were substituted for that of Greenberg which is by now irrelevant. According to Adorno the notion of a fundamentally oppositional art is a function of the bourgeois consciousness of freedom. Art, he argues,

> is not social only because it derives its material content from society. Rather it is social because it stands in opposition to society. Now this opposition art can mount only when it has become autonomous. By congealing into an entity unto itself — rather than obeying existing social norms and thus proving itself to be 'socially useful' — art criticizes society just by being there. Pure and immanently elaborated art is a tacit critique of the debasement of man by a condition that is moving towards a total-exchange society where everything is for-another. This social deviance of art is the determinate negation of a determinate society.[38]

According to Adorno the hardened autonomy of the modernist work of art bears a mimetic relation to the condition of the subject under a rationalizing and instrumentalizing modernity. However it also serves as a determinate negation of technological means-end rationality, and the only glimmer of anticipation of utopia which is available under such conditions. I am not saying that we have to agree with Adorno, but rather that a critique of his strong case for autonomy would lead to a more interesting and fruitful argument than that which takes Greenberg's theory of modernism as its target. It is possible to disagree with Adorno's mandarin opposition to popular and mass culture, comparable to Greenberg's rejection of kitsch as aesthetic false consciousness, while accepting that no form of emancipatory social transformation can be envisaged without some degree of autonomy being allowed to the subject, and consequently a gap between the subject and discourse. Indeed without granting some autonomy to the subject there would be no point in imaginging such a transformation, as how could its goals be established. Thus a politically radical art cannot be based on theories which dissolve the subject either into discourse or into a residue of amorphous desire.[39]

The problem for political theory and praxis is how to reconcile the claims of autonomy with the claims of collectivity. In the absence of a substantive change in society art could conceivably offer at least a model of ways of mediating between the two. A condition would be a rethinking of the kinds of theoretical and strategic polarization which inhibit this mediation from occuring. While the discourse which privileges the artist as the sole origin of the work of art must continue to be criticised, together with its social and historical determinants, the artist cannot simply be killed off or considered an epiphenomenon of discourse, but remains as a morally responsible social agent with the capacity for self-knowledge and innovation without which any kind of social transformation and cultural renewal are inconceivable.

Allegory

The concept of allegory has enjoyed a revival in the criticism of recent art. Largely responsible for this is American critic Craig Owens' brilliantly choreographed two-part article, 'The Allegorical Impulse: Toward a Theory of Postmodernism' which appeared in the theoretically formidable *October* magazine in the issues of spring and summer 1980. In an aside Owens refers to the 'poststructuralist counterparts' to postmodernist artists, and his article does indeed comprise a most thoroughgoing attempt to use poststructuralist philosophy and literary theory to identify and define a distinctive category of postmodernist art. Strongly argued as it is, there are in my view problems with Owens' attempt to maintain a radical critical theory of the postmodernist art which he describes, problems which are also common to other criticism using the same sources.

The revaluation of allegory in recent criticism contests the theories of art since Romanticism which privilege the formal and expressive element over the discursive. Postmodern allegory replaces the redemptive, purified and organic concept of form with textuality and the arbitrariness of meaning as it is read into an already existing fragment rather than emerging from an original totality. For Owens the expressivity of the artist—genius is supplanted by a supplementarity supplied by the reader. Allegory is a mode of reading the already-written:

In allegorical structure, then, one text is *read through* another . . . the paradigm for the allegorical work is thus the palimpsest . . . Allegorical imagery is appropriated imagery; the allegorist does not invent images but confiscates them. He lays claim to the culturally significant, poses as its interpreter. And in his hands the image becomes something other (*allos* = other + *agoreuei* = to speak). He does not restore an original meaning that may have been lost or obscured; allegory is not hermeneutics. Rather he adds another meaning to the image. If he adds, however, he does so only to replace: the allegorical meaning supplants an antecedent one; it is a supplement.[40]

Owens' own essay is itself an allegorical reading of a text on allegory: he takes as his object–text fragments of Walter Benjamin's book *The Origin of German Tragic Drama* and reads it through other, post-structuralist texts, Barthes, Lacan, Derrida and Paul de Man's *Allegories of Reading*. Owens' extension of literary allegory into a theory of art is happily confirmed by the priority of language in the French structuralist tradition, which allegory both requires and reaffirms. The opposition of structuralism to the phenomenology of experience parallels the postmodernist critic's implicit opposition to Greenberg's formalism. As in the baroque emblem books, allegory proposes a reciprocity between the visual and the verbal: 'words are treated as purely visual phenomena, while visual images are offered as script to be deciphered' so that in allegory 'the image is a hieroglyph; an allegory is a rebus — writing composed of concrete images'. This reciprocity maintains the priority of language, however, since it is on the basis of legibility and not the phenomenological experience of script. Also Owens' allegory would seem a continuation of the 'theatre' between the arts which Michael Fried condemned in minimalism, as against the modernist purification of the respective mediums: the allegorical work 'is synthetic; it crosses aesthetic boundaries'.

It is not merely a matter of allegorical readings of works of art, but of works of art which incorporate allegory into their very structure. Owens considers allegorical in this way the work of a variety of artists including Robert Rauschenberg, Robert Smithson, Laurie Anderson, Sherrie Levine, Robert Longo, Troy Brauntuch and Cindy Sherman. Most of these artists 'generate images through the reproduction of other images', the image in their work is in many cases an appropriated fragment. Photography is a primary medium for allegory because, according to Owens, it does not so much represent the world as 'our desire to fix the transitory, the ephemeral, in a stable and stabilizing image' — a desire for fixity and identity which by definition is never satisfied, so 'that desire becomes the *subject* of the image'. Perhaps the potential of the concept of allegory for a description of the processes involved in contemporary art, a potential which was not yet quite realized by Owens' article (although it has been developed in his subsequent writings), becomes clearer if we rephrase this to suggest that the subject, in the sense of human subject, is constituted in that desire which tears open the stitching between the self and the field of the Other, of the Symbolic, even as it sews. If we push Owens' theory a little further than he takes it here, we can see that allegorical reading is not something that an already identified, secure subject does to a work which is external to subjectivity, but rather allegory as a structural element of the text constitutes its reading subject — the viewer in the case of the work of art — in the act of allegorical interpretation. It is this that I take to be the implication of Owens' assertion that allegorical works of art employ a discursive elocutionary mode.

Owens gives allegorical works not only a constitutive function but a critical one as well. In this I think his theory marks an attempt to continue the avant-garde tendency of modernism, specifically of conceptual art. Earlier allegory was as much a way of concealing as of revealing; however the tenor of Owens' remarks suggests that he sees allegory as a critical, emancipatory strategy. Owens is however unwilling to accept the great narratives of either Marxism or modernism, and their concommitant aesthetic vanguardism (he argues for a continuity of allegory in art and popular culture). Thus he considers allegory to be not representation but a deconstructive rhetorical trope which involves an 'impossible complicity' with what it seets out to deconstruct. The example with which Owens concludes his essay is that of Cindy Sherman's photographs of herself posed according to the stereotypes of cinema, her *Untitled*

Film Stills (1977–80) which paradoxically accomplish the 'deconstruction of the supposed innocence of the images of, women projected by the media' by their painstaking reconstruction. According to Owens it is the complicity of these works which accounts for their allegorical mode 'For if mimicry is denounced in these works, it is nevertheless through mimetic strategies that this denunciation is made. We thus encounter once again the unavoidable necessity of participating in the very activity that is being denounced *precisely in order to denounce it*' (his italics). We might not concur, however, with the presumption that mimicry is being denounced: the reading-in of a critical intent confronts the same problem of an undecidable irony that we find in the work of Warhol, whose inscrutibility is the model for the postmodernist stance which permits both complicity and critical credibility.

Postmodernism does not allow the clean avantgardism associated with modernist radicality, and its critical componant is difficult to disentangle from careerism and a complicity which could be read not so much as deconstructive as opportunist. That is the weakness of postmodernism and its vulnerability to the diatribes of those who set themselves up as moralists. To return to Owens' article; this vulnerability of postmodernism to the accusation of too great a degree of complicity (is there *any* art which is not complicit?) is connected with its deconstructive purpose. The boundaries are more blurred than is the case with autonomous art:

> This deconstructive impulse is characteristic of postmodernist art in general and must be distinguished from the self-critical tendency of modernism. Modernist theory presupposes that mimesis, the adequation of the image to a referent, can be bracketed or suspended, and that the art object can be substituted (metaphorically) for the referent. This is the rhetorical strategy of self-reference upon which modernism is based . . . Postmodernism neither brackets nor suspends the referent *but works instead to problematize the activity of reference.* When the postmodernist work speaks of itself, it is no longer to proclaim its autonomy, its self-sufficiency, its transcendence; rather, it is to narrate its own contingency, insufficiency, lack of transcendence. (my italics)

Thus against 'the symbolic, totalizing impulse which characterizes modernist art', postmodernism 'tells of a desire that must be perpetually frustrated, an ambition that must be perpetually deferred', presumably the desire for origin and finality, the ambition for authentic, self-created 'full' meaning. The pursuit of the deferred desire of postmodernism leads Owens to the Lacanian psychoanalytic emphasis of his more recent critical writings.

The post-structuralist reading of Walter Benjamin's early book *The Origin of German Tragic Drama* reverses the direction that Benjamin's writings subsequently took. Although Owens recognizes at the beginning of his article that 'a conviction of the remoteness of the past, and a desire to redeem it for the present — these are (allegory's) two most fundamental impulses', and associates allegory with history painting, the post-structuralist basis of his argument tends to turn Benjamin's tragedy *of* history into an escape *from* history. Owens quotes Benjamin,

> In allegory the observer is confronted with the *facies hippocratica* of history as a petrified, primordial landscape. Everything about history that, from the very beginning, had been untimely, sorrowful, unsuccessful, is expressed in a face — or rather in a death's head. And although such a thing lacks all 'symbolic' freedom of expression, all classical proportion, all humanity — nevertheless, this is the form on which man's subjection to nature is most obvious and it significantly gives rise to not only the enigmatic question of the nature of human existence as such, but also of the biographical historicity of the individual. This is the heart of the allegorical way of seeing . . .

The tragedy of Baroque allegory involves the confrontation of man's mortality with the withdrawal of the possibility of redemption from the world. Thus Pascal writes of the universe in his fragmentary *Pensées*, 'the eternal silences of these infinite spaces fills me with dread'. Owens breaks off the quotation from Benjamin when it becomes concerned with the secularization or disenchantment of history within which any attribution of significance only serves to emphasize mortality:

This is the heart of the allegorical way of seeing, of the baroque, secular explanation of history as the Passion of the world; its importance resides solely in the stations of its decline. The greater the significance, the greater the subjection to death, because death digs most deeply the jagged line of demarcation between physical nature and significance . . . Significance and death both come to fruition in historical development.[41]

Benjamin's messianism was not only theological but also political: he was strongly influenced by Lukacs' book *History and Class Consciousness* (1923), and subsequently by his encounter with Brecht, and turned increasingly to an interpretation of the subjective effects of Capitalist social relations, mediated through the arts and other cultural phenomena. His drafts for a book on Baudelaire were concerned with the relations between the poet, with his sense of a classical tradition, and the city as the site of the circulation of commodities and the reification of the body.

A recently translated fragmentary text by Benjamin 'Central Park', showed how his concern with allegory was applied to the commodity:

The emblems recur as commodities.
Allegory is the armature of the modern.

And 'the commodity has taken the place of the allegorical way of seeing.'[42] The implication is that by interpreting commodities, and other social phenomena like fashion, allegorically the whole might reveal itself. Admittedly Benjamin's Marxism was rabinnical and Nietzschean, but he did remain concerned with social and economic processes, as well as with redemption. By re-reading Benjamin in terms of Derridean deconstruction and Lacanian psychoanalysis, Owens reverses the trajectory towards Marxism of Benjamin's concept of allegory. Even though Owens draws attention to the continuity between the allegorical modes of the mass media and postmodernist art, his theory doesn't allow any purchase on the institutional conditions and social effects of either. It thus lays itself open for its own re-appropriation for purposes of legitimating and promoting a postmodernist 'movement' rather than, as Owens clearly intends, as a critical way of 'reading'.

Nevertheless Owens' identification of allegory as a mode of contemporary art is of great importance. As a successor to theories of expression, allegory allows a way of structuring and deciphering works of art without recourse to the notion of a constitutive transcendental subject whose intentional meaning, the 'signified' is transmitted through the 'significant form' of the signifier. Allegory, instead of presupposing a self-identical, transcendental subject, allows for the constitution of subject positions which are dynamically entered into, or even repudiated by the viewer/reader/interpreter who participates with the 'author' in the creation of the work. The problem arises when this process is theorized purely according to a (Lacanian) psychoanalytic model, which has the effect of vacating it of history and the social. A theory of allegory is useful in the understanding of the distinctive features of contemporary art, but only if it is considered in terms of situation, of the repertoires of knowledge of particular constituencies of receivers, and the ideological pressures which privilege particular readings or ways of reading, including those of a 'postmodernist' type.

Fascination and the Uncanny

Like the allegorist, the 'fascinated' artist is also an appropriator or, better, a collector. Joseph Cornell, a latter-day Symbolist for whom the culture of *fin de siècle* Paris was an exotic Orient, might be conceived as the antetype of the postmodernist *fasciné* as well as the *bricoleur*. He catches just that moment when the Surrealist encounter with the *objet trouvé* meets the desire-arousal of mass-consumerism, and he manages to create paradises of Symbolist reverie, miniaturized and marginalized amid the domination of the market: doll's house theatres enclosed, with inadvertant irony, in the 'packaging' of a box. What is new, after Cornell and from Rauschenberg and Warhol onwards, is the interface between collecting and consuming.

Fascinare, the Latin for to lay under a spell, to enchant, to effect by witchcraft; *fascinum*, a spell; and, as the Oxford

Dictionary defines the English derivation, 'deprive (victim) of power of escape or resistance by one's look or presence (esp. of serpents); attract irresistibly, enchant, charm'. The collector is fascinated, seeking a nearness-within-distance: as Blanchot writes, 'Whosoever is fascinated does not see properly speaking what he sees. Rather it touches him in an immediate proximity; it seizes and ceaselessly draws him close, even though it leaves him absolutely at a distance'.[43] John Stezaker has described his collecting of mass media photographic imagery as an 'arrested' consumption, from Duchamp's description of his found objects as 'arrests', although the problem of what is or is not art does not arise for such a fascinated collector.

While the discourse of film theory and post-conceptual photo-works comes from Marx and Freud through the early structuralist Barthes, Althusser and Lacan — leading towards a critical and iconoclast attitude to desire; the discourse of the fascinating photo-image, where it is theorized, comes partly from the post-systematic Barthes of the 'third meaning' of the film still. Here there is reference to the 'obtuse' meaning which is beyond language and metalanguage; 'the passage from language to *signifiance*'; the 'inside' of the fragment;[44] and the *punctum*, the punctuation of a strange, unassimilable detail which Barthes describes in *Camera Lucida*, his last, Proustian narrative of the rediscovery of the image of his mother. This kind of response to the image is not one of critical distance but of *jouissance*, and is to be allied with the irreducibility of the 'figural' in Lyotard's opposition *Discours/Figure* (1968) and the desire-flow of *Anti-Oedipus* (1972), both in implicit Nietzschean opposition to a Lacanian conception of desire as a product of Law. The fascinated artist is therefore closer to the transavantgardist in the pursuit of intensity. Sharing the allegorist's sense of the loss of an immanent symbolic order, such an artist however, discerns in images not the perspicuity of discourse but a certain opacity which promises a sudden revelation, the mystical illumination sought by the Symbolists or the re-enchantment of the fragment of imagery.

The photograph in this order of experience is not so much an arbitrary fragment, a demonstration of textuality, as uncanny. This is the case with the work of the American

Richard Prince who re-presents rephotographed advertising images, excluding the contextualizing captions and without adding any text which would interpose a 'critical distance' between the viewer and the image.[45] His images have the quality of *déjà vu*, of repetition, which renders them strange, like the cadaver brought back to life in a horror story. The uncanny image is the fetish which, according to Freud, is at once *unheimlich* and *heimlich*, homely and unhomely (the German word for uncanny), desired and disavowed giving an experience of *déjà vu*. The work of Prince and recent Stezaker affirms the possibility of intense, arrested experience within the consumer image, but at the cost of the implosion of critical distance and the reinforcement of fetishism. This points to a real difficulty, at least within the area of mass-reproduced imagery or possibly of photographic 'mechanical reproduction' in general, in any argument for the possibility of simultaneous affirmation and critique within postmodernism.

Bricolage

Bricolage has been used to describe the combination of fragments of quotation from other works in a single work of art, or more specifically the use of found objects and fragments of material in recent sculpture. In French it is a slightly derogatory term for tinkering or pottering about, doing odd jobs, which Lévi-Strauss uses as a metaphor for mythical thought in the first chapter of his book *The Savage Mind* (1962, trans. 1966). He wants to argue for a common Reason at work in both science and mythical thought which are distinguished, by analogy with Saussure's linguistics, according to diachrony and synchrony, 'the scientist creating events (changing the world) by means of structures and the *bricoleur* creating structures by means of events'. The *bricoleur*-mythmaker draws from a stock of elements, Saussure's *langue*, to make the *parole* of the mythic statement. In the theorization of postmodernism, Lévi-Strauss' emphasis on the already-used aspect of the *bricoleur*'s elements is of interest: 'in the continual reconstruction from the same materials, it is always earlier ends which are called upon to play the part of means: the signified changes into the signifying and vice versa'.

Lévi-Strauss appears to be attempting to use structural-ism to bridge the 'divided representation' of modernity, and in the process creates a closed, if infinitely meaningful, universe:

> Mythical thought for its part is imprisoned in the events and experiences which it never tires of ordering and re-ordering in its search to find them a meaning. But it also acts as a liberator by its protest against the idea that anything can be meaningless with which science at first resigned itself to a compromise.[46]

This is an evocative description of the predicament of the postmodernist artist: in its emphasis on the conversion of diachrony into synchrony *bricolage* is a tempting category to apply to the visual arts. Lévi-Strauss' approach to anthro-pology seeks to overcome the theoretical dichotomy between nature and culture by demonstrating, through the application of the structural linguistics of Saussure, the processes of differentiation and structuration by which nature becomes culture. For the postmodern *bricoleur* nature is already culture and culture is a second nature: the city and the mass media are forests of signs. If nature makes a reappearance, it is as a representation within culture, doubly cooked, a signifier rather than a referent external to the sign.

Bricolage might be seen as a possible paradigm for the constitution of the 'decentred' subject and its products, and more specifically the collections of quoted images and appropriated fragments which make up the postmodernist art work.[47] However if this follows Lévi-Strauss' usage it could lead to a contradiction. Lévi-Strauss aims to demonstrate a transcendental universality in mythical thought, although without the constitutive transcendental subject as its precondition. Lévi-Strauss' critique of the anthropology of cultural evolution is, superficially at least, parallel to the rejection of historical teleology by theories of postmodernism. His anthropology of synchronic structures was widely criticized by French Marxists as a rejection of history, or more specifically of the notion of the individual as embedded in historical process.[48] Those critics who use the term *bricolage* to apply to recent art usually do so as an assertion of its radicality, including an emphasis on irreducible difference.

But how can this be squared with the reactionary implications of Lévi-Strauss' theory? Only, I think, if the 'anthropology' of the fragment, its theatrical presentation as a shard of prehistory, is used as a critical comment on the present and not a flight from history. This involves an emphasis on the specific contextual or situational meaning of the elements and the work of art which moves in the opposite direction to Lévi-Strauss' sublation of particular elements of myth into a universal combinatory. At the same time a critical account of Lévi-Strauss' theory could be used to interrogate the implications of totality and universality concealed behind postmodernist assertions of fragmentation and difference.

Simulation

The term 'simulation' has entered the discourse around art and mass culture from the writings of the French sociologist Jean Baudrillard, who has filled something of the role over the past few years that Marshall McLuhan did during the 1960s.[49] It is often used rather vaguely to indicate a general extension of the domains of reproduction — the mass media, fashion, packaging etc. — in a way which avoids talking about ideology; in other words, to take such discussions out of the context of Marxism, given a perception of the failure of proletarian and student revolution. Thus, the currency of the term is one of the outcomes of 1968. What is often lost is the genealogy of Baudrillard's 'theory' — if it can be called that — of simulation in both structuralism and metaphysics. In its rhetorical twists, Baudrillard's writing is perhaps best understood as strategy: he is our postmodern sophist.

In the structuralist project, phenomena or events — social, cultural, narrative — are formalized into sets of relations. This is a rationalist procedure of abstraction. These relations are part of the combinatory of which the phenomena are only one possible outcome among others, generated according to a code which is internal to the system. Thus a myth, in the form of a narrative, is abstracted by Lévi-Strauss into relations between its figures and events which form a synchronic structure: time, as we have seen with *bricolage*, is converted into space. A central criticism of structuralism was that it ignored the social and historical *production* of signification. This at once brings to mind the alternative, marxist practice of analysis, and attempts were made, notably by Althusser, to develop a structuralist Marxism. But if Marxism is rejected, what becomes of this 'temporal' inadequacy of structuralism? The problem of production is turned into a problem of force or of *difference*, differentiation and deferment. Force is conceived according to Neitzsche's 'will to power': will becomes positive desire in Deleuze and Guattari, and power receives a negative valuation in later Foucault. The problem for Deleuze and Guattari in *Anti-Oedipus* is that there must be a revolutionary force which can overcome the Law as a repressive agent: for Lacan, Law produces desire and desire reinforces the Law — Law becomes unsurpassable — whereas Deleuze and Guattari want to argue that desire is prior to Law and a force which might overcome it, in this they are Nietzschean. Derrida, whose concern is not with voluntarist revolution but with the (im)possibility of metaphysics, of writing philosophy in the language of the tradition which is at an end, converts the structuralist difference into *differance*, a movement of differentiation and differal: presence and origin can never be attained because as soon as they are written they are elsewhere: they are only inscribed in the traces which mark their absence and re-write them. Baudrillard remains paradoxically closer to structuralism and realism, simultaneously, than any of these moves.

Rather than interpreting phenomena in terms of structuralism, i.e. abstracting a structure, Baudrillard sees the contemporary condition as one in which phenomena themselves, as effects, are generated out of the structural code. This is what he means by simulation. Simulation is universalized both historically and socially. Simulation is implicit in a historical process whereby each order of value is superceded and absorbed as illusion by the next order of value which approaches closer to the 'truth' of the acknowledged supercession of the dichotomy truth-falsity by simulation. In Baudrillard's schema, the image draws progessively away from reality until it ceases to bear any relation to reality whatever (which may be where the image becomes postmodern).

> This would be the successive phases of the image:
> — it is the reflection of a basic reality
> — it masks and perverts a basic reality
> — it marks the *absence* of a basic reality
> — it bears no relation to any reality whatever: it is its own pure simulacrum . . .[50]

Baudrillard outlines this movement as a historical sequence: the hierarchically fixed image of feudal Christianity is superceded by the 'counterfeit' or false image (mirror, painting) of the renaissance and classical epoch, which is in turn superceded by the seriality of production in the Capitalist epoch, where phenomena are governed by equivalence rather than the priority of model and copy. The final and most recent development is when production is superceded by simulation: 'Whereas representation tries to absorb simulation by interpreting it as false representation, simulation envelops the whole edifice of representation as itself a simulacrum'. The representation of the real is replaced by simulation governed by the code. Baudrillard takes over where Marshall McLuhan left off:

> We are witnessing the end of perspective and panoptic space (which remains a moral hypothesis bound up with every classical analysis of the 'objective' essence of power), and hence the *very abolition of the spectacular* . . . We are no longer in the society of the spectacle which the situationists talked about, nor in the specific types of alienation and repression which this implied. The medium itself is no longer identifiable as such, and the merging of the medium and the message (McLuhan) is the first great formula of this new age. There is no longer any medium in the literal sense: it is now intangible, diffuse and diffracted in the real, and it can no longer even be said that the latter is distorted by it.[51]

Baudrillard extends this insight into a diagnosis of the postmodern condition:

The transition from signs which dissimulate something to signs which dissimulate that there is nothing, marks the decisive turning point. The first implies a theology of truth and secrecy (to which the notion of ideology still belongs). The second inaugurates an age of simulacra and simulation, in which there is no longer any God to recognise his own, nor any last judgement to separate true from false, the real from its artificial resurrection, since everything is already dead and risen in advance.

When the real is no longer what it used to be, nostalgia assumes its full meaning. There is a proliferation of myths of origin and signs of reality; of second-hand truth, objectivity and authenticity. There is an escalation of the true, of the lived experience; a resurrection of the figurative where object and substance have disappeared. And there is a panic-stricken production of the real and the referential, above and parallel to the panic of material production . . .[52]

Illustrations of simulation might be the Sci Fi novels of Philip K. Dick and the film *Blade Runner*, based on his *When Androids Dream of Electric Sleep*, where, within the total simulated reality of the movie, it is no longer possible to distinguish between humans and 'replicants'. Interestingly, the replicants' memories are fabricated by photographs, family snapshots.

'No more real', announces Baudrillard. But, firstly, isn't his model of realism a rather outdated one, a simple correspondence theory of words or images (icons) with an external reality of 'things'? And, secondly, isn't Baudrillard himself behaving like something of a realist?[53] He is arguing that 'simulation' as he delineates it corresponds with contemporary social 'reality', with the way things are: our reality is that there is no more real. It is as a commentator that he is most seductive — and according to Baudrillard, seduction is what simulation does. So perhaps his method of galloping metonymy — such that, for example, the clone produced from the genetic code (*ZG*, No. 11, Summer 84) or 'The Child in the Bubble' as a death by hygiene (*Impulse*, Winter 85) stand for the whole contemporary condition — is a way of pushing realism to a seductive limit where it, ironically and subversively, turns into simulation, generated by the code of 'True Stories' reportage. The real is displaced by a rhetoric of truth.

Following on from photography and painterly hyperrealism, we are now able to synthesize believable images by computer without any indexical relation to the real: the first totally synthesized science fiction movie is, I am told, currently in production. In such an age, Baudrillard's analysis might well seem seductive. To illustrate its application to art, recall the discussion of the work of Richard Prince in the section on 'Fascination' — he could equally well have appeared here — or consider the uses of plastic in the work of British sculptors Tony Cragg and Edward Allington. Cragg uses the universal 'industrial' substance, the medium of serial production, but asserts difference by the gritty contingency of the fragments, by distinguishing, viscerally, the qualities of different materials even as he installs them in a unified configuration; or draws attention to the social distinctions made between art/not art, and the different categories of value (use, exchange, commodity and aesthetic) and of production. The morality of his work is a materialist and perhaps realist one, even if the material is that of simulation.

In his book *L'Echange Symbolique et la Mort* (1976) Baudrillard compares plastic with the stucco of the Baroque, used for the creation of a wholly artificial nature. Edward Allington has used fake, *kitsch* plastic objects — fruit, fishes, flowers, animals and so on — together with gold-painted stucco shells, often very sexual in connotation. However the work is only partly 'jokey'. What is rarely sufficiently emphasized is the poignant and melancholy sense of loss which is conveyed. This commercial abundance is a mocking plenitude because it is sterile even as it parodies the cornucopia or 'horn of plenty': a comment on consumerism. What is also acknowledged, in the passage from Allington's *Ideal Standard Forms* to his current rococo and baroque modes, is that there never was an authentic truth or origin, that these are nostalgic constructions. Not only is the Parthenon, which he revered as a boy, a fibreglass imitation of itself, but its classical 'truth' was as gaudily *kitsch* as the simulated nature of today which is, therefore, in its artiface, the 'true' classicism.

Allington's reverberating ironies are somewhat analogous to those of Baudrillard. If the guarantee of the distinction between truth and falsity is, for Baudrillard, theological, then the 'death of God' leads him to what appears to be a Nietzschean nihilism. Actually, his view of realism is more Platonic, and his nihilism a reversion to sophism which remains within the terms of Plato, and deeply influenced, in my view, by the discussion of Plato's dialogue *The Sophist* in Gilles Deleuze's book *Logique du Sens* (1969). In the dialogue arguing the distinction between truth and falsity as the basis for the discourse of philosophy, Plato has the stranger say, disquietingly, 'once deception exists, images and likenesses and appearance will be everywhere rampant . . . And the sophist, we said, had taken refuge somewhere in that region, but then he had denied the very existence of falsity . . .' Deleuze extends the argument from the point of view of the sophist:

> The simulacrum is not degraded copy, rather it contains a positive power which negates *both original and copy, both model and reproduction* . . . no model resists the vertigo of the simulacrum. And the privileged point of view has no more existence than does the object held in common by all points of view. There is no possible hierarchy . . . Similarity and resemblance now have as their essence only the condition of being simulated, that is, of expressing the operation of the simulacrum. Selection is no longer possible . . . Simulation designates the power to produce an *effect*.

And he concludes 'Modernity is defined by the power of the simulacrum'.[54]

So we could say that for Baudrillard, simulation is a massive inversion of a totalized, post-structuralist difference into the identity of the Same: there is nothing which is not simulation. This is the macrocosm which is revealed in his microcosmic metonymies. Every separate phenomenon leads ineluctably to the same conclusion, without admitting criteria for verification since truth/falsity distinctions don't exist under simulation — and as Plato's dialogue shows, once the sophist admits the existence of falsity, he undermines his own argument. But without falsity what validity do his arguments have? Implicit assumptions of truth and the real lie behind Baudrillard's commentaries on contemporary society, and his fables are delivered in the tone of moral tales. Behind the façade of a structuralist

version of McLuhanism is another mask, that of an old
fashioned realist and moralist. Perhaps it is just this,
however, which lends to his descriptions of the extremes of
technology and consumerism, their vitality and seductive-
ness, even if his apparently joyful nihilism, the paradoxical
counterpoint to his moralism, offers no space for a
constructive critical practice.

Parody

Parody is so widespread in contemporary art that it is
tempting to regard it, together with appropriation,
allegory and bricolage, as one of the characteristic strategies
by which we might define a postmodernist art. However at
once the problem arises that parody has been employed
within the Western tradition of the arts since Classical
times. Parody is also a characteristic of paradigmatic works
of literary modernism, including Joyce's *Ulysses*, and
appears within the work of certain modernist artists (e.g.
Picasso, Picabia, Magritte) and even, it has been argued, in
the founding works of modernism in the visual arts, the
paintings of Manet. Is postmodernist parody, then, a
continuation of the 'long' tradition? Or of modernist
parody? Or can we specify a peculiarly postmodernist
approach to parody? If the latter is the case, how would be
distinguish it, if we can, from pastiche and appropriation?
Is there any justification for seeing such parody as radical or
subversive?

Linda Hutcheon defines parody as 'repetition with
critical distance, which marks difference rather than
similarity'.[55] If it is similarity which is marked, then we
are talking about imitation or pastiche: imitation where
such a procedure is culturally valued, pastiche where it is
not and imitation is derogatory in either intent or
reception. Parody is not just an internal relation between
the work and its model, but is necessarily pragmatic, in
that it assumes the audience will 'get' the reference, and
appreciate the double coding. It is self-consciously intertextual and sophisticated. Parody may be of a particular work,
or of the generic code as a whole. Hutcheon argues that
parody is distinct from satire in that the former is
'intramural' ('its repetition is always of another discursive

text') while the latter is 'extramural' (morally directed at an object outside the text).[56] This distinction may be hard to sustain, depending upon assumptions concerning the relation between artistic texts and social discourses, but it is true that it would he hard to specify a postmodernist satire.

This raises the question of norms. Does the effectiveness of parody depend upon the normative status of that which is being parodied, upon, specifically, its authority? And what happens to parody when this authority is *already* undermined? We could, I think, distinguish between parody which maintains the authority and the originary status of the model or generic code; parody which questions the *assumption* of authority and origin, so that the parodic text enacts their displacement or decentring; and parody which *begins* with the assumption of the impossibility of authority, origin, full presence and so on. Bearing in mind that this is over-schematic and over-generalized, I would like to propose as a working hypothesis that the first could be taken as a neo-classical or at least pre-Romantic conception of parody; that the second, following the assertion of originality and the sovereignty of the artist-creator in Romanticism, is a modernist (in my broader sense) form of parody; and that the third is characteristic of the discourse of postmodernism. I wouldn't wish to over-emphasize the periodicity involved (for example, *Don Quixote* could be read as of the second type) but rather to keep the distinction in mind as a regulative idea.

I would tend to see the difference between modernist and postmodernist parody as marking a shift from a strong to a weak form of nihilism. Strong nihilism involves a critique of supposedly 'higher' but in actuality repressive values. This nihilist critique involves a subversion by a minority of dominant cultural and moral values. Postmodern parody is closer to the cynical nihilism of fashion and the mass-culture industry: involving the implicit assertion that if everything is permitted then it makes no difference what we do and nothing is worth anything. Whether nihilism is or is not a radical position depends on the particular situation. Nietzsche's stance *vis a vis* 19th century morality was difficult and subversive. However I am not so sure whether nihilism as a component of postmodernism today is not collusive on some deep level with *laissez faire* neo-liberalism. It is possible that postmodern nihilism is the outcome of the loss of legitimation by the great narratives of the Enlightenment which Lyotard describes, and on a more mundane level the failure of the expectations of the 60s, including emancipatory and political ideals, and decline of faith in the welfare state. An alternative to nihilism in art might be negativity. Jeff Wall's back-lit cibacrome transparencies could be taken as an example of this for the way in which they 'refunction' both the advertising display (drawing attention to the way in which art is a branch of the 'culture industry') and narrative and realist painting, thus creating a ruined monumentalism. This double negation, of the fragmentation of modernist art and the monumentalism of the public display, which owes so much to the thinking of the Frankfurt School, is underwritten by a Hegalian Marxist concept of the dialectic, precisely the kind of 'great narrative' which Lyotard argues is delegitimated in the postmodern condition.

A fascinating 'test case' for postmodernist parody is provided by the paintings of Komar & Melamid which were exhibited during the winter of 1985 at the Fruitmarket, Edinburgh and MOMA, Oxford. The exhibition consisted of two groups of paintings: monumental paintings in a neo-classical version of socialist realism many of which included an image of Stalin; and eclectic sequences of smaller paintings attached together to make linear configurations. Whereas the former all referred to a unitary authoritative model and code (or rather the dual authority of revolutionary neo-classicism, darkened with age, associated with Jacques-Louis David and Soviet socialist realism), the latter parody a wide variety of genres and styles which are brought together into simultaneity. I would argue that these two groups of paintings re-enact the transition from parody which questions and subverts the assumption of authority and origin to parody which begins from the assumption of their impossibility. I would associate this shift with Komar & Melamid's move from the Soviet Union, which they left in 1978, to New York (via Israel) where all these paintings were made. In the catalogue to the show a strong case is argued by Peter Wollen that

Komar and Melamid's paintings are parodies in a satirical and then carnavalesque sense,[57] and that the politics of the recent work are not revolutionary and progressive, but 'symbolic and utopian'. I am not so sure.

Most of the large paintings include Stalin as a signifier, or, even where his image is absent, other signifiers of Stalinism — an exception, *Portrait of Ronald Reagan as a Centaur*, seems little more than a gesture of balance. In *I saw Stalin once when I was a child*, Stalin draws aside a curtain and glances out of the back window of a car; in *The Origin of Socialist Realism*, Stalin's shadow is being traced by a female artist-muse beneath two classical columns; in *Yalta Conference (From a History Textbook, 1984)*, Stalin sits beside ET, who has replaced Roosevelt and Churchill, while Hitler puts his finger to his lips behind. Like their neo-classical models, these paintings are all stagey, with in most cases a curtain or drape drawn aside to reveal the scene. The tonality is sombre, connoting 'seriousness' and evoking a doom-laden atmosphere. In each case, though, the decorum of the painting is punctured by an excessive or inappropriate signifier, for example Stalin with bare feet regarding himself in a mirror. These paintings are about the mythology of History created through representations which naturalize myth as 'realism'. Through parody they subvert the authority both of and in such representations, and reveal them as constructions of which reality is effect rather than origin. However, they are still parodies of the second type, because they remain dependent upon there being a recognition of an authority and authoritative style by the viewer, even if this acknowledgement is handled ironically. That the paintings including Stalin are the most successful indicates the extent to which parody requires authority. In this case it is doubly loaded, since Stalin is a father figure (an almost fairy tale figment of the artists' childhood) the ridiculing of whom might be taken as an oedipal act. The very invocation of Stalin in the ruined monumentalism of these paintings involves a return of the repressed, as the image of Stalin has to a large extent been suppressed in Soviet culture since the 22nd Party Congress of 1961 when his persecutions were attacked and he was accused of fostering a cult of personality. Stalin's embalmed body was removed from the mausoleum in Red Square.

Thus while there is in these particular paintings by Komar & Melamid an internal conflict of genre and subject matter, the effectiveness of their parody does not depend on this alone: context has to be taken into account. In relation to the experience of their producers, the paintings might be taken as a celebration of the freedom to parody what previously was taboo. However there is another question concerning their reception: What difference does it make to their meaning that they were painted and first shown in New York?

If I follow Wollen's argument correctly, he seems to be suggesting that it doesn't make any difference to their subversiveness as parody. He compares Komar & Melamid's paintings with Manet's *Le Dejeuner sur l'herbe*, as a parody of Giorgione, his *Olympia* as a parody of Titian's *Venus of Urbino*, and Hans Haacke's portrait of Margaret Thatcher, *Taking Stock*, 1983–84. Parody, he writes 'enabled Manet, by re-contextualising to re-function, by scandal and contrast to separate, to open up a space'. Surely it was of the utmost importance for the scandal of Manet's paintings that they were shown at the Salon, the very site of academic authority (whatever one might then want to argue about them being contradictory or illegible). Context is even more obviously involved in the effect of Hans Haacke's painting. The choice of the academic Victorian portrait genre is not just intended as a critique of Thatcher and her espousal of 'Victorian values': the context of Haacke's painting at an exhibition of his work at the Tate, bringing the interests of the museum into conflict with its liberal ideology, is essential to its meaning as parody. Therefore I think it must matter that Komar & Melamid's paintings were made and first shown in the United States, even if it could not have been otherwise: they satirize the social realist style, and the image of Stalin, in a country where the Soviet Union can be described as an 'evil empire'. Without a contextual basis, the parody of socialist realist style becomes a parodic subversion of any legitimation at all, and so leads to a shift, I would argue, from the parodic to the mimetic, since the refusal of *telos*, origin and narrative-historical legitimation, is orthodoxy in the art world where Komar & Melamid currently work and exhibit.

Where anything goes, what is there to parody? Or are

they parodying, in their more recent paintings, a situation where anything goes? If the latter is the case, the 'carnavelesque' argument, at least in its utopian sense, breaks down, since the parody would then be in the name not of a polymorphously perverse desire but of an *absent* authority, so their work might well circle back through decadence to authority. Hutcheon writes concerning Bakhtin's notion of carnival, to which Wollen wants to attribute a 'symbolic and utopian politics', that 'parody's transgressions ultimately remain authorized — authorized by the very norm it seeks to subvert. Even in mocking, parody reinforces: in formal terms, it inscribes the mocked conventions onto itself, thereby guaranteeing their continued existence'. Parody may be, in Kristeva's words, *'consolidation de la loi'*.[58]

Overviews

It is arguable that many of the terms of the discussion of postmodernism are collusive with rather than a critical comment on the conditions of social postmodernity. Raymond Williams in his book *Towards 2000* mounts a scathing critique of the typical forms and discourses of postmodernism. He insists on the need to take into account the *two* faces of 'modernism', to look

> at those innovative forms which destabilized the fixed forms of an earlier period of bourgeois society, but which were then in their turn stabilized as the most reductive versions of human existence in the whole of cultural history. The originally precarious and often desparate images — typically of fragmentation, loss of identity, loss of the very grounds of human communication — have been transferred from the dynamic compositions of artists who had been, in majority, literally exiles, having little or no common ground with the societies in which they were stranded, to become, at an effective surface, a 'modernist' and 'post-modernist' establishment. This, near the centres of corporate power, takes human inadequacy, self-deception, role-playing, the confusion and substitution of individuals in temporary relationships, and even the lying paradox of the communication of the fact of non-communication, as self-evident routine data.[59]

Williams argues that popularized versions of such assumptions as 'the insignificance of history; the fictionality of all actions; the arbitrariness of language' have become

> the routine diversions and confirmations of para-national commodity exchange, with which they have many structural identities. They are also heavily traded, in directly monetary forms, by their intellectual agents and dealers, some of whom, for a residual self-esteem, allow themselves a gestural identity with the exposed artists and theorists of the original innovative phase.

And he adds that 'Even substantial and autonomous works, of this tendency, are quickly incorporated into this now dominant minority culture'. At the same time there takes place 'the transfer of many of these deep structures into effectively popular forms, in film and television and heavily marketed books': Williams traces these modern epiphenomena to a deep structural paradox of modernism:

> Losing their relationships in depressed declining and narrowing communities, the innovating artists of the period went to the new material bases and the negative freedoms of those centres, in which, ironically, the very reductions and dislocations were the material and the means for a new kind of art which the metropolis, but it alone, could recognise.[60]

The shocks and dislocations of this art were transferred into the routines of a newly displayed normality.

> Thus the very conditions which had provoked a genuine modernist art became the conditions which steadily homogenised even its startling images, and diluted its deep forms, until they could be made available as a universally distributed 'popular' culture.

Williams' analysis bears some resemblance to that of Fredric Jameson,[61] in that both treat the cultural manifestations of postmodernism as symptoms of an underlying socio-economic process. For Jameson, the symptoms of postmodernist culture, which he describes in analyses of particular manifestations under headings including 'The Waning of Affect', 'Euphoria and Self-Annihilation',

'Pastiche Eclipses Parody', ' "Historicism" Effaces History', 'The Nostalgia Mode', 'Loss of the Radical Past', 'The Breakdown of the Signifying Chain', 'The Hysterical Sublime' and 'The Abolition of Critical Distance' — all of these are epiphenomena of 'multinational capital'. This term is borrowed from Ernest Mandel's thesis in *Late Capitalism* of the three stages: market capitalism, the monopoly stage or the stage of imperialism, and multinational capital which Jameson associates with 'a new and historically original penetration and colonialization of Nature and the Unconscious'.

Jameson's reading of Mandel, and for that matter of world history, is a Hegelian one: the three stages each 'mark a dialectical expansion over the previous stage'. What Jameson is attempting, then, is to incorporate a microanalysis of cultural phenomena using post-structuralism within a Hegelian macro-theory of history, so that the whole is to be read within the parts. Thus he reintroduces the concept of Totality, which many post-structuralist thinkers would wish to exclude. However Totality for Jameson is a historical reality, which he wants to hold together with a notion of 'cognitive mapping — a pedagogical political culture which seeks to endow the individual subject with some new heightened sense of its place in the global system'. So he concludes

> the new political art — if it is indeed possible at all — will have to hold to the truth of postmodernism, that is to say, to its fundamental object — the world space of multinational capital — at the same time at which it achieves a breakthrough to some as yet unimaginable new mode of representing this last, in which we may again begin to grasp our positioning as individual and collective subjects and regain a capacity to act and struggle which is at present neutralized by our spatial as well as our social confusion.

Without a Messianic vision of conclusive social transformation, the combination of Totality with a 'logic' of history leads to a pessimism[62] which Jameson is attempting to avoid. Yet it is hard to see how 'cognitive mapping' would be able to resist the totalizing logic of multinational capital — unless it were linked to specific social movements, in which case the Totality would break down.

Jameson's analysis is flawed on both sides: the actual world of politics, even if it takes place in 'the world' and involves multinational corporations cannot be subsumed under the Hegelian World-Historical Totality; and the adequacy of Jameson's sample of cultural phenomena, partly because there may well be — and I think are — other sites of resistance which he does not include, and most important-ly, because his examples are all limited to the United States. Thus Jameson's analysis, purportedly radical, ends up as another version of cultural imperialism, confirming a totality defined from the point of view of the USA.

*

It is clear that art did not 'die' with Kant and Hegel, but rather that what art *is*, its ontological status, became a problem. As I have suggested, it is possible to isolate two tendencies under modernity which could be taken as answers to the question 'What is art?'. One answers 'Art is Art': it is the tendency towards autonomy, 'art for art's sake'. The other answers 'Art is not-art': the category of Art is supposed to 'wither away' into social and political practice and/or theory. If we recognize anything as 'postmodernists', it is the impossibility of either answer. Art as supposedly autonomous remains dependent upon its Other for its very autonomy, and so is infected by heteronomy. And artists' repeated attempts to defeat art have either been re-incorporated into Art, its institutions and ontology, or else have forgone the radical potential that inheres in art's relative autonomy.

Perhaps the central problem for postmodernism in the visual arts is that, although we live in a culture of proliferating images, the future has no image. This is a result of both the loss of faith in the ideal of progress, and the changed nature of technology: the shell of the computer and its circuitry does not represent its data processing and communicational capacities. Jean-François Lyotard's ex-hibition *Les Immateriaux*, at the Centre Pompidou, combin-ing a McLuhanesque tactility with Borges' labryrinth, was an attempt to deal with this fact in a positive way which seemed similar in spirit to the exhibitions organized by the Independent Group, 'Man, Machine and Motion' (1955) and 'This is Tomorrow' (1956) which saw in an era of technological optimism.[63] The most difficult aspect of postmodernity to deal with is that which is unprecedented, even more so if it is unrepresentable. I would interpret the Sublime today not so much as an 'anamnesis of modernism',[64] as concerned with the unrepresentability of technology and the ineffability of the multinational corporation which can no longer be identified either with individuals nor any more with its monumental glass-box offices.

Even science fiction has forgone technological futurism for a bricolage of the anticipated ruins of our present times. The obverse of the Sublime, according to Kant affirming Reason even in its very unrepresentability, is the unreason of the apocalypse. The unrepresentable and unimaginable have turned us around to face backwards, like the angel of history in Walter Benjamin's well known ninth Thesis on the Philosophy of History which it is worth quoting once again, both as a prophetic anticipation of our postmodern condition, and to remind ourselves what we have lost in abandoning the perspective of at least the possibility, however faint, of redemption. Interpreting, allegorically, a painting by Klee called *Angelus Novus*, Benjamin writes:

> This is how one pictures the angel of history. His face is turned toward the past. Where we perceive a chain of events, he sees one single catastrophe, which keeps piling wreckage upon wreckage and hurls it in front of his feet. The angel would like to stay, awaken the dead, and make whole what has been smashed. But a storm is blowing from Paradise; it has got caught in his wings with such violence that the angel can no longer close them. This storm irresistibly propels him into the future to which his back is turned, while the pile of debris before him grows skyward. This storm is what we call progress.[65]

Notes

1. This is a much expanded version of the paper I gave at the ICA. Nevertheless it should still be read as a work-in-progress rather than as an attempt at any kind of definitive statement on postmodernism, for which it is still far too soon. I would like to thank Peter Dews for reading this paper

and making many helpful comments, and Lisa Appignanesi for her editing.

2. *Art in America*, May–June 1971, p.19.
3. Jean-François Lyotard argues that in post-industrial society and postmodern culture 'The grand narrative has lost its credibility, regardless of what mode of unification it uses, regardless of whether it is a speculative narrative or a narrative of emancipation'. *The Postmodern Condition: A Report on Knowledge*, Manchester: Manchester U.P., 1984, p.37.
4. 'The Politics of Theory: Ideological Positions in the Postmodernism Debate', *New German Critique*, 'Modernity and Postmodernity' issue, No.33, Fall 1984, pp.53–65.
5. See Clement Greenberg, 'Modernist Painting', reprinted in *The New Art*, New York: Dutton & Co, 1966.
6. For an argument towards a continuation of this tradition, see Benjamin H.D. Buchloh, 'Allegorical Procedures: Appropriation and Montage in Contemporary Art', *Artforum*, Sept. 1982. This is an important, strongly argued article with which I concur: the remarks which follow are not intended as a criticism of it, but rather of other arguments to be considered in the lexicon section of my paper.
7. Martin Heidegger, *Neitzsche*, Vol.1, 'The Will to Power as Art', London: RKP, 1981, p.84.
8. T.W. Adorno, *Aesthetic Theory*, London: RKP, 1984 (first published in German in 1970), p.5.
9. 'Architecture and the Conflict of Interpretation', *AA Files*, Annals of the Architectural Association School of Architecture, No.8, Jan 1985.
10. See Joseph Rykwert, *The First Moderns: The Architects of the Eighteenth Century*, Cambridge, Mass./London: MIT Press, 1983, chapter 2 'Positive and Arbitrary'.
11. The argument in this section is partly derived from Peter Bürger, *The Theory of the Avant-Garde*, Manchester University Press/University of Minnesota Press, 1984.
12. See Benjamin H.D. Buchloh, 'Figures of Authority, Ciphers of Regression', *October*, No.16, Spring 1981, which looks at the political parallels between the return of representation after Cubism and the 'postmodernist' return to figuration in painting.
13. See Marshall Berman, *All that's Solid Melts into Air: The Experience of Modernity*, London: Verso, 1983; the criticism of it by Perry Anderson, 'Modernity and Revolution', *New Left Review*, No.144, March–April 1984; and T.J. Clark, *The Painting of Modern Life: Paris in the Art of Manet and his Followers*, London: Thames and Hudson, 1985.
14. *Charles Baudelaire: A Lyric Poet in the Era of High Capitalism*,

London: New Left Books, 1973.

15. 'Modernism and Mass Culture in the Visual Arts', in *Modernism and Modernity: The Vancouver Conference Papers*, ed. Buchloh, Guibault, Solkin, The Press of the Nova Scotia College of Art and Design, 1983.

16. See my article 'Rauschenberg Re-evaluated', *Art Monthly*, No.47, June 1981.

17. Clement Greenberg, 'Avant-Garde and Kitsch' (published 1939), reprinted in *Art and Culture*, London: Thames and Hudson, 1973; Theodor Adorno and Max Horkheimer, *Dialectic of Enlightenment* (first published 1944), London: Verso, 1979.

18. 'Art and Objecthood', *Artforum*, June, 1967, reprinted in *Minimal Art*, ed. Battock, New York: Dutton & Co., 1968; for Judd's views on wholeness in sculpture, see 'Questions to Stella and Judd', interview by Bruce Glaser, in the same collection.

19. See Buzz Spector, *Objects and Logotypes: Relationships Between Minimalist Art and Corporate Design*, catalogue, The Renaissance Society at the University of Chicago, Jan 20–Feb 22, 1980.

20. Jeff Wall's essay 'Dan Graham's Kammerspiel' (*Dan Graham*, catalogue, The Art Gallery of Western Australia, 14 Sept–4 Nov 1985, reprinted in *Reallife Magazine*, New York) breaks important new ground in the critical discussion of Conceptual art: parts of this section are influenced by his argument.

21. '1975', *The Fox*, No.2, 1975, p.89.

22. A number of artists and critics in North America remain strongly influenced by the Frankfurt School.

23. The quotations from Achille Bonito Oliva are all taken from *The Italian Transavantgarde*, Milan; Giancarlo Politi Editore, 1980.

24. Gilles Deleuze and Felix Guattari, *Anti-Oedipus*, New York: The Viking Press, 1977, p.84.

25. Roland Barthes, *Image–Music–Text*, London: Fonata, 1977, pp. 146, 149.

26. *The Order of Things*, London: Tavistock, 1970, p.308.

27. See Norman Bryson, *Vision and Painting: the logic of the gaze*, London: Macmillam, 1983.

28. Michel Foucault, *Language, Counter-memory, Practice*, Ithaca NY: Cornell University Press, 1977, p.137.

29. *Ibid.*, p.117.

30. Jacques Derrida, *Writing and Difference*, Chicago: The University of Chicago Press, 1978, p.227.

31. Jacques Lacan, *The Four Fundamental Concepts of Psychoanaly-*

sis, Harmondsworth: Penguin, 1979, p.199.

32. Louis Althusser, *Lenin and Philosophy*, New York and London: Monthly Review Press, 1971, p.174.

33. See *Barbara Kruger: We won't play Nature to your Culture*, ICA catalogue, 1983.

34. Althusser, *op.cit.*, pp.180–81.

35. Stephen Heath, 'On Suture' in *Questions of Cinema*, London: Macmillan, 1981, p.79.

36. Victor Burgin, 'Photography, Phantasy, Function' in *Thinking Photography*, ed. Burgin, London: Macmillan, 1982; and 'The Absence of Presence: conceptualism and postmodernism' in the catalogue *1965 to 1972 — when attitudes became form*, Kettle's Yard, Cambridge, 1984; Mary Kelly, 'Re-Viewing Modernist Criticism', *Screen*, vol.22, no.3, 1981.

37. See Mary Kelly, *Post-Partum Document*, London: RKP, 1983. Part of Kelly's work-in-progress, *Interim*, was on show at the Fruitmarket Gallery, Edinburgh, during early 1986.

38. T.W. Adorno, *Aesthetic Theory*, p.321.

39. I would not wish to suggest that either Burgin or Kelly are doing this, since they attempt the difficult task of maintaining coherent theories of discourse and the unconscious together as a continuation of the project of the left to reconcile Marx and Freud. Rather, I am arguing that the theory of discourse and *désirant* subjectivity imply each other, an implication that Burgin and Kelly are trying to avoid in the ways that they use Freud and Lacan.

40. Quotations by Craig Owens are from 'The Allegorical Impulse: Toward a Theory of Postmodernism', part 1, *October*, No.12, Spring 1980; part 2, *October*, No.13, Summer 1980. For the implications of these ideas in the discussion of the work of a contemporary artist, see also my essay 'Allegories of the Subject: The Theme of Identity in the Work of James Coleman' in the catalogue *James Coleman*, Chicago: Renaissance Society and London: ICA, 1985.

41. Walter Benjamin, *The Origin of German Tragic Drama*, London: New Left Books, 1977, p.166.

42. 'Central Park', *New German Critique*, No.34, Winter 1985; see also Lloyd Spencer, 'Allegory and the World of the Commodity' in the same issue.

43. Cited in an unpublished paper on fascination by Paul Davies. See Maurice Blanchot, 'The Two Versions of the Imaginary' in *The Space of Literature*, University of Nebraska Press, 1982.

44. 'The Third Meaning' in *Image–Music–Text*, London: Fontana, 1977.

45. See my article 'Richard Prince and the Uncanny', *Art Monthly*, No.72, Dec 1983–Jan 1984.

46. *The Savage Mind*, London: Weidenfeld and Nicolson, 1966, p.22.

47. Dick Hebdige uses the concept of *bricolage* to explain how subcultural styles are constructed in *Subculture: The Meaning of Style*, London: Methuen, 1979, pp.102–6.

48. See David Pace, *Claude Lévi-Strauss: The Bearer of Ashes*, London: RKP, 1983, chapter 6 'Out of History'.

49. The notion of 'simulation' has been taken up in particular by *ZG* magazine (London and New York).

50. 'The Precession of Simulacra' in *Simulations*, New York: Semiotext(e), 1983, p.11.

51. *Ibid.*, p.54.

52. *Ibid.*, pp.11–12.

53. For a brilliant critique of Baudrillard, to which I am indebted, see Meaghan Morris, 'Room 101 Or A Few Worst Things In The World' in *Seduced and Abandoned: The Baudrillard Scene*, ed. Frankovits: Glebe, Australia: Stonemass, 1984.

54. From an excerpt from the book translated as 'Plato and the Simulacrum', *October*, No. 27, Winter 1983.

55. Linda Hutcheon, *A Theory of Parody*, London: Methuen, 1985, p.6.

56. *Ibid.*, p.43.

57. To define Mikhail Bakhtin's theory of the carnival Wollen quotes the following passage from *Rabelais and his World*, MIT, 1968, (written in the 1940s, published in Russian in 1965): concerning carnival laughter, 'It is, first of all a festive laughter. Therefore, it is not an individual reaction to some isolated "comic" event. Carnival laughter is the laughter of all the people. Second, it is universal in scope; it is directed against all and everyone, including the carnival's participants. The entire world is seen in its droll aspect . . . Third, this laughter is ambivalent: it is gay, triumphant and at the same time mocking, deriding. It asserts and denies, it buries and revives. Such is the laughter of carnival.'

58. Hutcheon, p.75.

59. Raymond Williams, *Towards 2000*, London: Chatto and Windus, 1985, p.141.

60. *Ibid.*, p.142.

61. 'Postmodernism, or the Cultural Logic of Late Capitalism', New Left Review, no.146, July–August 1984.

62. As it does, for example, in Adorno and Horkheimer's conception of the 'culture industry' in *Dialectic of Enlightenment*, London: Verso, 1979, see especially the chapter 'The

culture Industry: Enlightenment as Mass Deception'.

63. For information about these exhibitions, see Richard Hamilton, *Collected Works*, London: Thames and Hudson. 'Cybernetic Serendipity', held at the ICA in 1968, also anticipated Lyotard's exhibition.

64. This phrase was used by Lyotard during the conference.

65. *Illuminations*, London: Fontana, 1973, pp.259–60.

TELEVISION AND POST-MODERNISM
John Wyver

I want to offer just a footnote to Martin Jay's encyclopaedic paper, with special reference to television, and to make what I hope are one or two useful comparisons with Angela McRobbie and Michael Newman's arguments. My thoughts are only tentative, and they do not really engage with the philosophical dimensions of postmodernism so interestingly offered up here. I hope, however, that they do have some relation to the political questions raised. I should also say, given the presence of our French colleagues, that I apologise for the fact that all my examples are drawn from British television.

Until I heard Martin Jay I was struggling to find the centre for any argument I could make about television and postmodernism. For I was unable to identify any tradition of modernism within television, against which there might have been a reaction, as it is agreed there has been in architecture at least, and in the visual arts. Television, after all, was a latecomer to the modern period, and it is hard to make claims for it, or for any of its genres, or for its programme-makers, in terms either of contributions to the Enlightenment project or of the more limited idea of the cultural modernism of, say, Manet, Joyce, Le Corbusier and Stravinsky. It is difficult, too, to conceive of a notion of an avant-garde within broadcast television. My difficulty was also connected with the fact that television has been far less theorised about than any other cultural form, and there is always a sense in any discussion of it of almost inevitably starting from point zero.

Martin Jay persuasively contributed another characterisation to the melée of modernisms and postmodernisms when he argued that a defining feature of the modern period was the primacy given to the sense of sight. He suggested that from the mid 19th century onwards, recent challenges to the primacy of vision were of fundamental importance for postmodernism and he identified these not only in philosophical discourse but in certain inventions developed around the turn of the century, including X-rays and the cinema.

Later, in considering further 'that most quintessentially modern of art forms' the cinema, he noted the suspicion and critique of the power of vision in the writings of French film theorists like Metz. In the Anglo-American tradition he could similarly have cited the work associated with the British journal *Screen*.

In an influential 1974 discussion in that journal, Colin MacCabe sugssted that realism was 'centrally defined by a certain formal hierarchy of discourses whereby the narrative discourse is placed in a situation of dominance with regard to the other discourses of the text'.[1] In classical cinema, this narrative discourse, MacCabe argues, is carried by the camera, or, as he says, 'the camera shows us what happens — it tells the truth against which we can measure the discourses'. This primacy of vision, the argument then runs, extends throughout dominant models of cinema, especially those epitomised by Hollywood's output from the thirties through to the sixties.

Like Martin Jay's impressive rosta of critics, MacCabe is deeply unhappy with this, particularly since in his formulation the classic realist text cannot deal with the real as contradictory. So he searches for models of cinema as challenges to this. What I want to take from this absurdly schematic summary of MacCabe is the sense that his thesis tends to support Jay's argument, and to establish that dominant narrative and illusionistic cinema has, in line with the modern project, underpinned and reinforced the primacy of sight.

To some degree, this hierarchy of discourses has been carried over into television. The name itself — tele/vision: far/sight — is unequivocal, as were the first descriptions of television as 'window on the world'. From the beginning the most influential and the most watched aspect of the medium has been the 'relay' of pictures from elsewhere. In Britain one of the earliest series was called 'We Bring You Live Pictures' and any individual's mythic moments of television usually contain — in Britain at least — the Coronation, Kennedy's assassination, Churchill's funeral and Neil Armstrong setting foot on the moon.

While noting all the problems suggested by the word
'relay' Stephen Heath and Gillian Skirrow have extended
this analysis to television current affairs and documentaries.
In their detailed reading of a 1977 'World in Action'
programme, they suggest that

> what is specific to television — the possibility of 'live
> broadcasting', the present electronic production of the
> image — becomes the term of its exploited imaginary, the
> generalised fantasy . . . that is, that the image is direct,
> and direct for me . . . which fantasy — and the very title
> 'World in Action' pays tribute to its power — is then taken
> for the ground reality of television and its programmes.[2]

It is important, of course, to recognise this as what Heath
and Skirrow call 'the generalised fantasy', that is, part of
the ideology of television. They quote from a handbook
called *The Work of the Television Journalist* which lays out
part of this ideology: 'Film has its own pace and logic,
sometimes faster than words, sometimes slower, and the
commentary must follow it. Cutting film to match words is
possible, but it never works for long. The picture is
naturally dominant.' And as Heath and Skirrow comment:
'The empirical rule of the dominance of the picture is a
rationalisation of the ideology of the document, the
window on the world.'

We need also to note the myriad problems associated
with the word 'relay' which, again as part of the ideology of
television, suggests the unmediated transmission of the
Real, but which, of course, always involves a highly
specific social, technological and political construction.

In other of its forms, television is closer to MacCabe's
classic realist text, most obviously in the cinema-derived
drama series now so common on our screens. There is one
subsidiary aspect of this that might be noticed in passing,
with regard to the primacy of vision and what is known as
costume drama. Here historical, and hence dramatic,
authenticity is believed by the institutions to be guaranteed
by obsessional accuracy in the reproduction of sets,
furniture, props and costumes. It is the *look* of historical
drama that is important, whether that drama is a nostalgic
lament for the aristocracy ('Brideshead Revisited') or a tale
of working-class resistance like 'Days of Hope'.

The primacy-of-vision argument, however, is to some extent contradicted by other elements of television's operation. There are areas of the medium where the narrative discourse is undeniably carried by a voice, by a narrator, who will subsume — or at least attempt to subsume — the images within her or his flow. Mostly the images chosen are unspecific enough to allow this, but on occasions the convention breaks open, and this can throw into crisis the whole political legitimacy of the medium.

The recent miner's strike provided a number of examples of this, including one which a BBC journalist presented inadvertently to last year's Edinburgh Television Festival. A clip was shown there of a mass picket clashing with police; the newsreader's voice spoke of 'the miners surging forward' at precisely the moment when the pictures clearly showed police horses charging into the miners. The vocal disbelief of the television festival audience must have had a pre-echo throughout the country when that bulletin was first broadcast.

But where can all this lead us in a discussion of postmodernism? Martin Jay suggested that one, perhaps *the* feature of postmodernism, was the challenge to the primacy of vision. Vision per se is unlikely to be challenged by a medium which relies so heavily upon it, but we can perhaps recognise one or two examples of challenges to the forms of vision which it has been suggested are characteristic of the ideology of television, namely that of the relay, direct, and direct to me. That these examples also seem to share certain features of what is regarded as postmodernism in the visual arts — that is, appropriation of imagery, the borrowing of the surfaces of historical styles, the breakdown of the lines between high art and mass culture — is, to say the least, intriguing.

Postmodernist TV

My first example is that of rock promos, which in less than five years have established themselves as central to television, and a collage of which, I noted, was the most popular element of Jean François Lyotard's 'Les Immateriaux' exhibition. Traditional television entertainment relied on the relay model, (in Heath and Skirrow's formulation) a show pictured direct, and direct for me. The first rock videos were similar, but they rapidly broke from this to achieve a full liberation of the signifier. Promos are worlds of fantasy and imagination, often it must be said within dispiritingly narrow and retrogressive terms, but certainly offering a challenge to the dominant form of television.

The challenge of course is a limited and exceptionally circumscribed one, and one which has been easily assimilated by the medium itself. But it is there nonetheless, just as it is within certain television advertisements, title sequences and on-air promotion segments. None of these make any pretence to be showing me, offering me sight of, the *Real* occurring elsewhere.

Nor does one very particular group of documentaries, best exemplified now as the 'Arena' group. Documentaries traditionally do 'look at life', relay direct and direct for me, what is happening in Ethiopia, in the Lebanon, in the police force or on a Marines training course. But the 'Arena' strand which began with 'My Way' and has included 'The Private Life of the Ford Cortina', 'It's All True', 'Chelsea Hotel' and 'Ligmalion', has no such pretensions. These are highly structured, even if presented as naïve, collages centred around a theme or object. Within each brief segment they make no challenge to the relay model, but their mixing of forms and strategies (including, for example, fictional elements) is a resistance to television's dominant form of vision.

I'm aware, of course, that 'Arena' does not have a monopoly on this style, and that there are historical precedents that go back certainly to Humphrey Jennings, but 'Arena' does seem best to exemplify it at present.

Both these 'Arenas' and rock promos do, as I have suggested, share certain features which have been identified as postmodern. These include the forms of pastiche and parody (think here of Divine's current video for 'Walk Like a Man', which pastiches the Western, and of 'Ligmalion's' recent parody of rock promos); appropriation of imagery (Paul Hardcastle's current video to '19' which re-works Vietnam archive footage); the mixing of historical styles (the recent rebarbative homage to neo-classicism and National Socialism done by Freddie Mercury); and the collapse of the distinction between high art and mass culture (Malcolm McLaren's 'Madame Butterfly' is our best example here).

Both rock promos and 'Arena', if it is useful at all to think of them as postmodern, should, I would argue, be recognised as exemplars of symptomatic postmodernism. That is, even while they do offer some challenge to the dominant model of vision, they share certain features of the television culture as a whole, and they certainly do not offer the kind of challenge which I now want to go on to outline. What I wish to set against them are a couple of examples of what I might refer to as oppositional postmodernism, or in Hal Foster's phrase, of a 'postmodernism of resistance'.

For this stage of the argument I want to turn to and lean heavily upon Raymond Williams. In his recent book, *Towards 2000*, Williams analyses the original innovations of modernism as 'a response to the complex consequences of a dominant social order, in which forms of imperial-political and corporate-economic power were simultaneously destroying traditional communities and creating new concentrations of real and symbolic power and capital in a few metropolitan centres'.

Williams notes the paradox that the same processes controlled and centralised the new means of universal distribution — the cinema and later broadcasting — which were at the same time being discovered and developed. Thus, Williams says, and I regret that I have to telescope his argument, 'the very conditions which had provoked a genuine modernist art became the conditions which steadily homogenised even its startling images, and diluted its deep forms, until they could be made available as a universally distributed "popular" culture'.

Crucial to this argument is Williams' resistance to both technological determinism and cultural pessimism; crudely, his rejection of the ideas that advances in cable and satellite television will necessarily bring wall-to-wall 'Dallas', and that this is necessarily a Bad Thing. The real enemies, Williams asserts, 'not only in culture but in the widest areas of social, economic and political life, belong to the dominant capitalist order in its paranational phase'.

No surprises there; but the question remains: How do we resist this enemy, and in particular, its current cultural manifestations? Two suggestions; the first with a resistance to the dominant model of tele-vision, using a form which, following Benjamin, might be called 'dialectical images' or, after Berger, 'a dialogue of images'.

The best current example is undoubtedly Channel Four's series 'About Time'. In the first film of the six, images and arguments are used against each other to *open up* questions and debates. There is no pretence at relaying a *Real*, nor of ordering in a hierarchy the discourses on offer. The result is one of the richest and most suggestive pieces of recent television. I don't want to make a full critique of that film but I should note how different it is from the subsequent film which was authored and presented by John Berger. Here, although a wide range of images and sounds were called upon, they were strictly controlled and subordinated to Berger's presence, and offered only a very reduced opportunity for dialectic. Again, quite how useful it is to label (at least some of) 'About Time' as postmodernist, I'm not sure, but it does seem to me to use a strategy which has parallels with certain contemporary visual artists, who similarly appropriate and re-order to create a dialectic.

The strategy is also one used by certain artists working in the gap between broadcast television and the visual arts, in the area which is often called video art. Artists here as diverse as Joan Jonas, Gary Hill, Dan Reeves and Ed Mowbray share features of this strategy of resistance. Reeves's twenty-five minute tape 'Smothering Dreams', for example, mixes newsreel footage, children's games, auto-biography, clips from westerns, model reconstructions and much else to explore the personal and political experience of Vietnam.

These examples are what we might call objective ones, where the dialectic is created, or at least deliberately offered, by the piece itself. I want to end with the suggestion of another type of dialectic, a subjective dialectic which each and every one of us develops in our relationship with mass culture. I'm all too aware that I don't have even the beginnings of a theoretical psychoanalytical model for this. Indeed if it didn't sound hopelessly sentimental, I'd say that my only support for the idea is some kind of faith (but then of course that's a word banished from the postmodern vocabulary) in the individual (and that's certainly another).

Williams alludes to something close to what I'm searching for when he identifies 'an area diametrically opposed to an incorporated "modernism" '.

> It is a simplicity of every kind, which is quite differently sustained . . . It is there in the intense vitality of some kinds of popular music, always being reached for by the market, but repeatedly renewing its impulses in new and vigorous forms. It is there also (against many of our pre-conceptions) in some kinds of popular 'domestic' drama and fiction, in that always edged-towards-sentimental embodiment of everyday lives and situations . . . It is in this very general area of jokes and gossip, of everyday singing and dancing, of occasional dressing up and extravagant outbursts of colour, that a popular culture most clearly perists. (*Towards 2000*)

For me this is unfortunately and dangerously close to a vision of a happy, contented England dancing round a maypole and thereby, somehow, making a stand against international capitalism. Yet Williams, I'm sure, is right. We live in a mass culture to which we do not simply submit. We take its images, its narratives, its formulations of desire, and measure them against our real experiences of a real world. At the same time we re-work and re-use them, in our conversation and gossip, in our fantasies, in every aspect of our lives. And this re-use is our own individual form of resistance.

Humanism, I'm afraid, has finally gotten the better of me, despite my real respect for and interest in, theories of the look and postmodern challenges to the primacy-of-vision. I'll end, then, with another chunk of that well-known humanist, Raymond Williams:

> The direct energies and enjoyments of this popular culture are still irrepressibly active, even after they have been incorporated as diversions or mimed as commercials or steered into conformist ideologies. They are irrepressible because in the generality of their impulses, and in their intransigent attachments to human diversity and recreation, they survive under any pressures and through whatever forms, while life itself survives, and while so

many people — real if not always connected majorities —
keep living and looking to live beyond the routines which
attempt to control and reduce them. (*Towards 2000*)

Notes

1. Colin MacCabe, 'Realism in the Cinema: Notes on some
   Brechtian Theses', *Screen*, vol. 15, no. 2, Summer 1974.
2. Stephen Heath and Gillian Skirrow, 'Television: A World in
   Action', *Screen*, vol. 18, no. 2, Summer 1977.

POSTMODERNISM AND POPULAR CULTURE
Angela McRobbie

The 'Soweto Dash'

Rather than starting with a definition of postmodernism as referring either to a condition of contemporary life, or a textual, aesthetic practice, I want to begin by suggesting that the recent debates on postmodernism possess both a positive attraction and a usefulness to the analyst of popular culture. This is because they offer a wider, and more dynamic, understanding of contemporary representation than other accounts to date. Unlike the various strands of structuralist criticism, postmodernism considers images as they relate to and across each other. Postmodernism deflects attention away from the singular scrutinizing gaze of the semiologist, and asks that this be replaced by a multiplicity of fragmented, and frequently interrupted, 'looks'.

The exemplary text or the single, richly coded, image, gives way to the textual *thickness* and the visual *density* of everyday life, as though the slow, even languid 'look' of the semiologist is, by the 1980s, out of tempo with the times. The field of postmodernism certainly expresses a frustration, not merely with this seemingly languid pace, but with its increasing inability to make tangible connections between the general conditions of life today and the practice of cultural analysis.

Structuralism has also replaced old orthodoxies with new ones. This is apparent in its re-reading of texts highly placed within an already existing literary or aesthetic hierarchy. Elsewhere it constructs a new hierarchy, with Hollywood classics at the top, followed by selected advertising images, and girl's and women's magazines rounding it off. Other forms of representation, particularly music and dance, are missing altogether. Andreas Huyssen[1] in his recent introduction to postmodernism

draws attention to this 'high' structuralist preference for the
works of high modernism especially the writing of James
Joyce or Mallarmé.

> There is no doubt that center stage in critical theory is held
> by the classical modernists: Flaubert . . . in Barthes; . . .
> Mallarmé and Artaud in Derrida; Magritte . . . in
> Foucault; . . . Joyce and Artaud in Kristeva . . . and so on
> *ad infinitum*.

He argues that this reproduces unhelpfully the old
distinction between the high arts and the 'low', less serious,
popular arts. He goes on to comment,

> Pop in the broadest sense was the context in which a notion
> of the postmodern first took shape, and . . . and the most
> significant trends within postmodernism have challenged
> modernism's relentless hostility to mass culture.

High theory was simply not equipped to deal with
multi-layered pop. Nor did it ever show much enthusiasm
about this set of forms, perhaps because pop has never
signified within one discrete discourse, but instead combines images with performance, music with film, or video,
and pin ups with the magazine form itself. As a *Guardian*
journalist recently put it, 'Rock and pop performers today
have to speak in multi-media tongues' (3.1.86).

With the exception of Barthes, 'heavy weight' criticism
has been focussed towards memorable texts, while light-
weight cultural analysis is given over to the more
forgettable images of everyday life. And the 'purity' of the
about-to-be-decoded-image is reflected in the pivotal
position occupied by semiology and structuralist criticism
in media courses up and down the country. Despite
gestures towards intertextuality and interdisciplinarity,
this centrality given to *the structualisms* in effect squeezes all
the other complex relations which locate the text, or the
image, and allow it to produce meaning, out of the picture.
These relations include those which mark out its physical
place within the world of commodities, its sequencing, and
its audience as well as consumers. Such issues are frequently
relegated, with some disregard, to the realm of sociology or
'empiricism' as though these were the same thing. And

while critics argue that this outside reality is really nothing more than a series of other texts, they are in the meantime happy to treat questions about consumers, readers, audience, and viewers, as intrinsically uninteresting, as though this entails hanging about street corners with a questionnaire and clipboard.

Postmodernism allows what were respectable sociological issues to reappear on the intellectual agenda. It implicitly challenges the narrowness of structuralist vision, by taking the deep interrogation of every breathing aspect of lived experience by media imagery as a starting point. So extensive and inescapable is this process that it becomes conceptually impossible to privilege one simple moment. So far only Dick Hebdige's[2] Subculture. The Meaning of Style has broken out of this inadvertent reproduction of the old divide between high culture and the pop arts, as well as between representation and reality. In Subculture, Hebdige recognises that familiar objects warrant analysis as signs and repositories of organised meaning, as much as linguistic or 'pure' visual signs. Under the conceptual umbrella of subculture, he brings together art, literature, music, style, dress, and even attitude, and places these on the same analytical plane. Hebdige also brings a speed and urgency to the business of interpreting the familiar marks of contemporary life.

It's surprising, then, that in a more recent article, where he engages directly with the question of postmodernism, Hebdige[3] disavows the playful element in Subculture . . . and, more manifestly, in the new fashion and style magazines. In contrast with what he sees now as an excess of style, a celebration of artifice and a strong cultural preference for pastiche, Hebdige seeks out the reassuringly real. He suggests that the slick joky tone of postmodernism, especially that found on the pages of The Face represents a disengagement with the real, and an evasion of social responsibility. He therefore insists on a return to the world of hunger, exploitation, and oppression and with it a resurrection of unfragmented, recognisable subjectivity. He only fleetingly engages with what Jameson[4] has described as an important characteristic of the postmodern condition, that is the death of subjectivity and the emergence, in its place, of widespread social schizophrenia.

Hebdige seems to be saying that if this rupturing of identity is what postmodernism is about, then he would rather turn his back on it. What I will be arguing here is that the terrain of all these surfaces Hebdige mentions — pop, music, style, and fashion — is neither as homogenous nor as limited as he (or *The Face*) would have it. This landscape of the present, with its embracing of pastiche, its small defiant pleasure in being dressed up or 'casual', its exploration of fragmented subjectivity — all of this articulates more precisely with the wider conditions of present 'reality' — with unemployment, with education, with the 'aestheticisation of culture', and with the coming into being of those whose voices were historically drowned out by the (modernist) meta-narratives of mastery, which were in turn both patriarchal and imperialist.

Postmodernism has entered into a more diverse number of vocabularies more quickly than most other intellectual categories. It has spread outwards from the realms of art history into political theory and onto the pages of youth culture magazines, record sleeves, and the fashion pages of *Vogue*. This seems to me to indicate something more than the mere vagaries of taste. More also, than the old Marcusian notion of recuperation, where a radical concept which once had purchase, rapidly becomes a commodity, and in the process is washed, laundered, and left out to dry. Later on in this paper I will locate this coming together of the worlds of intellectual analysis and pop journalism (as well as pop production) around postmodernism, by considering the role of education, and in particular 'cultural studies'. Here it is sufficient to point to the extensiveness and flexibility of the term.

Postmodernism certainly appeared in the UK like a breath of fresh air. It captured in a word, a multitude of experiences, particularly what Baudrillard[5] has called the 'instantaneity of communication'. This refers to the incursion of imagery and communication into those spaces that once were private — where the psyche previously had the chance to at least explore the 'other', to explore, for example, alienation. Baudrillard claims this space now to be penetrated by the predatory and globally colonialist media. But as the frontiers of the self are effaced and transformed, so too are the boundaries which mark out

separate discourses and separate politics. Baudrillard interprets the new associative possibilities thrown up by
'instantaneity' gloomily. 'Everything is exposed to the
harsh and inexorable light of information and communication', which in turn generates only an 'ecstasy of communication' . . . But need Baudrillard be quite so
pessimistic? Why must this speeding-up process, this
intensification or exchange be greeted with such forebod-
ing?

The remainder of this paper will be given over to arguing
the case for postmodernism. It will suggest that the
frenzied expansion of the mass media has political consequences which are not so wholly negative. This becomes most
apparent when we look at representations of the Third
World. No longer can this be confined to the realist
documentary, or the exotic televisual voyage. The Third
World refuses now, to 'us', in the West, to be reassuringly
out of sight. It is as adept at using the global media as the
old colonialist powers. Equally the 'we' of the British
nation no longer possesses any reliable reality. That
spurious unity has been decisively shattered. New alliances
and solidarities emerge from within and alongside media
imagery. A disenchanted black, inner city population in
Britain, can look in an 'ecstasy of communication' as black
South Africans use every available resource at hand to put
apartheid into crisis. Jokily, and within a kind of
postmodern language Dick Hebdige wrote, in *Subculture*,
that TV images of Soweto in 1976 taught British youth
'the Soweto dash'. Ten years later this connection has
amplified. The image is the trigger and the mechanism for
this new identification.

Implosion

Of course it's not quite so simple. The South African
government has recently banned journalists from the black
townships. And in less politically sensitive arenas, the
media continues, relentlessly, to hijack events and offer in
their place a series of theatrical spectacles whose points of
relevance are only tangentially on what is going on, and
whose formal cues came from other, frequently televisual,

forms of representation. 1985 was rich in examples. Reagan's illness was relayed to the public, overwhelmingly in the language of soap opera. A *Guardian* correspondent pointed out that nobody would have been convinced if his doctors had not appeared at the press conferences dressed in white coats. A few weeks earlier Shi'ite militiamen took over a TWA airline in Athens. In what was largely a bid for space on Western prime-time television, the captors could afford to appear smiling and jubilant as they offered their victims a Lebanese banquet, against a backdrop of random gunfire at the ceiling, before packing them off to the United States.

This easing out of the real in favour of its most appropriate representation makes it more difficult to talk about the media and society today. It creates even greater difficulties in assessing the relationship between images, or between popular cultural forms, and their consumers. The consciousness industries have changed remarkably over the last ten years, but so have the outlook and the expectations of their audiences.

Against a backdrop of severe economic decline, the mass media continues to capture new outlets, creating fresh markets to absorb its hi-tech commodities. Symbolically the image has assmed a contemporary dominance. It is no longer possible to talk about the image and reality, media and society. Each has become so deeply intertwined that it is difficult to draw the line between the two. Instead of referring to the real world, much media output devotes itself to referring to other images, other narratives. Self-referentiality is all-embracing, although it is rarely taken account of. The Italian critic and writer, Umberto Eco, recently contrasted what TV was (paleo-TV), with what it now is, (neo-TV). 'Its prime characteristic is that it talks less and less about the external world. Whereas paleo-television talked about the external world, or pretended to, neo-television talks about itself and about the contacts it establishes with its own public.'[6]

Self-referentiality occurs within and across different media forms. One TV programme might be devoted to the production of another (Paul Gambaccino 'on' the Tube), just as television films based on the making of other large-scale cinema productions are becoming increasingly common. There is a similar dependency for material and content, as well as a relatively recent redefinition of what is interesting, and what readers and viewers want, in the print media's use of *televisual stories*. *The Face* magazine ran a piece on The Tube, and more recently on Michelle, the pregnant schoolgirl, in East Enders . . . The *NME* carried a major feature on Brookside, and *City Limits* sent two journalists to the Coronation Street set, for a week. It's not so much that fiction is being mistaken for fact; more that one set of textual practices (in this case British soap) has become the reference point for another (reading the newspaper or glancing at a headline).

Media interdependency is both an economic and a cultural imperative. Childrens' TV on a Saturday morning evolves entirely around the pop music industry, offering an exclusive showcase for new 'promo' videos. The contents of these programmes are orchestrated around all the familiar pop business, phone-in to the stars, interviews, the new single, the talent competition for young hopefuls. This shows the feeding-off effect between mass media today. Where once the middle class world of Blue Peter documented childrens' initiatives for charity, now Capital, in the form of culture and visual communications, penetrates further into the youth market. In the *classless* world of these programmes this means pushing back the frontiers of young people as consumers by transforming children and even toddlers into fans and thus part of the record-buying public.

The implications of this endless cross-referencing are extensive. They create an ever-increasing, but less diverse verbal and visual landscape. It is these recurring fictions, and the characters who inhabit them which feed into the field of popular knowledge, and which in turn constitute a large part of popular culture. It would be difficult not to know about Victoria Principal, it would be impossible not to know about Dallas.

Texts have always alluded to or connected with others. Simone De Beauvoir's *Memoirs of a Dutiful Daughter* gives up many pages to all the other books she read during her childhood, adolescence and early adult years. Indeed this critical bibliography forms a major strand of the work. The difference now is that the process is less restricted to literature, more widespread, and most apparent in the commercial mass media where there are more spaces to be filled. And such an opening up doesn't necessarily mean an extension of rights of access, only rights of consumption. More often it means a form of cosy, mutual congratulatory, cross-referencing and repetition. (Wogan in Denver, Clive James in Dallas). Baudrillard greets these recent changes with some cynicism. He claims that more media offers less meaning in the guise of more information. 'All secrets, spaces and scenes abolished in a single dimension of information.' Eco follows this when he describes the scrambling effect of multi-channel choice on TV. 'Switching channels reflects the brevity and speed of other visual forms. Like flicking through a magazine, or driving past a billboard. This means that "our" TV evenings no longer tell us stories, it is all a trailer!'

Images push their way into the fabric of our social lives. They enter into how we look, what we earn, and they are still with us when we worry about bills, housing and bringing up children. They compete for attention through shock tactics, reassurance, sex, mystery and by inviting viewers to participate in series of visual puzzles. Billboard advertisements showing an image without a code, impose themselves, infuriatingly, on the most recalcitrant passer-by.

However what is often forgotten is that the media also enter the classroom. This remains an undocumented site in the history of the image. But in seminar rooms across the country, slides are projected and students prise open new readings. The educational incorporation of contemporary mass media represents something other than the simple consumption of images, but it is also part of the widening out process I mentioned earlier. People's usage of and experience of the media increases not just because there is more of it, but because it crops up in different places. Almost all the new disciplines in the arts and social sciences make use of pop imagery, whether in adult education, on degree courses, or on project work with unemployed young people. This gives rise to a rather more optimistic reading of the mass media than that offered by Baudrillard. The invasive impact of these new technologies, because they now occupy a place within these institutions provide a basis

for the production of new meanings, new cultural expressions. There is a myth that radical or challenging media
forms come 'from the street'. In fact it is in the media
workshops, in the creative writing classes and the college
studios that such work emerges. Art students specialising
in graphics and writing a dissertation on 'left imagery' go
on to work freelance for *The Face*; others opt for mainstream
advertising agencies while working unpaid for the Labour
Party, or the women's movement or for new black cultural
groups.[10] And of course the history of British pop music is
one which grew out of the expansion of the art schools in
the 60's and the flooding into them of bright young
working class boys.

It is not absolutely necessary for my argument that these
new forms of pop culture are and have been of a
homogenously high standard. It is much more important
that the work itself is considered both in terms of where it
comes from, who made it, and which groups have, in turn,
taken it up.

Twenty years ago Susan Sontag[11] offered an interesting
perspective on those forms of popular culture which are
good because they are so awful. This was reflective of a *camp*
sensibility, the essence of which is 'its love of the unnatural:
of artifice and exaggeration'. Until then this was a widely
felt, but as yet untheorised popular aesthetic. In her essay
Sontag stressed the importance of the knowing audience,
one which could allow itself absorption because it was
equally capable of detachment. This is useful to us here
because it offers a fruitful way forward in understanding the
more combatative side particularly to young peoples'
engagement with culture. We can use both the notion of
camp and that of the knowing audience to extend Jameson's
recent attempt to make sense of the ever-accumulating and
stultifyingly banal images which form such a staple part of
the media output.[12] He describes this as a new kind of
depthlessness, a 'waning in effect'. Jameson applies the
term pastiche to describe these circulating forms. This
certainly has an immediate resonance. In both pop music
and in the popular soap operas, pastiche is a dominant
motif. According to Jameson pastiche is 'without that still
latent feeling that there exists something normal compared
to which what is being imitated, is rather comic. Pastiche

is blank parody . . .'

In Dallas and Dynasty this is the most appropriate way of describing the heightening of reality which becomes in turn a deadening unreality. These soaps signal a realism in which they have absolutely no investment. The practiced sincerity of the pop performer, his or her anxiety to convey real, recognisable, and searing emotions, carries the same quality. In each case the reference back to real life or real emotions is purely formal or stylistic. A mannerism pointing nowhere. But Jameson's accurate account of this 'speech in a dead language', fails to engage with its reception. Perhaps this is because the bulk of his analysis of the 'postmodern condition' is focussed towards art rather than popular culture, and in this arena little academic concern has been shown for audiences or consumers. However in that field where Jameson's thesis is most markedly appropriate, in pop music and its subsidiaries, there is no question of denying the consumers or fans their place. But how this integration is understood conceptually remains more problematic. Sontag's linking pastiche with its favoured audience, gay men, is instructive because she shows how a relationship evolved around a social minority making a bid for a cultural form in which they felt they could stake some of their fragmented and sexually deviant identity. The insistence, on the way, on both style and pleasure made the product attractive to those outside as well as inside. The result was the absorption of camp style into the mainstream of popular taste. Sontag's approach is useful because she is talking not so much about pure or original 'artistic' invention. Rather she is describing how forms can be taken over, and re-assembled so as to suit the requirements of the group in question. This often means outstripping their ostensible meaning and ostensible function. In this capacity male gay culture has in the last few years had a remarkable impact. It has been explicit and outspoken, while holding onto both an aesthetic and a political discourse. In pop m usic, groups like Frankie Goes to Hollywood and Bronski Beat as well as performers like Marc Almond and Boy George have utilised many of the pastiche elements which Sontag describes, achieving main-stream success without blunting the edges of a celebratory homosexuality.

The advantages of Sontag's comments are that they emphasise *agency*. She brings the audience, the consumers, the 'camp followers' into the picture without sidetracking into 'empiricism'. The same would have to be done with pop music and contemporary youth culture. It is impossible to understand Boy George and Culture Club's rise to prominence without considering the punk, art-school, London, 'educated' subculture from which they emerged.

And, if media forms are so inescapable 'if unreality is now within everyone's grasp' (Eco),[13] then there is no reason to assume that the consumption of pastiche, parody or high camp is, by definition, without subversive or critical potential. Glamour, glitter, and gloss, should not so easily be relegated to the sphere of the insistently apolitical. For the left, necessarily committed to endorsing the real and the material conditions of peoples' lives, there remains still an (understandable) stiffness about Neil Kinnock's appearance in a Tracy Ullman video. This need not be the case.

If, as Jameson suggests, life has been dramatised to the level of soap, if love is always like a *Jackie* story, then yes, the sharp distinction between real life and fictional forms must give way to a deep intermingling, unmeasurable and so far captured most precisely in fictive or cinematic forms. Scorsese's *King of Comedy* traced this 'overdetermination by the image', as did Woody Allen's *Stardust Memories*, as well as his more recent *Zelig* and *The Purple Rose of Cairo*. But Gore Vidals novel *Duluth* outstrips all of these.[14] It is a model of postmodern writing. Gore Vidal has his tongue firmly in his cheek. *Duluth* is a witty multi-layered fiction which moves from the town of the title, to the soap series based on the place, outwards to the novel of the soap, backwards into the historical romances favoured by the town's top woman cop, and forwards into a science fiction setting where Roland Barthes makes a guest appearance. Obligingly Vidal ends the novel by handing over to a word processor.

All of this comes close to what Baudrillard infuriatingly calls implosion.[15] It's a vague but appropriate term. It implies an outburst of energy which is nonetheless controlled and inclining inwards. Baudrillard, Eco and Jameson all see this as a totalising and all-immersing process. But none of them consider the new associations and resistances which have come into prominence by way of these processes in the last fifteen years. Many of these share more in common with the shattered energy of implosion, with Jameson's fragmented schizophrenic consciousness, than with the great narratives of the old left,

> It was especially the art, writing, film-making and criticism of women and minority artists, with their recuperation of buried and mutilated traditions, their emphasis on exploring forms of gender- and race-based subjectivity in aesthetic productions and experiences, and their refusal to be limited to standard canonizations, which added a whole new dimension to the critique of high modernism and to the emergence of alternative forms of culture.[16]

In the British context one would want to append to this formidable production not just the proliferation of pop culture and the challenge it has mounted to the mainstream arts, but also the involvement of youth in the creation of an egalitarian avant-garde. Of course this is no longer an avant-garde proper, since the privileging of the forms have been abandoned in favour of a cross referencing between forms, and notably between pop music and 'art', between aesthetics and commerce, between commitment and the need to make a living. This leads directly to a further failing in Jameson's account. There is no recognition that those elements contained within his diagnosis of postmodernism — including pastiche, the ransacking and recycling of culture, the direct invocation to other texts and other images — can create a vibrant critique rather than an inward-looking, second-hand aesthetic. What else has black urban culture in the last few years been, but an assertive re-assembling of bits and pieces, 'whatever comes to hand', noises, debris, technology, tape, image, rapping, scratching, and other hand me downs? Black urban music has always thrived on fake, forged identities, creating a façade of grand-sounding titles which reflect both the 'otherness' of black culture, the extent to which it is outside that which is legitimate, and the way in which white society has condemned it to be nameless. Who, after all, is Grandmaster Flash or Melle Mel? Or who was Sly and the

Family Stone? Who mixed the speech by Malcolm X onto a haunting disco funk backing track? Reggae also parodies this enforced namelessness. Many of its best known musicians suggest a deep irony in their stagenames: Clint Eastwood, Charlie Chaplin, and so on.

In America graffiti remains the best example of fleeting, obsolescent urban aesthetics. It gives its creators fame once they get into the galleries but otherwise only faint notoriety,

> It is a cultural identity which half mocks, half celebrates, the excesses of mainstream white culture. The graffiti painter is the Spiderman of the ghettos, projecting pure fantasy. A terminal vantage point on white consumer culture. Hip hop is a subculture which feeds for its material upon the alien culture which needs make no concession to blacks. The spray paints and comic book images of graffiti painting, to the disco beats and found sounds of rapping, are diverted from their mainstream domestic use and put out on the streets as celebration. For the white middle class kid, the comic heroes occupy a space of boredom. For the black ghetto kid they are transformed by graffiti art into fantastic visions invested with secret meanings.[17]

Alongside these largely male forms, must be placed the writing of black women, the great explosion of the written word which writes a history otherwise condemned to remain only within popular memory. Toni Cade Bambara's[18] prose is closest in rhythm to the jazz sounds of the city. It is breath-taking, agile writing, insisting on the pleasures, the wit and the idiosyncracies of a community more often characterised as monolithic and deprived. All of this is taking place within the cracks of a crumbling culture where progress is in question and society seems to be standing still.

There *is* no going back. For populations transfixed on images which are themselves a reality, there is no return to a mode of representation which politicizes in a kind of straightforward 'worthwhile' way. Dallas is destined to sit alongside images of black revolt. And it is no longer possible, living within postmodernism, to talk about unambiguously negative or positive images. But this need not be seen as the end of the social, or the end of meaning, or for that matter the beginning of the new nihilism. Social agency is employed in the activation of *all* meanings. Audiences or viewers, lookers or users are not simple-minded multitudes. As the media extends its sphere of influence, so also does it come under the critical surveillance *and* usage of its subjects.

The reason why postmodernism appeals to a wider number of young people, and to what might be called the new generation of intellectuals (often black, female, or working class) is that they themselves are experiencing the enforced fragmentation of impermanent work, and low career opportunities. Far from being overwhelmed by media saturation, there is evidence to suggest that these social groups and minorities are putting it to work for them. This alone should prompt the respect and the attention of an older generation who seem at present too eager to embrace a sense of political hopelessness.

Notes

1   Andreas Huyssen, 'Mapping the Postmodern', *New German Critique* 1984.
2   Dick Hebdige, *Subculture, The Meaning of Style*, Methuen, 1979.
3   Dick Hebdige, 'The Bottom Line On Planet One', *Ten 8*, No. 19.
4   Frederic Jameson, 'Postmodernism and Consumer Society', *Postmodern Culture*, ed. Hal Foster Pluto Press 1985.
5   Jean Baudrillard, 'The Ecstasy of Communication', *Postmodern Culture* ed Hal Foster see above.
6   Umberto Eco, 'A Guide to the Neo Television of the 1980s', *Framework no. 25*.
7   Simone De Beauvoir, *Memoirs of a Dutiful Daughter*, Penguin 1984.
8   Jean Baudrillard see above.
9   Umberto Eco see above.
10 This was certainly my experience teaching art students at St Martin's School of Art in London.
11 Susan Sontag, Notes on 'Camp', *Against Interpretation*, Eyre & Spottiswoode 1967.
12 Frederic Jameson see above.
13 Umberto Eco see above.
14 Gore Vidal, *Duluth*, Heinemann 1983.

15 Jean Baudrillard, *Towards a Political Economy of the Sign*.
16 Andreas Huyssen see above.
17 Atlanta and Alexander, 'Wild Style . . . Graffiti Painting', *ZG* no. 6.
18 Toni Cade Bambara, *Gorilla, My Love*, The Women's Press 1983.

BRIEF REFLECTIONS ON POPULAR CULTURE
Jean-François Lyotard

First of all, I must say that this afternoon I felt as though I
were taking a rejuvenation treatment. I think it's a good
strategy to be generous towards one's adversary. But I do
think that the great problem posed by the three presentations is that of the popular itself. In other words, the
question of what is the *demos*. Do the words 'popular' and
'democratic' mean today what the traditions of folklore and
of democratic politics have transmitted to us? There's an
ambiguity because 'popular' used to refer to the old
regional nations anchored in their traditions, and 'democratic' which meant the set of enlightened citizens, able to
reason, and in particular to have taste. Now in the notion of
'pop', which synthesizes and condenses the two, I think
there's neither the one nor the other. For example, it's very
difficult to imagine that pop music today belongs to a
folkloric tradition, in the strict sense. And I don't think
that the democratisation or democratism of TV (even
British TV) means that it is addressed to enlightened
citizens, and that it answers their desire. I think that on the
contrary, 'pop' is a product: I'm not talking about popular
culture, but about the pop viewer or spectator or public in
general. That public is a product of the only thing that all
types and levels of culture have in common, let's say, for
the sake of simplicity, the commodity. It's the commodity
which produces its public. Of course one can say that this
commodity satisfies the public, since the public is made for
the commodity, and by the commodity. I'd have a lot of
reservations about that, although I recognize that we
mustn't have a negative attitude with respect to this
problem. I think that the presentations were possibly a
little hasty with their concessions to what is positive in
these forms of pop culture or mass culture.

The question everybody raised was that of knowing how
to introduce resistance into this cultural industry. I believe

that the only line to follow is to produce programmes for TV, or whatever, which produce in the viewer or the client in general an effect of uncertainty and trouble. It seems to me that the thing to aim at is a certain sort of feeling or sentiment. You can't introduce concepts, you can't produce argumentation. This type of media isn't the place for that, but you can produce a feeling of disturbance, in the hope that this disturbance will be followed by reflection. I think that that's the only thing one can say, and obviously it's up to every artist to decide by what means s/he thinks s/he can produce this disturbance.

ICA DOCUMENTS 5

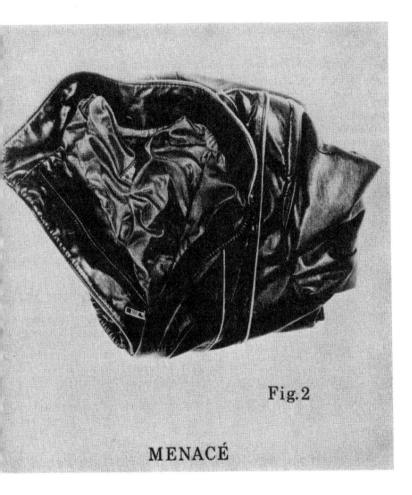

Fig. 2

MENACÉ

Mary Kelly, From Interim, 1984

NAMES: PROPER AND IMPROPER
René Major

In this paper I will present some aspects of the research I have been doing on a psychoanalytical theory of proper names.

Everyone knows about proper names, which seem quite simple but which are in fact very complicated. We all have a proper name and yet this proper name rarely belongs to only one person. We do not choose our own name (at least the name which is on our birth certificate) and yet it identifies us and distinguishes us from everyone else, to the extent that we identify ourselves by our own name.

Insofar as a proper name may designate several people (even people who do not know each other), it is quite 'improper' to single out one person.

Insofar as it refers to a real subject, the proper name is a mark related both to a sound (you respond to the sound of your name) and to the letter (you recognize your written name). The proper name is distinguished from the common noun in that it is not at all necessary to refer to the meaning (of the signifier) in order to designate its referent. However, proper names distinguish one person from another. The proper name is thus a mark without meaning (an un-meaning mark), insignificant and yet remarkable, in both senses of the word. It allows us to recognize someone, but the mark can be used more than once and even endlessly. The mark is valid at the same time for one person and for all those who have the same name. This produces homonymy; names which have no relationship (in terms of what they designate) may coincide. As far as proper names are concerned coincidence may just as well make them homonymous.

Things become even more complicated if one takes into consideration the signifiers of a proper name or its imaginary properties. Thus there is a homonymous relationship between Mr. White and the colour white of a dress, white skin, white rage, Whitehall, White House,

White Hotel or white lie. From one language to another, we find a number of such imaginary relationships: for instance, between Freud (which means Joy in German) and Joyce, between Freud's name and the pleasure principle, between Freud as a proper name and Psychoanalysis as a proper name.

A theory of proper names allows us to understand better the passages between the psychical stage, the theoretical stage and the institutional stage; it may also help us to throw light upon several delicate points concerning transference.

In the history of English thought, the theory of proper names has been dealt with by philosophers, philologists, logicians and linguists such as John Stuart Mill, Bertrand Russell, Alan Gardiner and Saul Kripke, all of whom were basically trying to define the properties of the proper name as the referent of a real subject.

What interests me here is how the proper name and its referent can be separated from the signifiers and their imaginary component, how the name can also be separated from the referent by its capacity to distinguish the similar and the dissimilar, and also how the different functioning levels of the proper name can meet, become entangled or disentangled.

'Theatre is a passionate overflow/a terrifying transference of forces/from body/to body.' You may be acquainted with this affirmation of Antonin Artaud's. Not only does it state the general proposition, 'there is transference in theatre', but it designates the theatre as a place where transference makes itself felt through excess.

I will leave the question as to what 'transference' here means and equally whatever it is that is made manifest in the overflowing, that is to say what is indexed which can only be indexable through excess. Because the question turns on itself. The transference as a whole is the staging of an apparatus of representation, an apparatus which brings about disguised transports, sets down translations, literally 'brings to pass' demands and desires, from one place to another, through playing on misunderstandings (*quipro-quos*), through switching characters on and off stage and through smuggling into the situation signifiers marked in such a way as to be as insignificant (*insignifiante*) as they are remarkable. Proper names are exchanged and thereby lend one another elective identities and strange lives. This nomination and exchange of names assure the reproduction of representation, but the necessary split in representation introduced by repression takes place between desire and death. With Hamlet (which Freud considers to be the first modern play) it becomes exemplary. In contrast to what happens with Oedipus, Hamlet finds himself deprived, by his father's murderer, of any possible realisation of his 'own' parricidal desire. The fact of the father's already being dead only makes his burden the greater and obliges the conflictual task of avenging him to suffer a delay, because Hamlet has difficulty recognising his desire, which seems immured in his father's tomb, in this task. The relationship of this indecision to the undecidability of representation on the analytic stage is a trait which has not up to now been examined. The interval introduced into the speech of analysis transposes, via the action of the unconscious, whatever has the status of *saying* into that of a *doing*, once no withdrawal to the position of spectator has been left to the play of transference of desires. That means that the margin of interpretation (in the theatrical sense) is that much greater when the transference lacks play.

So, for Artaud, in theatre there is transference, a terrifying transference, a transference which is obliged to come to pass but which must not be reproduced: 'This transference,' he affirms or would have wanted to have been able to affirm, 'cannot be reproduced twice'. It repeats itself only once, as a repetition, or rehearsal, which isn't repeated, finding its origin and its end in this single repetition. In this way something beyond the principle of repetition is posited, in which one finds confused the production of the scene and its annihilation, the advent of the father and his effacement, the event of the murder which is just as real as it is imaginary in one single, self-identical moment.

Writing which would not delimit a space between the body and its disguises, speech which would not be dead once it is spoken out loud, that would be absolute performativity, the act and the word once and for all transporting ineluctable cruelty into the festivities. Such would be the reproduction, through rendering it exem-

plary, of the theatre of the dream. Exemplary, because
desire would there be realised without disguise. But not
only that. It would also have to produce, within the space
of its representation, the dreamer and his interpreter: a
dreamer knowing that he is not dreaming while dreaming
and an interpreter who doesn't engage in interpreting while
interpreting.

The thought of Artaud which I am referring to here is
only intended to evoke the problem that it raises of a place
of passage, a *passable* or *a linking passage* (*un praticable*), I'll
have to say, between the representing apparatus of the
psychic stage, that of the theatrical stage and another,
broader, that of the social stage. The 'broader stage' is one
of Freud's expressions, designating the stage on which the
events of human history are played, the devélopment of
Civilisation and the backlash of archaic experiences. This
stage is none other than 'the other stage', that of the
unconscious; it blends with it but also overflows it,
'reflects' it all the while through 'repeating' it and revives it
without repeating or rehearsing it. Certain reflections will
only be representable and visible in the repetition/rehearsal
of history. Distinct from one another, these stages (with
their internal and external limitations) will pass over into
one another, at the limit.

The Tragedy of Hamlet

In order to examine how this transference from one scene to
another is managed, there is nothing better than to review
the tragedy of *Hamlet*. In effect, this tragedy puts these
different stages in enclaves, through subjecting representation to the representation of representation.

Hamlet's fate of being an exception comes about through
his having his ear poisoned by the voice of a ghost —
nothing guarantees that it speaks the truth. It tells him of
'foul crimes' for which the debt that must be paid is a heavy
one:

> If thou art privy to thy country's fate
> Which happily foreknowing may avoid,
> O, Speak!
> Or if thou hast uphoarded in thy life

Extorted treasure in the womb of earth . . .
Speak of it!

Now, what misfortune is at issue, if not the one that has
already been sensed, which presages the end of a dynasty
(like that of the Labdacides who die out with Oedipus)?
Since it is a question for Hamlet, as for Oedipus, of being
the agent of it, this issue must be imputed to

. . . some vicious mole of nature
. . . wherein they are not guilty . . .
By the o'ergrowth of some complexion
Carrying the stamp of one defect
. . . the dram of evil
Doth all the noble substance of a doubt
To his own scandal

This injustice of nature will justify exceptional behaviour.

To discomfort Claudius or to convict him of the murder
of his father and to convince himself through convincing at
least one other (Horatio) of it, Hamlet introduces theatre
onto the stage of the reality of theatre. The scene that is
played refers back to a real scene which, itself played out,
refers back to another real scene. And so on. This
trans-scenariority builds up an uncanny structure through
the constant intrication of the genuinely alien and the
familiar. This representation within the representation
must be capable of producing the mark of truth in the play
of fiction. Hamlet has the actors perform The Dumb-Show,
the mime, and then the play which produces the scene in
which a character pours poison into the ear of the sleeping
King. But the pantomime only tells of the 'argument' of
the piece. It doesn't reveal its secret. The latter must be
uttered. 'The players cannot keep counsel; they'll tell all.'
Nonetheless, producing the play within the play is not
enough. From being an actor, the tragedy's King
(Claudius) has become a spectator. And in so far as he is a
spectator, he knows that the player-king doesn't die. He
can remain impassive. Claudius might have shown no
particular distress if what I call a *praticable* in French — a
linking dialogue — had not taken place between Hamlet
and himself, interrupting the unfolding of the play. Their
dialogue bears essentially on the title of the piece and the

name of the characters. The title: The Mouse-Trap. The subject: a murder committed in Vienna. There is nothing there to awaken any suspicion whatsoever. Claudius does not know that Hamlet knows that he is the murderer of his father. The court in attendance for the performance know nothing, nor does the Queen. These are all things the audience knows. For Hamlet, the nub is to make it known that he knows through making manifest in Claudius the uneasiness which will prove to him that what he knows is accurate and will assure him that from that moment on Claudius will be certain that he knows. To get to that point, there is only one means available: to get the names of the one play to pass over into the other. Hamlet replies to Claudius' questions: 'Gonzago is the duke's name; his wife, Baptista.' Lucianus is the character who pours poison into Gonzago's ear; 'the story is extant, and writ in choice Italian.' 'You shall see anon', Hamlet announces, 'how the murderer gets the love of Gonzago's wife.' With these words, whereby Claudius and Lucianus become equivalent, the king rises and leaves the show. An unusual situation: a spectator, who has come to the theatre to live an imaginary life, there finds a representation of his real life.

I am less preoccupied here, it should be understood, with the contents of the piece than with the theatrical form (even though there is some relation between the two) which multiplies and divides the marks with whose aid the passage from one scene to the other comes about. Now, another displacement of the mark will occur by means of nomination. By speaking of Lucianus, Hamlet has really and truly distilled a poison into Claudius' ear. In fact, he spelled out that Lucianus is the King's nephew. Through placing in the foreground a homonymic relation between the poisoners Claudius and Lucianus, Hamlet, the nephew of the reigning King, swaps roles with Lucianus, letting it be known, through this substitution, his regicidal desire: a desire Claudius has deprived him of, the first time around. He is so unwilling to accept this that, for him, the immortality of the old King Hamlet is not dead. It cannot become so, as long as his desire remains interred in the crypt. The old King does not know that he is dead.

Through the play of proper names which the Italian play introduces, the scenes become interchangeable. To the extent that Gonzago represents the old King Hamlet, Claudius, occupying Lucianus' place, may end up in Gonzago's place if Prince Hamlet, the nephew of Claudius, becomes the homonym of Lucianus, Gonzago's nephew. All the dramatic force of the piece consists in the fact that names that have no relationship come to coincide with one another. If one adds to the chessboard the death of Shakespeare's father around the time of the writing of Hamlet and the name of Shakespeare's son, Hamnet, dead at an early age, the circle is closed, running from Shakespeare's son to the play's spectator, identified with the Prince who dies by the poisoned sword. Across the centuries, Shakespeare continues to bring his son to life again and let him die, in each of us.

In the theatre, the spectator willingly becomes a stranger to himself, lending his name to those who, on the stage, know how to die. He gains through representing for himself the life that he dreams of living, and the multiplicity of lives that he imagines for himself, through becoming, on each occasion, the object of election. In doing this, he also encounters the manner in which he might be capable of dying or might wish to die, yet without ever encountering death 'in person'. If he can imagine his death for himself, it remains unpresentable in reality. He participates in it as a spectator, as he might in dreams, and it is as a spectator that he can see it being reiterated as a representation of the unrepresentable. The impossibility of seeing oneself dead in reality, like that of seeing oneself being born, is what underlies, through and through, the imaginary of the theatre, the repetition/rehearsal of the origin and of the end.

Beyond that of the proper name, one can distinguish two other functions which are set in motion by the staging of the staging: that of the election and that of the stranger;

The investing 'in its own right' (*en propre*) of Hamlet's role and the fate that he makes come to pass depends upon the 'historical truth' of the father's murder, that is to say upon the truth insofar as it is what the father makes him a gift of apropos of an event which has already taken place. Because there were no witnesses to the murder and no proofs of it, 'Truth' is based solely on the word of the father. This self-affirmation gives the speech of the ghost not its reality, but its 'historical' truth. It is speech which passes from an interior tribunal, the heart of hearts, to an exterior one, and on account of its atemporal character, assigns it the place of an anterior one. The ghost's voice elects Hamlet an avenger: a son who doubts the words of the ghost since he wishes to represent for himself the non-representable, his origins and his own death. What Hamlet conceives, in his heart of hearts, is the event that he cannot represent to himself and which is nonetheless inscribed within him as constitutive of an anteriority forming the basis of his election. That is what remains 'extorted treasure uphoarded in the womb of earth'.

Hamlet is a stranger to whatever it is that sustains the father's desire to kill the brother who robbed him of his crown. It is not as the heir to the throne that Hamlet, held back by the repression of his own parricidal desire, plans to assassinate Claudius. To stage his desire, he chooses a foreign play, 'writ in choice Italian'. This alarming representation earns him his exile and he reappears as a foreigner after having thwarted the plot which would have had him assassinated. So, confronted with Laertes, whose father he has killed, a Laertes in despair over the death of Ophelia, Hamlet finally comes to declare himself a Dane. 'This is I, Hamlet the Dane'.

These 'terrifying' transferences on to the Prince, who fascinates the gaze of those who can only desire what they desire via him, without taking account of what they truly desire, through desiring all the while to desire it, through knowing all the while that they know it without wanting to know how they know it, mean that the name 'Prince' is just a deception. Whether he is a good or a cruel Prince, all his name does is hollow out the gap between the life and the death he makes for himself, and the life and the death which falls to us. But it is also in his relation to the proper name that this discrimination of the fellow and alien beings is to be found.

The various modes in which the proper name, the election and the stranger function are reproduced in the tragedy of Hamlet thanks to the reduplication of the theatrical representation and to its being consigned to the abyss. The name of Hamlet renders those of Gonzago, of King Hamlet and of Claudius homonymic. Even though they have no relationship with each other, it makes them coincide. Yet their encounter remains a contingent one as long as the places are interchangeable. It becomes a necessary one, and hence one that is completely knotted, when it is untied with its dénouement. That means that the tying together of the three registers of functioning of the proper name is what holds the name back from being inscribed in the lineage. With the name Hamlet — this is alos true for Oedipus — there is an end to a dynasty, which gives these names an exceptional significance.

The Analytic Stage

The derealising function of the apparatus for representation put into play in analytic practice has been compared to that of the theatre. This comparison may be underlined through a reading of Freud, in particular his 'Psychopathic characters on the stage' (1905), except that the question of mimesis in Freud is linked to that of catharsis in an unexpected fashion, namely that the tragic 'pleasure' is a pleasure which is essentially masochistic and narcissistic. What is more, with Freud there takes place a rupture in the Aristotelian analogy between play and *Schau-spiel*, the play not implicating the apparatus of the spectacle but lending itself to an effective and direct mimicry at the same time as a renunciation, albeit a possibly provisional one, of pleasure: this 'frustration' introduces a fracture of the economic system in favour of a deferred economy.

In reality everything in the apparatus of the analytic stage aims at welcoming the power of the theatrical apparatus in order to hold it in suspense. Analysis establishes a protocol according to which speech comes to be spoken in an unheard-of fashion: the absence of substitute satisfactions makes manifest the sexual reality of the unconscious in the very act of speech. The space thus given a place establishes, through this fact, that so-called reality is shot through and through by the imaginary. The theatricality of the imaginary hence comes to be temporarily deployed with the subject having no a priori assignable or decidable place and without the pleasure which is linked to the representation of the self in this or that place receiving any specular guarantee. Nonetheless, withdrawing this space from the laws of reality is only prescribed in function of a real whose laws it is a matter of learning. The decision as to the real thenceforth finds itself submitted to the articulation of an internal ideal of undecidability and of an external ideal of decidability. The paternal word, which cannot be carried out in the tragedy of Hamlet, will, in the analytic space of its representation, be accomplished, recessed back from the mark which, socially and visibly, determines it.

The text is Freud's, written at the same time as 'Thoughts for the Times on War and Death' (in which the division of representation is organised as a function of desire and of death). The text is less concerned with certain questions concerning theatricality than it is with raising the problem of the closure which delimits those scenes in which are produced the limits of the representable and the specific psychic traits which demarcate its contours. In 'Our Attitude Towards Death', Freud affirmed that when it comes to our unconscious — and hence when it comes to primary repression and the radical splitting of consciousness which constitutes representation — 'the idea of our own death is as inaccessible to us as is that which inclines us towards murderous impulses when confronted with strangers'. In the text which follows on from it, apparently taking an entirely different point of departure — I'm referring to 'Some Character-types met with in Psychoanalytic work' (1916) — Freud considers some surprising traits which show themselves to be an obstacle to the renunciation analysis requires of every direct and immediate pleasure (such as those one may discover in the theatre). Yet it is from theatre that he takes his main examples. The bearers of these peculiar traits refuse, by declaring themselves to be exceptions, to submit to the necessities which in general force themselves on everyone. It is true that each of us would like to be an exception and thus be accorded 'special' privileges, but precisely because of this, Freud tells us, 'there must be a particular reason, and one not universally present, if someone actually proclaims himself an exception and behaves as such'. Now this reason can only be due to an experience of profound suffering, which the subject knows himself not to have been responsible for. Which is precisely what defines injustice.

Does not the future Richard III, right from the beginning of the play, declare, in no uncertain terms:

> I, that am curtail'd of this fair proportion,
> Cheated of feature by dissembling Nature,
> Deform'd, unfinish'd, sent before my time
> Into this breathing world, scarce half made up,
> And that so lamely and unfashionable,
> That dogs bark at me as I halt by them;
> . . .
>
> And therefore, since I cannot prove a lover,
> To entertain these fair well-spoken days,
> I am determined to prove a villain, . . .

Freud interprets these lines of Gloucester's by paraphrasing them as follows:

> Nature has done me a grievous wrong in denying me the beauty of form which wins human love. Life owes me reparation for this, and I will see that I get it. I have a right to be an exception, to disregard the scruples by which others let themselves be held back. I may do wrong myself, since wrong has been done to me.

The sympathy one feels for the character stems from those reasons that each of us may possess, even in the smallest degree, for demanding reparation for wounds inflicted to our self-love.

The critical attitude of the spectator is deflected to such an extent that he can, without ceasing to identify with the hero, hear:

> The secret mischiefs that I set abroad
> I lay unto the grievous charge of others.
> . . . and, with a piece of Scripture,
> Tell them, that God bids us to good for evil:
> And thus I clothe my naked villany
> With old odd ends stol'n out of holy writ,

So such characters are exempt from guilt. But not from shame. It is even upon shame that their shameful behaviour is built. Yet this shame is not experienced as such. It remains unconscious, like the sense of guilt of the person who can give it the name shame. Hence the mother of Richard III, the Duchess of York, says to him:

Bloody thou art, bloody will be thy end;
Shame serves thy life, and doth thy death attend.

In Freud's text on Richard III (a text which is followed by a
study of *Macbeth*), there is no warning given of the
exceeding of the limits granted to the theatrical space
through an allusion to the obvious analogy between these
characters who claim to be exceptions and 'the behaviour of
whole nations whose past history has been full of suffering'.
The passage is no longer brought about through a
transference of concepts from one stage to another —
'concepts cannot without danger be torn from the sphere in
which they were born and in which they developed' he will
say in *Civilisation and its Discontents* — but through the
transference of the proper name. For obvious reasons, Freud
cannot communicate the cases which would have shown
such a character trait. He must necessarily shield their
identities. However, names which do not have a relationship can coincide from one stage to another, can be in a
homonymic relation with each other. Now, to be an
exception is to be a stranger to the law which governs the
behaviour of one's fellowmen. It is also to bear a name
which cannot be the same as any other. But it is exactly this
non-coincidence of the unique trait or mark — it is not
universal — which can allow it to pass from one context to
another, from one apparatus of representation to another.

I would have liked to have expanded upon the 'obvious
analogy' between those characters who are exceptions and
those, the 'unpresentables', who have played leading roles
on the political stage of the 20th century. I would have
been led into constructing other homonymic relations, but
also some synonymic relations; that is, the conditions under
which the three functioning levels of the proper name come
together inextricably in order to produce the certainty of a
proper name. That would make a long story, the telling of
which I will have to forgo today, and agree to save it for
another setting.

So as to bring these brief remarks to a provisional close
with the author who permitted me to open them, the very
author who dreamed of producing and annihilating the
theatrical stage, I would like to emphasise that the
statement which flowed from his pen, 'I, Antonin Artaud,

I am my son,/my father, my mother,/and me' only has body through his proper name. There is nothing more uncertain for each of us than his proper name and nonetheless this very certitude, in Artaud's statement, holds together all the transferences which through being entwined, never cease to terrify.

Translated by John Forrester

THE ROLE OF THE INTELLECTUALS IN FRANCE
Jacques Leenhardt

How can an intellectual speak about intellectuals? This is not a rhetorical question: in fact, this lecture reflects my ambivalent situation.

As a French intellectual of the eighties, I had in mind when I proposed the title of this lecture, to account in a classical sociological way for the dilemma of the French intellectuals via à vis the socialist power in their country. Two years ago, we had a large public discussion about why the intellectuals — a large majority of whom used to be 'leftists' — had suddenly become mute, if not altogether allergic to the new socialist government in France. I was thus prepared to develop some thoughts on this puzzling situation and to criticize the subsequent versatility of those intellectuals.

However, in analysing the leading lights of that period, it became increasingly clear that a sociological approach tended to explain away any fundamental shift in the intellectuals' self-consciousness. Everything could then just be grasped at the superficial level of 'opinion' and easily criticized.

I was forced to confront a new dilemma: should I resign myself to facing the question of the compromise of the intellectuals at the level of the expression of their opinions, or should I try to find, behind these flattering opinions, a more profound and long term dilemma which would be at once sociological and philosophical? Here, I will try to develop the second alternative.

I can well imagine the total confusion experienced by anyone confronted by the French intellectual scene today. What a mess! No sooner have foreign publishers had enough time to translate Philippe Sollers' latest Maoist book, than he has become a convinced Catholic. No sooner is Jean-Marie Benoist's pamphlet accusing America of

cultural and political imperialism out of print, than
Benoist subscribes to Reagan's philosophy and threatens to
sue someone who has quoted a sentence from his anti-
American book. How can people find their way around?
How can anybody follow so many frequent intellectual
reversals! How is it possible to understand that renowned
intellectuals, former members of the French Communist
Party, willingly sign a petition in Le Monde advising the
U.S. Congress to vote in favour of military aid to the
Nicaraguan Contras in order to defend freedom and
democracy? Is it possible to make sense out of such
recantation, of what is in effect a permanent palimpsest of
epistemological, ethical and political assumptions? In this
tragi-comic waltz, can the sociologist save the philosopher
who is loosing ground, or perhaps, the philosopher save the
sociologist?

I shall try to answer this question by sequentially
tackling different types of phenomena. First of all, in the
evolution of the intelligentsia of the past decades, I will try
to locate some elements which account for the sudden
changes of attitude. I will then investigate what is at stake
in these reversals, taking into consideration that this
constitutes a central problem of the history of French
intellectuals since 1945. Finally, I will try to show how our
intellectual life has undergone a profound transformation of
its fundamental paradigms. To do this, I propose to refer to
only one major figure, one meaningful thinker of the last
years, Roland Barthes, and leave aside those epigones who
flourish thanks only to the media.

Traditionally intellectuals in France have represented a
form of opposition to the establishment. They founded the
legitimacy of their discourse on their relative autonomy as a
social group made up largely of academics, writers, artists.
Even though it may have been an illusion on their part or a
myth on the part of society (the so-called 'freischwebende
Intelligenz'), one must admit that their legitimacy was based
on the supposed and accepted universality of their point of
view.

After World War II, this situation deteriorated rapidly.
The causes are many and well-known. Let me only
emphasize two:

  1. the radicalized split between East and West and the

dominant role of the Communist intellectuals;
2. the increased participation of the intellectuals in the political and ideological post-war debate.

Although some of the leading French thinkers, like Sartre, have tried to avoid a strict polarization within intellectual life, a 'Yalta of the mind', this split nonetheless contaminates three decades of our intellectual life.

It was a time during which intellectuals armed themselves with categorical truths. Everyone had to make a choice, and there were actually only three: the Communist party under the banner of proletarian science; Americanism; or retreat from the world, which attitude I would qualify as tragic. For some it was fuelled by a rebirth of the Catholic faith; for others by a pagan agnosticism, as in Camus' case. In fact, Camus remained marginal; the Christians became divided, and this third alternative as proposed by the leftist group surrounding the review, *Les temps modernes*, and by the young nationalists of the rightist *Defense de l'occident*, which attempted to maintain a universalism of thought against political demands, were doomed to failure. The intelligentsia had to disavow its existence as universal consciousness in the face of the political and take a stand or enroll. As the political monopolised questions and answers, everything had to be fitted into the manichaean mould of either/or.

This situation was to prevail for twenty odd years and one could say that it came to an end only with the Hungarian revolution of 1956 and Soviet intervention in that country. At this point an essential change occurred. To a large extent it took intellectuals away from the political debate and led them to a more careful reading of *society*. The doctrinarians become sociologists. The social sciences develop and ideology ceases to be a weapon in order to become an object of scientific investigation. The critic of enlightenment and of the faith in teleological progress becomes, above all, the social critic. This criticism moves away from the ends and goals of history and from the so-called 'meaning' of history in order to deal with the social, its transformation and its structures.

Inasmuch as this attitude rejects norms defined by a constant reference to the long-term goals of history in favour of a knowledge of what is near at hand, it irrevocably puts an end to the 'universalism' intellectuals had claimed for themselves up to this point. Hence, their intervention appears more as a component of the system, a manner of improving its functioning. By leaving aside their transcendental approach, intellectuals have become, in their own consciousness, managers of the social.

It is at this point that the question of the autonomy of thought vis à vis the social system becomes more acute. If the intellectual is nothing more than a civil servant of the consensus, what legitimacy can he or she henceforth claim apart from being a mere *reproducer* of society as it is? The 1960s were characterized by this fear: if all transcendental values — such as reason, history, the proletariat, truth, man, and, of course, God — are dead, then history has reached its stage of repetitive eternity. The full rationality of such a state finds its expression in the structuralists' theories, conceived as the ultimate theory of the self-reproduction of structures. One talks then of mirrors, repetition, lack of movement and the death of the subject.

Althusser, Bourdieu, Foucault, during these years conceived of thought as entirely determined by structures. That is, all forms of thought are reduced to the thought of the structure. All phenomena, having lost their autonomy, are understood as symptoms. In the most desperate expression of this attitude, Baudrillard formulates its ultimate consequence: there is no more social, no more value, no more substance. Everything is a sequence of arbitrary simulacra for which it would be vain to seek a ground.

Althusser's theory of the Ideological State Apparatus, the work of Bourdieu and Passeron — both *The Inheritors* and *The Reproduction* — testify to the uneasiness of intellectuals in the French philosophy and sociology of the seventies. Having become a social group specialized in the elaboration of knowledge, and knowledge having become an essential part of post-industrial society, the intellectuals feel reduced to serving the society. The new situation worries them, since it ends with their self-representation as universal consciousness.

The Idea of Reversal

In the light of the development I have just briefly

described, I would like to turn now to the function of 'reversal'. As I tried to show in the first part of this paper, the intellectual conjuncture of the years 1975 to 1985 cannot be understood independently of the context which preceded it: the era of thinkers armed first of all with truth and then with knowledge. The extraordinary development of the social sciences in the sixties — anthropology, linguistics, psychoanalysis, sociology, etc — provided intellectuals with a degree of self-confidence comparable to that of the progressive intellectuals of the years 45–55, who were motivated by the sense they had of possessing the transcendental truth. The result has been a similar dogmatism, devoid of eschatalogical hope because a-historic, but fraught with intellectual as well as institutional arrogance.

In this context, the idea of reversal takes on a meaning which goes far beyond recantation. As early as 1946, Camus had defined the question which pervades the French intellectual scene of the years 1975–85. Faced with the frightful revelations of Nazism and Stalinism, he is driven to recognize that dialectical argumentation is powerless, because it belongs to the same logic as that which led to these monstrosities. Indeed, through the logic of the philosophy of history, we are led to judge as *normal* what we simultaneously reject as monstrous. It is a *normal* development, because it is logical within the logic of history itself. Thus monstrosity cannot be thought with the means of that logic, because it will be denied in a process of *Aufhebung*. Nazism and Stalinism have meant a return to faith and obscurantism of beliefs which led to a denial of life, says Camus.

> We are living in terror because persuasion has become impossible, because man has fallen entirely into the hands of history and he can no longer turn toward the part of himself which helps him discover the beauty of the world and of human faces — a part of himself which is as authentic as the historical part.

The reversal to which Camus then invites his friends Aron and Sartre means abandoning Hegelian historical reason in favour of an approach which he, himself, qualifies as *naïve*. By a naïve approach, he does not mean a stupid one, but rather one which seizes reality in its immediacy and not through the code of a totalizing vision. Against a major totalizing synthesis, Camus suggested a minor approach. This does not imply that he aims at marginality, but rather that he rejects the overwhelming quality of thought systems.

In the seventies, when the intellectuals hit against the conceptual walls which they had themselves erected, they rediscovered — some of them with a surprising ingenuity — the philosophical and sociological sources of this 'other approach' to which Camus had alluded. All fields were then affected by this phenomenon of what I have called *reversal*. This approach leaves aside Plato and Hegel, Lenin and Mao, and instead goes to Nietzsche and Protagoras, the Sophists and the Cynics. The body asserts itself against discourse and the immediacy of pleasure and suffering prevails against logocentrism. Freud is reduced to ashes in *L'Anti-Oedipe*; Marx faces defeat amongst intellectuals. The master-thinkers vanish and symptomatically Jean-François Lyotard writes about 'the strength of the weak'. Sociology turns to social movements rather than to social structure. In literature, the individual as subject comes back and countless biographies of writers — including those reputed for their formalism and rejection of subjectivity, such as Robbe-Grillet — are published. Finally, sociology itself elevates biography to the height of method. Small is beautiful.

But once again, let us not dwell on conjunctural movements and intellectual fashion. Beyond these, the essential concern of the intellectual strata remains: what can discursive logic do against the monstrous reality of the world? In the last part of this paper, I would like to explore this problematic, through one significant example: that of Roland Barthes. I quote this author, because he had the curious fate of dying in the fullness of intellectual maturity and because his last book, in spite of that coincidence, can be seen as an epistemological testament.

Camera Lucida is not only a book about photography. It is a work in which Barthes cast a retrospective glance at his own work and chose to end with an epistemological questioning fed by ethical preoccupations.

In the opening pages of *Camera Lucida*, Barthes formulates the position of the scientist in the social sciences. The intellectual act, he says, comprises existential experience, the formulation of that experience in a theoretical discourse and a meta-theoretical questioning: what is my discourse worth in the context of this experience? And he adds, "I am torn between two languages. The one expressive, linked to existential experience; the other, critical, based on knowledge" (Sociology, semiotics, psychoanalysis).

Barthes points to a new epistemic subject who is neither the subject of knowledge as it is built up in culture, nor the blind and mute subject of intimate experience. The new epistemic subject arises through a critical appraisal of knowledge reached through a consciousness which experiences the world. 'Me voici donc moi-meme, mesure du "savoir" photographique'. 'Thus, I am, myself, the measure of photographic knowledge.'

The transformation which Barthes imposes on his thought is remarkable. The search for universality must go through a stage in which knowledge is tied to the experience of the cognitive subject. In order to have access to the truth of his object, that is to say in order to truly become 'knowledge', the *studium* — the methodical approach — must go through the emotional experience produced by the external world in the cognitive subject. This is what Barthes calls the *punctum*, what disturbs.

This new requirement shows us that in Barthes' eyes, the *truths* to which the social critic of the *Mythologies* led him in the fifties, and then the semiotician of *The Fashion System* in the sixties, are not likely to satisfy the researcher in the aftermath of moral and scientist triumphalism.

The abandoning of the recourse to the language of pure reason in the approach to truth has the effect of splitting the structure of the knowing consciousness into a gnoseological consciousness on the one hand, and an ethical consciousness on the other. If the humanities lose human truth, says Barthes, it is because theirs is a gregarious (i.e. cultural) knowledge, as is gregarious their notion of man as an object — whereas the truth of the latter is singular.

The ethic of pity which Barthes borrows from Rousseau allows him to gauge the correctness of knowledge by the recognition of the human condition in its singularity, and not the other way around.

If it is Rousseau who helps Barthes, at the moment when Barthes feels obliged to abandon a type of rationalist discourse, it is because Rousseau was the first eighteenth century thinker to found the human sciences on an experience which precedes rationality, but without falling back into religion. For Rousseau, pity represents in us the whole species, and not our singular being. Its expression, he says, is prior to any *reflexion*. Hence, the presence of pity changes and reorganizes any project of knowledge. If, for Rousseau and Barthes, pity is not a societal effect, but on the contrary, precedes all socialisation and all culture, it is on pity that the science of the singular subject must find its foundation — before semiology and sociology come into play.

I have only been able to gloss over the slow evolution that takes place from the Barthes of *Mythologies* to his semiotic phase and from there to *Camera Lucida*, via the *Pleasure of the Text* and *A Lover's Discourse*. The last sentence of *Camera Lucida* is illuminating once we situate it in that evolution.

'It is up to me to choose whether to subject the spectacle (a given photograph) to the civilized code of perfect illusion, or to confront in it the rise of an unbearable reality.'

The man of knowledge faces a choice that he must make: either he barricades himself behind the discourse of pure knowledge and translates the spectacle before his eyes in the 'civilized codes of perfect illusion' — that is, he participates in the reproduction of illusion by hiding what he sees; or else, he initiates a deeper relationship with the species which appears in him under the 'obsolete name of pity', as Barthes terms it, and therefore faces the 'rise of an unbearable reality'.

In the eighties, this cannot perhaps be anything but the awakening from the dominant scientific dogmatism. This is a strange, indeed to some extent, paradoxical, but rich conclusion to draw from the last book of one of the founding fathers of semiology.

It would be possible to trace a similar trajectory in the work of Michel Foucault. In him, the epistemological question is contained in the notions of power, submission, violence, etc.

Finally, to conclude. I have tried to show that *reversal*

takes on quite different forms and densities, depending on whether one looks at the thinkers or at their media epigones. But seen as a whole, the French intelligentsia has been marked by the need to rethink its own rationalism, whether dating from its first historicist period (philosophy of history) or from its later scientistic phase (structuralism and generalized semiotics). Barthes and Foucault are in this respect exemplary.

In the cases of other, perhaps more visible intellectuals, the movement of thought seems erratic and parodic, because it is detached from a mature examination of an object and therefore takes on the unstable form of mere opinion. One day Leninist, the next day liberal; one day Maoist, the next day, Christian. And so on . . . The great difficulty in analysing intellectual movements resides in the fact that we cannot follow them all on the same plane. There have been basic changes over the last years, but not all the books thereby affected give us equal access to the essence of those changes. Because intellectuals are also the agents of the media system of burnt-out, rapid obsolescence, they disseminate themes that have been taken out of their epistemological context. The game of opposition between media figures becomes more important than the exchange of ideational commodities. Nevertheless, the totality of these exchanges, through which values and signs circulate without distinction, indeed constitutes the framework of our intellectual life.

The dilemma is therefore permanent, not only with regard to the options that one has vis à vis an object of knowledge — and I have tried to show how deep the transformation is on that level — but each intellectual daily finds him or herself in front of another dilemma: to which intellectual arena or market will he or she offer his or her work? To the exchange of signs of intelligence and subtlety in the vanity fair of the media, or, on the other hand, to the *concern with oneself* and the return to the unbearable reality, which leads to less immediate glory, but gives greater value to the work?

It is not by chance that our two main intellectual figures of the sixties and seventies, Barthes and Foucault, have faced precisely this dilemma in their last works and thus reacted against a certain intellectual rot.

ON COLLEGES AND PHILOSOPHY
Jacques Derrida with Geoff Bennington

Geoff Bennington: *Jacques Derrida has been called the leading French philosopher of the day. Clearly his work is most easily associated in this country, and I think in the Anglophone world in general, with a movement, or a pseudo-movement called deconstruction or sometimes 'deconstructionism'; but it is also true that over the last 10 years at least, there has been a whole other strand to his work which is perhaps less easily assimilated to what we tend to think of these as deconstruction or deconstructionism. That other strand is associated with the analysis of philosophy as an institution, with philosophy in institutions and with the philosophy of institutions. Some of this work has been published, but I think it's much less well-known here — or perhaps it's well-known that that side of his work is less well-known.*

Early on, this work was associated with a group called 'LE GREPH' which stands for Groupe de Recherche sur l'Enseignement philosophique *— a research group in the teaching of Philosophy; and it is also associated with the creation of the Collège International de Philosophie, which we are going to start off by talking about. Derrida was one of the people put in charge of creating the project for that Collège and was in fact its first Director.*

I've asked him to begin this evening by talking fairly specifically about the College which I think is an interesting institution. Then I'll try to engage him in conversation about some of the implications of the College — the philosophical implications: what is philosophically at stake in the creation of such an institution. I hope that the evening will move in a concentric way from the specific focus of the talk to a broader range of concerns in the question time.

Jacques Derrida: I bring good news. The Collège International de Philosophie *does* exist and there are many proofs of this existence. It has a legal existence and the legal status of this institution is that of a private association, supported by the government, but as a free, private and autonomous insitution. It exists, it is visible and has been so for two years as a series of seminars — about 50 or 60 seminars, taking place all the time. It was officially created on 10 October 1983 on the basis of a report which we — four people who were asked by the French government — had written. We were asked to prepare the foundation of this institution. We can come back later to the legal, current activity and goals of the institution.

I will first emphasise the main idea of the College, the main concept, what we call the regulating idea. The College is supposed to organise research on objects — themes, which are not sufficiently represented in existing institutions in France or outside France. Objects and themes which are marginalised or repressed or not sufficiently studied in other institutions; philosophical or not philosophical objects. Of course, the determination of these objects requires strange analysis because certain people are supposed to identify these objects. The College does not represent a philosophical doctrine even if, of course, it has some privileged links with certain streams of thought in philosophy, science, art or critical theory. Yet it is not supposed to represent any school of thought, as such. What we wanted to do was to displace and to question the dominant model, let us say of the western University.

What is this model? What do we think it is? It is a model of the classical or modern university in which philosophy has a very strange, very particular and very privileged place. I refer here to philosophical discussions at the beginning of the 19th century in Germany around the creation of the University of Berlin in 1810, philosophical discussions which defined the role of philosophy in the university. I think this model, directly or indirectly, dominates all the western universities in Europe, the USA and even in England, even if it has had to negotiate with previous models of mediaeval universities. According to this model we have a pyramid in which philosophy, as a department, or spread through all the departments from the top of the pyramid, is supposed to define the objects and the fields of the whole institution, the whole building of the university. For example, the philosopher is the one who is supposed to know what physics is, the essence of

physical being; what the psyche is, what society is. He or she is supposed to know the essence of the objects of the sociologist, the physicist, the psychologist, the historian, the lawyer and so on. So the concept of the university is a philosophical concept, and the organisation of the university is a philosophical organisation. At the top of this pyramid the philosopher watches, or is supposed in principle to watch the whole field of the different disciplines, but at the same time he is confined in a department. So — and this is a paradox which was stressed by Kant and by Schelling — how is it possible that *one* discipline — philosophy — may at the same time think and have the concept of the *whole* academic space?

We'll come back to this paradox later on — but it explains why in this academic hierarchy, philosophy is queen, the philosopher is the king and emperor, and yet his space is reduced to almost nothing — just to a point. The history of philosophy during the 19th and 20th century — the history of what we call the death of philosophy or the crisis in philosophy and in the philosophical institution — has to do with this structure which recognises the authority and the hegemony of philosophy and yet at the same time reduces the space of philosophical teaching and philosophical research. What we wanted to do in this college, the main concept of the institution, was to question this general structure and if possible to displace, to transform the situation from that point of view. That's why, within the College, we are interested, among many other things, in the history and the structure of the philosophical institution as such, and of philosophical teaching as such. In France, as you know, the teaching of philosophy has many peculiar aspects. It exists in the secondary schools, in principle. At the time when the College was created and some four or five years before, under the previous majority, the teaching of philosophy in secondary schools was threatened by new rules and new policy. Geoff Bennington was referring to GREPH as an association which was created, on the one hand to study philosophical teaching in France and specially in secondary schools, and on the other hand to oppose government policy which threatened this teaching. Not simply to keep things going as they were, but, while preventing this political threat, trying to transform the situation. This platform was one of the premises of the creation of the Collège International de Philosophie. In the College we insisted that we should have many representatives who were philosophy teachers in secondary schools — that's one of the originalities of our institution.

Now — why is the College a college? College is an old word, well known in this country. We made the choice to name this institution a college for two reasons. First to show that there should not be any stable hierarchy within this structure, among the people who teach, give seminars and organise research. Then, there should not be any academic title, and people elected or co-opted to the College could apply from anywhere in France or outside and even from outside academia on the basis of their projects. The projects should conform to the regulating idea of new objects, new themes and themes and objects which are not studied enough in universities and other current institutions. We do not mean by this that things that are taught and studied in the universities are not interesting, but as soon as they are recognised and identified as legitimate objects in other institutions, we are not specially interested in them. We are not at war with other institutions, but we select themes and objects that are marginalised or excluded or disqualified in other institutions. There will not be any permanent tenure in the College, and the people who teach or organise research in it will do so for a limited period; so there will be no chairs. The College will be a mobile model and light structure.

'College' too because it has to be a liberal institution. Which implies that it should be totally autonomous and totally free with regard to its relation to the state on the one hand and on the other to — let's call it civil society. That's a very useful distinction which we can question later on, but let's start with these trivial distinctions. Of course we are not totally dreaming, not totally sleeping and we know that we need the help of the State (we live on the money of the State, a very small amount, almost nothing), but on condition that we remain totally free in the choice of our themes, subjects and so on, and in the choice of the people who teach and do research in the College. That's why we called it a college — to insist on the liberal structure of this institution. Of course we do not believe in the opposition between liberal and non-liberal, we know it is very complicated and more and more complicated, and this complication is one of our concerns — not only in our minds but in the seminars which we organise. We do not believe simply in the distinction between public and private universities. I think tht today the problem is that there are no more *private* institutions and no simply *public* institutions: this pair of concepts has to be re-elaborated and that is another of our themes — one of our difficulties too. We know that we cannot simply decide at the beginning that we won't be simply a liberal or a private or a public institution; but we keep in mind, that this is a problem and that we want to change this situation and have a new approach to these problems.

Now — what about '*Philosophie*' in the title? Of course we would not like to reproduce philosophy and the status of philosophy as it is in other institutions. It's not simply a critique of or a fight against other institutions: we want to transform the vertical structure, this pyramid into something that will be more horizontal, with a new sort of relationship between philosophy and other fields, other disciplines. Constituted disciplines or disciplines to be constituted — new disciplines. It is not just a matter of what they call interdisciplinarity. We have nothing against interdisciplinarity: it is a very necessary thing which makes for progress in some institutions: but not enough. It is now a classical concept and it has been a classical concept for some time. With or without this name it is something which is recommended by Hegel, and by Fichte and Schelling, and so on. What we want to do is not simply inter-disciplinarity, which implies that we have already identified objects and competences — that we know what these objects are and what a competent teacher or researcher is in relation to these objects. Interdisciplinarity associates different people, competent in their different fields, to co-operate or collaborate on identified objects which require a multi-theoretical competence.

We want to discover objects which are not already identified. On the borders of different disciplines, new objects which are produced by new situations — technological, economical, historical situations, and we give a priority to those new objects which do not require simply a given competence, but require a new training for a new competence. And this implies that philosophy opens itself to these new objects in what is called Science, Arts, Architecture, Music and without any goal-oriented organisation of the research. That is one of our main concerns.

The idea of the College was formed at a very specific moment in France when, some ten months after the arrival of the new majority, there was a major colloquium on Science and Technology. It was very interesting and productive, but everything was understood as goal-oriented. In France we oppose this type of research to 'fundamental' research which is not programmed as something which could be used by state or civil society — medicine, army, industry and so on. 'Fundamental' in the old sense refers to philosophy, mathematics etc. as not being goal-oriented researches; whereas chemistry or technology or physics may be goal-oriented — as may even sociology, even psychology.

Of course, once more, I do not believe in this opposition. I think that today everything can be reappropriated (or recuperated) as goal-oriented research. Even the most fundamental research in physics, linguistics, theory of literature and philosophy. But, nevertheless, the first step we have to take, even if we don't believe in the last analysis that these oppositions work, is to claim that we want to undertake no-goal-oriented research, to remain free of any programme that could be imposed on us, not only by the state but by many other forces in society. and first we should analyse what this traditional opposition means and to what extent it works.

What are the ruses for re-appropriating fundamental research? The most general form of our themes in philosophy would have this title: Philosophy and its Others. Which means anything — not only the fields which are traditionally related to philosophy, but fields which are not — for example, Architecture. But when we say Philosophy and *Its* Others, we remain in a traditional structure in which — I quote Hegel here — it is philosophy which defines its others. It defines its relation to something which is not philosophy and which can be reappropriated, becoming philosophy in its turn. It is

interesting, and in our times it may lead to interesting and
new things, different from Hegel's times. But the general
scheme is *its*. That's why I would insist on another
dimension, that is philosophy and another which cannot be
its other, which resists philosophy as totally heterogenous
and, resisting philosophy, provokes philosophy into new
moves, a new space in which philosophy does not recognise
itself.

Speaking of the arts for instance, architecture, and not
only what we call the major arts (music, painting and
literature etc), but new sorts of arts defined as minor arts,
cinema and so on — speaking of these arts I would
emphasise the fact that in the college we would like not
only to study these arts in the traditional discursive mode,
studying the theory of music and architecture and so on but
also to *perform*. We would like practitioners in music and
painting not only to discuss with other people, philosophers and others, but to work; creating, composing,
writing, carrying out experimental research and practice.
That's the performative or performing dimension of
research in the college. We have already done some of these
things.

Now, why is the College 'international'? If we had time I
could quote some things from the report which is the
constitution, the charter of the college. It's a secret
document, of course; but if we have time I could quote
some of it. It's not supposed to be published. It was
submitted to the government, so it is written in special
language! Well, in this document we try to justify the
international dimension of this new institution. Of course,
every western institution pretends to be international. We
invite foreign visitors, we translate, we travel and this is, of
course, the international appearance of every institution.
What we wanted to do was to develop something else —
that non-French members of the College, professors,
researchers, artists, and students of course, would not only
be invited by the college but would also be making
decisions, be organic members of the college. We have
already done this to some extent, not enough, but to some
extent. The College would therefore be a really international institution, located in France at the beginning;
but not *just* a French institution open to foreign scholars.

How did we justify this necessity, this claim? First, some of us were interested — I'm limited myself specially here to the philosophical aspects of the College which is not *only* a philosophical institution — in what happens today between different philosophical traditions, not only the German and French but Continental and non-Continental, European and American and within every country many different national traditions which cannot communicate, which cannot translate themselves or one another, not only because of the language and not simply because of the structures of the academic institutions, but for other reasons which are more difficult to analyse. I don't think that language or institutions are the only obstacles here. This is something which is very difficult to locate and today there is more than ever an *apparent* communication between these countries and traditions, and at the same time a total misunderstanding: we wanted not only to analyse this phenomenon which is a scandal for a philosopher (since a philosopher thinks that philosophy must overcome these borders and these limits), but to transform it and to open new possibilities in the so-called dialogue between different philosophical traditions.

Of course, the Channel from that point of view, is something very important for us, because as you know if French and American and German philosophy, despite many difficulties, communicate with each other — the communication between British and French philosophy is more difficult. Some years ago we tried with Alan Montefiore to face this problem: it was very difficult and I think our attempt was not a total success. We would like now, with the help of British philosophers, to transform this situation. Of course in France there are some people, a small but growing minority, who are interested in British philosophy and the British tradition and I think that the College could give them and also British philosophers a place. But not only to official British philosophers or not only to official representatives of British literary theory for instance, but to people who in Britain or elsewhere are fighting in their own country and in their own institutions in the same way that we are fighting in France.

Now, there is a problem of language. We are interested in the general problem of translation and we would like the

College not only to teach foreign languages and to teach French to scholars and students coming to France but to teach other languages to French people so they can participate in common research within the College. In one report we stated that of course, if in the beginning the French language is dominant in the College, this fact should not be transformed into a law or a right. In principle, French should not be a privileged linguistic medium in the College.

GB: *My first question is a question about the element of 'philosophy' in your title. I think the same question could be asked of the other elements as well, probably with a little more difficulty of the college part, certainly of the international part. However complicated the relationship of the College and the GREPH before it, however complicated your own relationship to philosophy as traditionally constituted, I think a lot of people will still be surprised by the attachment you show for philosophy or at least for the* name *'philosophy'. I think a lot of people find it difficult not to think that philosophy has had its day, that it is finished, that its concerns have dissolved into other constituted or more-or-less constituted disciplines like linguistics, anthropology, sociology, types of history, psychoanalysis, and trans-disciplinary fields such as feminisim. To take an example: at the beginning of the conference at Cerisy in 1980 devoted to your work, Philippe Lacoue-Labarthe and Jean-Luc Nancy, who organised the conference, stressed in their opening statement that it should be a* philosophical *conference. There were cries of dismay from many participants, and specifically, I think, the American literary theory participants. Or, in a slightly different vein, I was reading a recent discussion of something which was set up in the wake of that conference, the Centre de Recherche Philosophique sur le Politique, again by Lacoue-Labarthe and Nancy. In this discussion, which is in* New German Critique, *it was suggested that this philosophical stress on* the political *rather than on* politics *implied a retreat from 'real issues', a refusal to engage in concrete struggles, and notably those connected with feminism. It's obvious that this sort of suspicion of philosophy is extremely widespread: it can come from all sorts of different places, and it creates extremely unlikely allies. And your own work, which as I've said is often not at all philosophical in a very recognisable sense of that term, has been received in the English-speaking world*

*largely not by philosophers (though perhaps increasingly so), but
among people working with literature and literary theory. So it
seems that the stress on this name 'philosophy' is, to say the least,
provocative. I wonder if you could say a bit more about what is
philosophical today, where is philosophy, why remain attached to
the name philosophy?*

JD: I won't be able to answer this question, but before
trying to say something I would like to make two points
very clear. First, even if I have been involved with the
College from the very beginning, it does not represent
anything specially attached to me and I have tried to do all
I could to avoid using the College as a place for
representing any group to which I am attached, or
representing myself. I remain at a distance in the Report,
insisting that the College should not express a special
philosophy and of course should not represent deconstructionism. That's the first point. That is my ethics in this
situation. It's very difficult because at one and the same
time I want to defend what I think is truth, and not to
influence the evolution of the College. It's very difficult
and I have to negotiate this every day.

The second point is that I never said a word against
philosophy. I insisted on the contrary that philosophy was
not dead and that the closure of philosophy was not the
death of philosophy. Now — why do I and my colleagues
in the college insist on the world 'philosophy'? What is
their, or my strategy here? As soon as you give up
philosophy, or the word philosophy, what happens is not
something new or beyond philosophy, what happens is that
some old hidden philosophies under other names — for
instance the name of literary theory or psychology or
anthropology and so on — go on dominating the research
in a dogmatic or implicit way. And when you want to make
this implicit philosophy as clear and as explicit as possible,
you have to go on philosophising. And even if you
deconstruct philosophy or if you want to think of the limits
of philosophy, of the special kind of limits of philosophy,
you have not only to philosophise in a general and a
historical way but to be trained in the history of philosophy
and to go on learning and teaching philosophy. That's why
I am true to philosophy.

At the beginning of this report we tried to analyse

schematically the historical situation in which this new institution was rooted. One of the main features of this institution is what we call the need for philosophy or the re-awakening of philosophy, not only or specially in the philosophical institutions but outside or beyond, in fields which are not philosophical. Everyday you see more and more physicists and medics or architects — even soldiers and the military — asking for philosophy. They reach a point where the type of reflection they need is the philosophical type; and so there is a demand for philosophy coming from outside the institutions. You can perceive this everywhere I think, especially in France where it is obvious that, sometimes with very strange and worrying implications, people are asking for philosophy — in the newspapers, in the media, even in rock groups. The College should be a place where this demand can express itself and have a place to organise itself and make itself known. In the last ten or twenty years what happened in France was a so-called establishment of non-philosophy. Philosophy was supposed to be dead and now the place was free for sociology and psychology — the human sciences. I have nothing against the human sciences, but in this new space another kind of philosophy was programming everything. That's what we wanted to question.

GB: *It might still be thought that in spite of all the provisoes you've just made, there is still a sort of covert universalism of philosophy being posited. One might ask the same sort of question of the international element in the College's title, because in a sense the statement that the college would start in French and move on might possibly be linked to a notoriously difficult case. I'm thinking of the French declaration of 1793 — or possibly also the American declaration of 1776 — where there is an inevitable tension between the specific name of a country, as in the name of the French or Americans, and yet an obvious universal claim behind it. There are some interesting recent analyses by Jean-François Lyotard about those sorts of tension. I would ask whether, given the 18th century references, this might still possibly be seen as part of what Lyotard would call the grand narrative of the Enlightenment. In* The Postmodern Condition, *which is obviously a book where he is simplifying a lot of things, and possibly simplifying them beyond a level which you would want to take up — there is a footnote where he links the GREPH explicitly to that sort of Enlightenment project. This would obviously then link into the current debates which have been going on here and in many other places about the postmodern, postmodernity, a possible dispersion and fragmentation of philosophy as opposed to universalising tendencies. There's the debate on these issues between Lyotard and Habermas, who I guess is no philosophical ally of yours, but might perhaps in that sort of presentation seem closer to your position than Lyotard — who, incidentally, has become the next director of the College: so there are a number of complicated intersections to be negotiated. Perhaps you might want to comment on that type of debate; on the Enlightenment problematic, the suspicion in the project of the College of a sort of universalism, an internationalism which would be a very Enlightenment type of thing, and the sort of things that are being said in the name of postmodernity and postmodernism.*

JD: First, I would make a distinction between internationalism and universalism. It is not a universal College. It is an international college, which means that we do not want to dissolve the national identities, the national languages, the national idioms into a universal medium, erasing all the differences into a transparent medium of communication. That's why we insisted in the report on the fact that the internationality would respect different idioms; and the kind of translation we are interested in is not translation in the conventional sense of the term — scientific translation in which unequivocal terms are available for everybody, erasing all the idiomatic values. We are interested in poetics and poetic language, language which remains irreducibly idiomatic: the translation should take this into account and so we are not being universal in the classical sense of the Enlightenment. More especially, the historical problem of the English language is very important today for us because we all experience it. When a German and a Frenchman meet, if they don't speak each others' languages, they speak English. When I gave a lecture in Frankfurt I gave it in English — it was the only possibility.

So you see that although we have nothing against Enlightenment and Universalism we are not simply Universalists in this sense.

Now, as to the Enlightenment, I would make two gestures. Of course in some situations I am totally on the side of the Enlightenment. It depends on the analysis of the situation — the forces against which we have to fight in terms of Enlightenment as rationality, criticism, absolute suspicion against obscurantism, etc. But, on the other hand we know that the philosophy of Enlightenment, reduced to its common features, implies many things that I think we have to suspect and deconstruct. The kind of rationality, teleology, universalism in the sense we were referring to, a certain sort of optimism etc.: we also have to deconstruct, to take the time to deconstruct, Enlightenment. But when I say we have to deconstruct a thing, I do not say we are *against* it, or that in any situation I will fight it, be on the other side. I think we should be on the side of Enlightenment without being too naive, and on some occasions be able to question its philosophy.

GB: *You quite rightly said that the College does not represent you and I think we should respect that. Nonetheless I am going to link something of the college's project to some of your work and then perhaps make this my last question and open it to the floor. I am going to do something extremely unfair, which is to quote from a text of yours. This is a seminar you gave in 1975 — the first time that you explicitly talked about GREPH in your seminar and linked your teaching to questions of institutions.*

JD: It was the beginning of the GREPH.

GB: *The quote goes as follows:* 'The university is philosophy, a university is always the construction of a philosophy, and it's difficult but not impossible, as I shall try to show, to conceive a programme of philosophy teaching (as such) in a philosophical institution (as such) which would consistently follow from or even survive a rigorous deconstruction.' *This is part of an argument in which you make the sort of gestures you have just been making and say that if one thinks philosophy is dead, in fact one is just falling back in a hasty way into unanalysed philosophies and so on. But you also say that this moment in your own work of addressing institutional questions isn't an accidental thing that's come about, but part of a systematic enterprise of deconstruction.*

You say that deconstruction has for a while engaged principally with a sort of 'internal' analysis of the Western metaphysical tradition of onto-theology, phal-logocentrism and so on, but certainly you give the impression in that text — I am summarising it slightly unfairly to provoke you a bit — that the time has come to address questions of the institution. Obviously this can be linked very closely with an impression, which is I think partly false, and a demand which is certainly oversimplified and very common on this side of the Channel: the impression that for a while deconstruction was involved with that sort of internal semantico-conceptual analysis, destructuration and so on, the sort of work we are mostly familiar with and that has been met with interest. But also a demand for, roughly speaking, some politics. This is a demand I am sure you are very familiar with, and it goes along with the idea that this is all very well and very interesting, but the time has now come to deliver the politics. To what extent does the College constitute such a delivery in your own terms and to what extent does it not?

I'd like to link that with another question and run the two together: This one comes from a recent text which you delivered at Columbia University, where you state that any text or any part of a text always projects or prescribes an insitutional model or a model of a possible community of interpretation and reading. You say that this is part of the law of the text. This is a very complicated argument and I'll have to leave some of the complications out, but you do say that this means that something like a negotiation of political questions is implied in the very structure of the text as such; *you say that not only does a text invite or prescribe a certain model of an institution, but that any actual interpretation in its very* performance *of that interpretation also proposes such a model. There's never a simple coincidence between the model prescribed by the text being read and the model implied in the performance of the interpretation of that text. You say that this brings questions of negotiations between models, and therefore political questions, into the heart of the deconstructive enterprise. and you say that this explains why deconstruction is seen to be far too political a business for some people but also not nearly political enough for others.*

JD: These are not unfair questions. First, not to forget the last point, I will insist that there is no such thing as a deconstructive *enterprise* — the idea of a *project* is incompatible with deconstruction. Deconstruction is a situation. Of course sometimes it takes the shape of a project, of a text signed by somebody and so on. But what we call deconstruction in its academic or in its editorial form is also a symptom of a deconstruction at work everywhere in society and the world; so the 'enterprise' is not the essential thing in deconstruction.

'The time has come' — first in 1975 I had already insisted on the aspect of institution. It was before I was involved in some groups and some actions; but even in those early works in which 'internal' deconstruction was predominant there was some stress put upon the institution — deconstruction as politics. Of course it was less visible, but I could demonstrate that it was already at work. I'm not justifying myself; it's just a small point.

'The time has come': what does that mean? Of course I was not *delivering* — I think I've never delivered anything — I was not delivering the politics of deconstruction. As for saying that I don't think that anything could survive deconstruction. I don't say that *nothing* can survive deconstruction. Deconstruction is life to me, so it is survival in itself. But I don't think that anything, especially an institution, could survive deconstruction in the classical form of a new wonderful building, built after the negative moment of deconstruction. If somebody thinks that — that first we have to deconstruct everything and then we'll have a new kind of society, a new kind of university . . . that would be the reproduction of the oldest schemes. What survives deconstruction should have new forms. It couldn't be a new system for instance, because the idea of system is one of the targets of deconstruction. It wouldn't be a system, a new happy totality of a university, a society or anything else. But the fact that this form, this structure, has been deconstructed doesn't mean that after deconstruction (if there is such a thing as 'after deconstruction') we will have nothing, or chaos. We are in the process of deconstruction and there are new things and things which fall apart and new forms — we can perceive many things which survive, not survive but *live through* deconstruction. I would say in a very rough scheme that everything which is living today lives through deconstruction, especially the academy. This is not surviving, but 'living on'. Of course, the fact that we cannot identify the old forms and shapes, the old organisation of departments and disciplines doesn't mean that now it's only disorder: it's not a new order but it's a permanent process of disordering order. I don't think that 'the time has come' for anything.

GB: *Except for me to ask for questions from the floor.*

Mark Cousins: *I'd like to ask about the persistence of the use of the term philosophy. When you were asked about it, in a sense you*

*gave a negative case for maintaining the term philosophy. You
said, and I'm sure most people would agree with you, that one
reason for retaining philosophy is that every time it's claimed to be
dead what is given rebirth to is an old-fashioned philosophy. That
seems to me an argument for saying that* thinking *ought to
continue, and my question would be: what is the relationship
between philosophising and thinking? I ask it because obviously
philosophy and philosophising involve thinking: but they not only
involve having a head, but also having a corpus — a body. There
is a corpus of philosophy which would include, say, Plato and
Aristotle. You've talked about a kind of training — a training in
philosophising normally means making certain remarks about that
corpus. Now does that corpus remain in your conception of
philosophy; and if it does, then where does that place the question
of the international aspect of philosophising? Where does that
specifically European corpus or philosophy as we know it relate to
the question of the international aspect of the institution? Does
philosophy in that sense leave that corpus intact? Will it persist in
what is called philosophising or is it in some sense a corpus that can
be left to one side? Why in fact continue to use the term philosophy?*

JD: That is a very central and difficult set of questions. Of
course I wouldn't content myself with a negative answer to
your question. I think that the word and activity of
philosophising must be kept in life for affirmative reasons.
I use the word 'palaeonomy' to explain the way we should
use an old word; not simply to give up the word, but to
analyse what in the old word has been buried or hidden or
forgotten. And what has been hidden or forgotten may be
totally hetereogenous to what has been kept. This would
mean that under the name of philosophy, something could
have been totally forgotten in a very strong sense of
'forgotten', and using the word 'philosophy' would help us
to remember what has been totally forgotten. This would
be true for other words as well as 'philosophy'. Very often,
and especially in this report, I use the word 'thinking'. It's
a very difficult word. We can understand it in a
Heideggerian way but not only in a Heideggerian way. I
am referring to Heidegger but not only to Heidegger, in
saying that *thinking* is something which is not limited to
science, technical philosophy and so on, and in asking the
questions we asked in the founding of this institution —
questions about philosophy, about the limit of philosophy,

about the relationship between philosophy and the sciences and so on.

The questions about all those closures are, I would say, thinking questions. In that case, thinking is not reducible to philosophy in the classical sense. Thinking is perhaps something which has been forgotten under the name of philosophy. But philosophy is, as you recall, a Greek name, and for us, since we have to start from the place where we are, I think that in Europe the thread which leads to thinking has been essentially philosophical even though I think that philosophy is not simply thinking. Nevertheless, in Europe one of the essential ways of thinking thinking, for having an access to thinking, has been called philosophy. Of course I was maintaining that we have to study the corpus of the tradition, Plato, Kant — but we are not very clear on what the philosophical corpus is. There have been violent interpretations which have imposed Plato, Descartes, Kant, Hume, etc., as major philosophers and there are other minor philosophers and others who are not even studied or known or published in our libraries. So I am interested in the transformation, the deformation, of the corpus. The corpus is not finished, not because we are writing new texts but because in Greece, in the Middle Ages and in the 18th century some things were written and not published and recognised as major pieces of the philosophical corpus. So, the question is an open question, even in Europe.

Now, beyond (but what is beyond Europe?) there are cultures, texts, ways of thinking, in Asia for instance, or Africa, there is thinking at work which is not philosophy in the European sense. The international dimension of the College should bring us to those forms of thinking which are not strictly philosophical. The adventure of thinking — and this is something which is not reducible to philosophy in the western sense — found its way in different ways in other civilisations. For me philosophy has been the major way of thinking, or forgetting what thinking should be. But that's our memory and our forgetfulness. In other cultures there is another memory and another forgetfulness.

Homi Bhabha: *I wanted to talk about the way the 'International' survives after deconstruction. In your 'Babel' essay* *you talk about translation and I would think that one of the ways in which you can talk about survival is in that concept of translation. What you say there is very important. I would like you to gloss it. You say that translation is non-mimetic, non-dialectical but, echoing or doubling on Benjamin, you say that there is a kind of 'differential harmony' of becoming a language. This seems to be a way of describing the notion of the international post-nation and post-internation and I would like you to talk about this.*

JD: In this text I was speaking in the wake of Benjamin when he says that translation is simply survival, which doesn't mean that *überleben* comes *after* life but that the life itself is already survival: that the original text, before being translated, demands translation and that is its way of surviving and living on. I agree that this scheme has an essential link with what I was saying and with the project of the *Collège International*. To the extent that I have something to do with the College, it is in that direction . . . It's a problem of course. Survival is a problem. All this is very problematic. The survival of the college is a real problem, I could show you how problematic it is — within weeks it may not be surviving any more. I'm referring not only to technical and financial and political difficulties in the classical sense, but also to inner, essential difficulties, so when I say deconstruction is survival, is surviving, its not un-optimistic — it's surviving through many problems, and it's a finite survival. It's not redemption or eternity — it's surviving.

Jacqueline Rose: *I was amused by your saying that 'everything lives', 'everybody who is living, lives through deconstruction' at the end of your paper, because about two years ago Julia Kristeva, sitting in exactly that place, ended her talk by saying that everything that lives, lives through love and psychoanalysis. My question is about your very complicated relationship to psychoanalysis, which would of course be a whole discussion in itself, but I'm thinking of the journey that runs say from 'Le facteur de la vérité' to* La Carte Postale. *As I understand it, in the present text, your critique is of what can be called Lacan's concept of the symbolic, of the* point de capiton *and anything which produces a closure of fixity of identity. You talk of ummasterable anxiety as the place from which, in a sense, you are trying to speak against the closure of the Lacanian structure. And again, what you are criticising in that piece is the structure of sexual different. This is* *a feminist question. Is the structure of sexual difference grounded in that notion of identity?*

JD: That is the kind of question that I won't be able to even try to answer in English. First: it's a huge question. I never criticised the *'point de capiton'*. I never said that we should get rid of it. On the contrary the question is to know what to do with it. How the theory is constructed with the 'point de capiton'. The way Lacan uses these facts, because I think he is right in saying that this is a necessary structure. I never said that sexual difference should be deconstructed.

JR: *No, but your critique is addressed to the privileging of sexual difference in psychoanalytic difference.*

JD: What are you referring to? That I was *accusing* psychoanalysis of privileging sexual difference?

JR: *Yes, in your critique of, say, the Oedipus complex, as something which privileges one moment of psychic structuration over the others.*

JD: That's something else. Privileging the Oedipus complex is not privileging sexual difference. My point is not against sexual difference. It's against the transformation, the identification of sexual difference with sexual binary opposition. But I've nothing against sexual difference. It's also a problem of course. You have to survive it too. On the contrary — it's in the name of sexual difference that I was criticising sexual binary opposition, because what I think (but I could not demonstrate this in such a short time) is that the way sexual difference has been interpreted by philosophy and by psychoanalysis, transforming sexual difference into sexual opposition, leads to erasing the difference, and now we have a classical logical scheme, with Hegel for instance — as soon as you use oppositions in a dialectical way then at one moment or another you erase the difference and you enter homogeneity. I think that this can be demonstrated and that was my point: not against opposition but beyond opposition. Sexual difference beyond opposition and beyond binary structure. This is quite different from what you are charging me with. Did I answer your question?

JR: *Well, I think it's a big discussion — but when you say that sexual difference is also a problem which we're having to survive with, I would want to say that that was the domain of psychoanalysis.*

JD: Yes of course. I have nothing against psychoanalysis.

There are so many sorts of psychoanalysis — so many trends, so many theories. So when you discuss *a* theory in psychoanalysis, does that mean you are against psychoanalysis? No. Even if you discuss Freud, I think discussing some aspects of his work, or Lacan's work or others, you are not against it.

JR: *Can you say something about 'invagination' and why you use that term?*

JD: That's a question I am asked in the name of feminism everywhere I go. I don't speak simply of invagination — I speak of double chiasmic invagination. Of course I was not totally naive in using this term, but as you know it's a medical or biological term describing a general structure: the vagina is only an example of this general structure. The outer limits become the inner limits: you have an interiorisation or introjection of something which is outside and when you have a structure in which the outer limit becomes an inner limit then you have an invagination. It's a very complicated structure, and I was using this word in the analysis of Blanchot's narratives. Of course, in this narrative the question of the woman is at the centre, but in such a way that there is nothing against woman — on the contrary it is a discourse on woman as affirmation. To me it is the most subversive discoure on woman and that's why I used this word which has many other connotations, many other meanings, in the analysis of a text which is to me the most interesting about woman — and not anti-feminist at all. Not feminist either. I am not against feminism, but I am not simply for feminism.

NOTES ON CONTRIBUTORS

Geoff Bennington is Lecturer in French at the University of Sussex, co-translator of *The Postmodern Condition*, and joint editor of the *Oxford Literary Review*.

Jacques Derrida, one of France's leading philosophers, is author of *Writing and Difference*, *Of Grammatology*, and *Dissemination* amongst many other books.

Peter Dews is the author of articles on post-structuralism and Critical Theory, and the editor of a volume of Jürgen Habermas's interviews.

Kenneth Frampton, Professor at the Graduate School of Architecture and Planning, Columbia University, is the author of *Modern Architecture*.

Martin Jay, Professor of History at the University of California, Berkeley, is the author of *Adorno*, and *Marxism and Totality*, amongst other books.

Philippe Lacoue-Labarthe teaches at the University of Strasbourg and is the author of *Portrait de l'artiste en général* and *Le Sujet de la philosophie*.

Jacques Leenhardt teaches at the Ecole des Hautes Etudes en Science Sociales. His books include *La Force des Mots* and *Lecture Politique du Roman*.

Jean-François Lyotard, currently Director of the Collège International de Philosophie, is the author of numerous books, including *The Postmodern Condition*, *Economie Libidinale* and *Discours, Figure*.

René Major is a practising psychoanalyst and editor of the important magazine, *Confrontation*, as well as author of *Rêver l'autre* amongst other books.

J.G.Merquior, is author of *Foucault* and *Western Marxism*.

Angela McRobbie teaches Sociology at Ealing College of Higher Education and is currently writing a book on popular culture, *'Working as a Waitress in a Cocktail Bar'*.

Michael Newman, freelance art critic and curator, has published widely in *Art Forum*, *Art Monthly* and other magazines and has written various catalogues, including the recent James Coleman for the ICA.

Demetri Porphyrios, Director of the History and Theory Studies in Architecture at the Polytechnic of Central London, is author of *Sources of Modern Eclecticism* and numerous articles.

John Wyver, author of a book on Trevor Griffiths and former *Time Out* television critic, is an independent television producer currently working on a series of programmes on contemporary art.

This new edition of *Postmodernism: ICA Documents* was commissioned by Robert M. Young and produced by Martin Klopstock and Selina O'Grady for Free Association Books. It was finished in June 1989.

This edition was printed on a Miller TP41 on to 80g/m^2 vol. 18 Bookwove.